A SHORT HISTORY OF

JAPAN

Dr Curtis Andressen is a senior lecturer in the School of Political and International Studies at Flinders University, South Australia. He has been a willing student of Japan for over two decades and has spent several years living there. Curtis Andressen has published widely on a variety of aspects of contemporary Japanese Society and is co-author of *Escape from Affluence: Japanese students in Australia* and author of *Educational Refugees: Malaysian students in Australia*.

Series Editor: Milton Osborne
Milton Osborne has had an association with the Asian region for over 40 years as an academic, public servant and independent writer. He is the author of eight books on Asian topics, including *Southeast Asia: An introductory history*, first published in 1979 and now in its eighth edition, and, most recently, *The Mekong: Turbulent Past, Uncertain Future*, published in 2000.

A SHORT HISTORY OF

JAPAN

FROM SAMURAI TO SONY

Curtis Andressen

ALLEN&UNWIN

For my parents, Thorsten and Marilyn Andressen

First published in 2002

Allen & Unwin
83 Alexander Street
Crows Nest NSW 2065
Australia
Phone: (61 2) 8425 0100
Fax: (61 2) 9906 2218
Email: info@allenandunwin.com
Web: www.allenandunwin.com

National Library of Australia
Cataloguing-in-Publication entry:

Andressen, Curtis A. (Curtis Arthur), 1956– .
    A short history of Japan: from samurai to Sony.

    Bibliography.
    Includes index.
    ISBN 1 86508 516 2.

    1. Japan—History. I. Title.

952

Figures from *A Brief History of Chinese and Japanese Civilisations*, Second Edition by Conrad Schirokauer, © 1989 by Harcourt, Inc. reproduced by permission of the publisher.

Set in 11/13 pt Sabon by DOCUPRO, Canberra
Printed by South Wind Productions, Singapore

10 9 8 7 6 5 4 3 2 1

CONTENTS

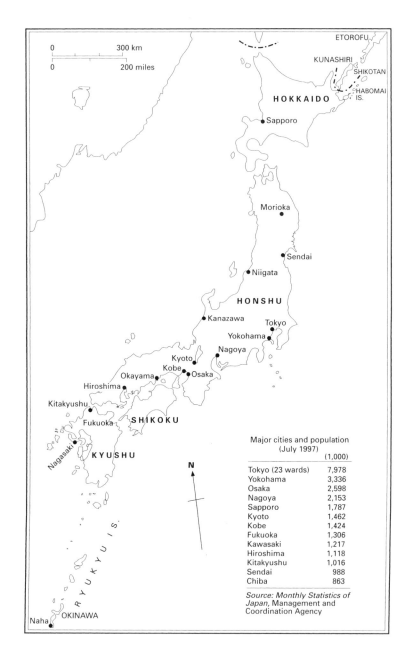

Major cities and population (July 1997)	
	(1,000)
Tokyo (23 wards)	7,978
Yokohama	3,336
Osaka	2,598
Nagoya	2,153
Sapporo	1,787
Kyoto	1,462
Kobe	1,424
Fukuoka	1,306
Kawasaki	1,217
Hiroshima	1,118
Kitakyushu	1,016
Sendai	988
Chiba	863

Source: Monthly Statistics of Japan, Management and Coordination Agency

Japan's lands and cities.

ACKNOWLEDGMENTS

No book is written without a lot of support. Many Japanese friends and colleagues over the years provided valuable insights into their society. Keen Western observers of Japan also helped me to understand Japanese culture, and prominent here is Peter Gainey. A number of people provided a great deal of help in the editing stage, including my hardworking parents and Andrew MacDonald. Peter, again, proved to be invaluable at this stage. Debbie Hoad was a dedicated and creative research assistant. I also owe a debt to Professor Colin Brown for his encouragement to undertake this task. Any errors or omissions, of course, remain the responsibility of the author. Finally, a special thank you to Blanca Balmes, for her love and unwavering support.

ABBREVIATIONS

ADB	Asian Development Bank
ANA	All Nippon Airways
APEC	Asia–Pacific Economic Cooperation forum
ASEAN	Association of South East Asian Nations
CEO	chief executive officer
DAC	development assistance committee
EEOL	equal employment opportunity law
EU	European Union
FTA	US–Canada Free Trade Agreement
GDP	gross domestic product
GNP	gross national product
JAL	Japan Airlines
JNR	Japan National Railways
JR	Japan Railways
LDP	Liberal Democratic Party
MITI	Ministry of International Trade and Industry
MOF	Ministry of Finance
NAFTA	North American Free Trade Agreement
NEC	Nippon Electric Company
NIC	newly industrialising country
NIE	newly industrialising economy
NTT	Nippon Telephone and Telegraph

ODA	official development assistance
OECD	Organisation of Economic Cooperation and Development
OPEC	Organisation of Petroleum Exporting Countries
POW	prisoner of war
PRC	People's Republic of China
SCAP	Supreme Commander for the Allied Powers
SDF	Self Defence Forces
SDPJ	Social Democratic Party of Japan
UNHCR	United Nations High Commission for Refugees
UNTAC	United Nations Transitional Authority in Cambodia

1
INTRODUCTION

FEW COUNTRIES HAVE BEEN the subject of so much scholarly attention yet remain so elusive. Who exactly are the Japanese? Are they peace-loving or war-like? Creators of stunningly beautiful art forms or destroyers of pristine natural environments? Isolationist or expansionist? Considerate of other cultures or arrogantly dismissive? Willing members of the international community or shy and fearful of engaging with others? Wildly successful or perched on the edge of economic ruin? Newspapers over the past few decades have provided all of these images.

In the late 1980s Japan appeared on the verge of an economic takeover of the world. The purchase of Columbia Pictures by Sony and the Rockefeller Center by Mitsubishi Real Estate at the time were two of the more dramatic examples of Japanese economic power. In Australia residents of Queensland's Gold Coast (with the notable exception of local real estate agents) protested the Japanese buy-up of prime real estate. The reaction in many parts of the world was fear. Movies such as *Rising Sun* intimated that there was a rather sinister plot by inscrutable kingpins to make Japan the next superpower by taking control of the global economy. Yet governments around the world at the time vied for the investment opportunities held out tantalisingly by Japanese megafirms.

So what happened? Since the early 1990s this image has been turned on its head. Suddenly Japan is a giant with feet of clay. Financial institutions are closing their doors, or merging, and their leaders are being marched off to jail or are hanging themselves in hotel rooms. At the same time, the Liberal Democratic Party (LDP), in power almost continuously since the end of the Pacific War, has managed to remain in control of the government, while voter apathy—reflected in the 1995 election of former comedians as governors of both Tokyo and Osaka—is at an all-time high. The recession in Japan, which has dragged on for more than a decade, seems to present a problem too large and complex for the government to handle. Politicians appear unable to dissociate themselves from long-standing interest groups, so stimulus packages designed to pull Japan out of recession continue to take the form of pork-barrelling, with massive contracts awarded to construction companies and the like who in turn fill LDP coffers. Unfortunately, the money is not spent effectively, public confidence has not been restored, and Japan's economy in the early twenty-first century continues to slump.

Part of the problem concerns the demographic profile of Japanese society. Voting is not compulsory, and those who vote are disproportionately older and more conservative, so outdated policies tend to endure. Japan also has a very rapidly ageing population, with high numbers of people entering retirement over the next ten to twenty years. At the same time the birthrate has dropped to its lowest levels ever, so there are fewer and fewer people to support an ageing population. Hence, when contemplating retirement, older Japanese workers have a tendency to save even more than usual. This lack of spending continues to inhibit economic recovery.

Japanese companies, too, which appeared unstoppable in the 1980s, are suddenly looking for international partners to help them out of their dire financial straits, hence the recent link-up between Nissan and the French automobile company Renault, preceded by the American company Ford's massive purchase of Mazda shares. At the same time many Japanese companies, which continue to make world-class products, are posting record profits, and through the 1990s recession Japan enjoyed huge trade surpluses. It is an unusual type of economic downturn. Furthermore, Japan continues to hold by far the greatest foreign exchange reserves of any country in the world, is second only to Germany in overseas assets and has been the world's largest creditor nation since 1985. The country provides nearly 16 per cent of the world's economic output and is therefore, for a range of reasons, watched carefully by other countries.

On the international front, however, Japan is relatively subdued. A few personalities have emerged on the international scene, such as Akashi Yasushi, the head of the United Nations Transitional Authority in Cambodia (UNTAC) during the UN reconstruction of that country in the early 1990s and, more recently, Ogata Sadako, present head of the United Nations High Commission for Refugees (UNHCR), especially prominent during the UN's recent intervention in East Timor. These are exceptions, though, and Japan continues to play a less visible role than is appropriate for a country that still has the second largest economy in the world. At the same time, it is a key source of funds and direction for many international organisations such as the UNHCR and the Asian Development Bank.

In part the Japanese reluctance to be more assertive is a reflection of the country's vulnerability. In many ways the label of 'fragile superpower' continues to hold true. In spite of massive investments abroad, trade surpluses and cutting-edge products, Japan remains vulnerable to fluctuations in foreign policies and economies. It continues to import 80 per cent of its primary energy requirements and is dependent on value-added exports for its wealth. When restricted to its home islands Japan is a poor, isolated, island nation. It must trade to create wealth, and this fundamental reality has moved the country into imperialism, war, destruction and global trade at various times over the last century. At the same time, given Japan's massive foreign investments and level of trade, other countries are dependent on its goodwill for economic growth. In this sense economic globalisation serves to protect Japanese interests.

There is a curious tension in Japan's foreign relations. Many in the region still remember Japan's wartime aggression; as a result, while investment is welcomed, the investor is watched with some wariness. In the history of the region the Pacific War did not end so long ago, certainly not long enough for fundamental cultural change to take place. Foreign trade, regardless, does not take place for altruistic reasons and Japan, like other countries, tries to maximise its benefits. Japanese companies also tend to recreate their structures overseas. They claim to need the quality products that only Japanese firms can provide. In other countries, though, Japanese companies are often seen as supporting each other while freezing out local suppliers. Hence, the extent to which Japanese investment produces long-term local benefits (particularly ones that are spread around rather than going mostly to local elites) is hotly debated.

For most people in the region the effects of Japanese trade and investment are highly visible. Whether it is downtown Bangkok, Sydney, Ho Chi Minh City, Shenzen or the Klang Valley outside Kuala Lumpur, the names of famous Japanese companies are everywhere. Automobiles bear Japanese brands, as do stereos, televisions, computers and a vast range of other types of consumer electronics. Goods that carry Japanese names, too, are often made (or at least assembled) in the low-wage countries of Asia. There are few countries in which Japanese companies are not playing a substantial role and in which their goods are not readily accessible.

While Japanese goods are moving around the world, so too are Japanese people. Tourist departures rose dramatically in the 1970s and 1980s, and even in the 1990s they continued at record levels. More than 17 million Japanese travelled abroad in 2000, more than 80 per cent of them as tourists. While there are increasing numbers of independent, especially budget, travellers, most still prefer package tours. Indeed, Japanese are renowned for their failure to blend into local cultures, remaining observers rather than participants (though younger Japanese seem to be challenging this trend). In part this is a result of the Japanese employment system, which gives few holidays to workers, and in part it reflects the essentially culture-bound character of the Japanese nation.

One group which is increasingly visible on foreign landscapes, however, is young Japanese women. They are the 'bachelor elite' of Japanese society. They tend to live at home and work full-time after completing their education, thereby saving substantial sums. Foreign travel is one of the preferred ways of spending this money. Indeed, they are a prized group for marketing companies. Does this indicate a substantial change in women's roles, though? Today there remains much debate about the extent to which contemporary changes are part of the mainstream. The Equal Employment Opportunity Law (EEOL) of 1986 (most recently revised in 1999) helped women to access management-track positions. This change has been driven to some extent by an increased assertiveness on the part of women, and partly by the demographic shift in Japan.

Although the economic downturn of Japan in the 1990s has meant relatively high unemployment levels, the ageing population will lead to substantial labour shortages in the not-so-distant future, and this should have a significant impact on women's participation in the labour force. At the moment, although it is clear that more women are being provided more opportunities in the labour force, the classic working-life profile, where women in their 30s and 40s quit working to raise children and re-enter the labour force later in life, is still evident. However, women are increasingly being given the option of a career path in Japanese companies, and this trend will almost certainly become stronger over time.

Participation in the labour force is, of course, linked to changes in the social roles of women in Japan. The average age of first marriage for women has increased three years over the past three decades and now stands at 27.5 years. At the same time the fertility rate has dropped, from 4.5 children per Japanese woman in 1947 to 1.36 today, well below the

*An increasingly rare
sight in modern Japan.*

replacement level of 2.1 children. This is having an impact
throughout the social system, from work expectations to
gender roles to demands for specialised services.

Japanese men, on the other hand, seem to be stuck in the
past, where the traditional life cycle is still very much the norm.
There are a few indications, however, that young Japanese men
are beginning to question the dedication and compliance that
such a life demands, and are considering alternatives. This
dissatisfaction is in part related to the increasingly visible costs
of the existing system. Indeed, one of the most recent issues
being publicly debated is that of *karōshi*, literally 'death from
overwork', though it generally refers to the problem of chronic
exhaustion. Former Prime Minister Obuchi, who died in 2000
while still in office, is its most recent high-profile victim.

The educational system also plays a key role in defining the roles of young Japanese. At least since World War II, the (ideal) expectation has been that a Japanese man should do well in his entrance examinations, enter one of the top universities in the country and, after graduation, secure a position in a well-known company or government department. He should work diligently, get along with his colleagues and stay with that organisation until retirement or death. A Japanese woman, on the other hand, should gain entry to a good education institution, secure a partner from among the well-heeled young men there, work a few years, then marry and have children, raise them and perhaps re-enter the labour force at a relatively low level when she reaches middle age. This model for Japanese women is presently undergoing significant change, though there is less change in the life cycle of males.

Although it reinforces very traditional roles, the education system has served the needs of Japan very well and has enjoyed widespread support in the postwar era. This is primarily because, in spite of some abuses of the system, and a bias towards higher income groups, the system is, at least in theory, a meritocracy—which has, however, come under increasing criticism in recent years. There have been charges made by a range of writers about the focus on rote learning, pressures to conform, lack of flexibility, censorship of textbooks and little emphasis on creative thinking. Violence in schools, directed at both students and teachers, has become a particularly pressing problem. Perhaps the most contentious issue, however, and one which is very difficult to change, is the use of entrance examinations throughout the educational system. One of the key roles of the education system in Japan is to stratify society, and this is done most visibly at the end of the final year of high school (though arguably much earlier), when students sit entrance examinations for various universities. The university one attends is linked to status, field of employment and hence upward mobility. Competition to enter the top universities in Japan is intense (as exemplified by the term *shiken jigoku*, 'examination hell'). Preparation can begin as early as kindergarten. Indeed, a segment of private industry, the *juku* ('cram school') has been developed primarily to help students pass these examinations, and such schools are increasingly visible. High incomes and a high standard of living are leading to this approach to education and social stratification coming under increasing pressure, however. The decline in the school-age population also means that accessing elite universities has recently become somewhat easier.

There have been some changes in the education system in recent years, one of the most important developments being the support for internationalisation, the key feature of which is study-abroad programs for high school and university students. There is also a variety of programs that facilitate Japanese students taking part of their tertiary education in an overseas educational institution, ranging from obtaining a foreign degree either partially or wholly in Japan (or overseas), securing credit towards a Japanese degree while studying abroad for a year or more, or taking short-term courses overseas for credit. Altogether some 180 000 Japanese studied abroad in 2000, an increase of nearly 100 000 over the 1988 figure. These programs serve a number of purposes. In a shallow sense they allow the educational institutions concerned to improve their attractiveness at a time of significantly declining enrolments. They are, in this case, a marketing tool that dresses up a tourist trip as a study-abroad program. Other programs are organised with more profound pedagogic intent, and give students the benefits of traditional programs of overseas study with individuals meaningfully interacting with people from different races and cultures.

There is no doubt that young Japanese people are caught in a transitional period. Their parents created Japan's economic miracle, and young people generally want for little in a material sense. However, not having experienced the country's devastation during the Pacific War, with the costs of dramatic economic growth becoming clearer, and a number of leaders calling for changes in the way in which the economic and social systems are organised, it is understandable that younger Japanese are questioning their goals. Indeed, in the late 1980s it was official policy to spend more on consumer items which would enhance quality of life (and in the process, help to reduce the trade surplus). The recession of the 1990s has tended to slow such changes. But the traditional systems are still firmly in place and those who are searching for alternatives are still on the periphery, although women have much more flexibility in this regard than do men. Given the profound nature of the changes which are occurring in Japan, however, it may be expected that those who are now the trendsetters will be part of a significantly modified mainstream in the future.

In the meantime the people who continue to hold power in Japan are mostly older men, conditioned by the hardships they faced in the 1940s and 1950s, who have seen Japan defeated, impoverished and at the mercy of foreign powers. They owe their success to the existing system, are part of a web of obligations and naturally have a vested interest in maintaining the status quo. This is a powerful force in resisting fundamental change.

Change is also inhibited by the way in which power is distributed within Japanese society. Just who governs Japan continues to be debated, especially by Western political scientists. Conventional wisdom has it that there is an 'iron triangle' of power in Japan—politicians, the bureaucracy and big business—and these groups balance each other. No one group has overall control. This is especially puzzling given that the structure of government is easily recognisable to anyone from a Western country. It functions, however, in a uniquely Japanese manner.

A key point here is that the different centres of power in Japan are locked together. Politicians, for example, look to Japan's large business conglomerates for funding and they in turn expect appropriate support. Politicians find themselves so busy raising funds for the favours expected by business and electorate alike that they have little time to gain expertise within a portfolio and therefore to formulate new laws. This is essentially left to the bureaucracy, which gives this group enormous authority: over time the bureaucracy has come to be a centre of power, often seemingly independent of politicians.

However, competition between departments tends to both balance power and, at the same time, inhibit change. Bureaucrats in turn are tightly connected to the businesses for which they set the policy frameworks, and mutual obligation is apparent here. For example, after retirement a bureaucrat who has shown himself to be suitably sympathetic to the needs of a particular company can expect a plum job advising that company on business strategy and gaining favours from the government, especially using his connections with his juniors who continue to work within the bureaucracy. The term for this is *amakudari*, or 'descent from heaven' (high-level people coming down to earth). There is thus a network of dependencies within these centres of power, reinforced by informal personal connections usually begun at university. It is not surprising that outsiders find it difficult to determine exactly how policies are made in Japan, which leads some writers to conclude that there is a secret plot within these power structures to push Japan ahead at all costs.

In the 1980s this system of power-sharing appeared to work wonderfully well. Numerous books were written on how social and economic structures operated. Bureaucrats in particular were seen as the guiding geniuses of the economy, charting future directions and negotiating secret deals between competing companies for the greater good of the nation. This was never so clear-cut, of course, but it was difficult to argue against the incredible successes of the country in the economic arena. The growth of the bubble economy in the late 1980s, however, and the subsequent recession, has dealt a tremendous blow to this picture of invincible and omniscient leaders, and raises questions about the educational and employment systems which nurtured their outlook and behaviour.

In a sense the way in which the power structures are set up in Japan is merely a reflection of fundamental characteristics of Japanese society. Some authors have argued that to understand Japan one must consider its origins as a civilisation built on wet rice agriculture similar to, for example, Indonesia or Vietnam. Because such an agricultural system demands close cooperation, whether for the construction of paddies and

3 EASY WAYS TO TRY SCUBA TODAY!

PADI

BUBBLEMAKER

...ling all young adventurers! Bubble-...ker opens the floodgates to the ...ll of breathing underwater. Between ...ving gum and drinking straws ...y kids love blowing bubbles. Now ...you have the SEA-DOO® SEA-...OTER™ Dolphin, let us teach you ...o blow bubbles the PADI way!

PADI SEAL TEAM

Young divers – get tanks full of air and pull off exciting stunts. On an aquamission you will dive into an adrenaline-pumping adventurous underwater journey. After you complete the PADI SEAL TEAM Course you'll feel more confidant using your new SEA-DOO® SEASCOOTER™ Dolphin.

PADI JR. OPEN WATER DIVER

If you are between 10 and 14, the PADI Junior Open Water Diver program is for you. Throughout the course, you'll learn fundamentals of scuba diving, including dive equipment and techniques. Once you've completed your certification you'll discover new ways to use your SEA-DOO® SEA-SCOOTER™ Dolphin.

$25 OFF

THE PADI JR. OPEN WATER DIVER COURSE

To receive your $25 rebate you must first complete the PADI Jr. Open Water Diver cou
then send in this coupon with your name, address and copies of your
SEA-DOO® SEASCOOTER™ Dolphin and PADI Jr. Open Water Diver receipts to:

SEA-DOO Rebate • PADI Americas • 30151 Tomas Street • Rancho Santa Margarita,

supplying them with water, planting or harvesting, the resulting society will strongly value cooperation and have a network of mutual obligations at its core. In Japan this has been modified by Confucianism, with all of its attendant obligations and demands for respect and obedience at different levels. Viewing Japan from the perspective of its citizens being part of a complex network of dependency and obligation is one useful tool for analysing the way in which Japanese society functions. A complementary view is one of exploitation, akin to a Marxist perspective. Indeed, it is difficult to reject the idea that Japan's miracle economic growth was not achieved without severe sacrifice on the part of ordinary Japanese workers. A trip to Japan today is a powerful reminder of the demands made of labour. An early morning walk through one of Tokyo's major train stations dramatically underlines the point that Japanese companies put high demands on their employees, as they pour lemming-like out of jammed commuter trains and race for their offices. Indeed, much of contemporary journalistic writing on Japan likes to focus on the dysfunctional aspects of the employment system—the incredibly long working hours, the expected bouts of super-expensive after-hours drinking/singing/bonding by 'salarymen' (white-collar wage earners) and, increasingly, female office workers, or the long and dreary commuting trips home late at night.

More to the point is that Japanese companies tend to organise their workers into a military-like structure, where small groups are assigned tasks that must be completed on a daily basis. Coupled with the obligations between the workers in these groups, employees who call in sick without a very good reason, or shirk their duties are rare, since the resultant burden will fall on their co-workers. At the same time, the system of seniority, which is connected with age and contains substantial penalties for people who switch companies, means that the system is very stable, and employees must usually think in terms of long-term employment (though there are signs that this system is loosening up, especially with the recent economic problems in the country). In smaller companies the military analogy is not so apt, though different forms of exploitation are evident, such as where larger companies effectively control smaller suppliers.

The rather unusual ways in which the Japanese social and economic systems function has for decades generated tremendous interest in other countries, an interest kicked off by Japan's dramatic recovery following the devastation of the Pacific War. Quick to respond to the economic miracle were a variety of writers who analysed virtually every aspect of Japanese society. Contributing in no small way were the Japanese themselves, who held forth on the issue to foreigners as well as to fellow citizens. (It appears that many were surprised at how quickly the economy had grown.) The result is a body of literature entitled *nihonjinron* ('discussions of the Japanese'), and its proponents have come up with a variety of explanations (ranging from reasonable to bizarre) for why the Japanese are different from everyone else and how this has allowed them to enjoy such spectacular economic growth. Hence, we have former Japanese Prime Minister Yasuhiro Nakasone expounding on Japan's monsoon (as opposed to desert) culture. Shizuma Iwamochi, former head of the Association of Agriculture Cooperatives, once told a group of foreign journalists that Japanese could not digest foreign beef because their intestines were different from those of Westerners. Others discuss the nature of the Japanese brain, which is said to make people more group-oriented than people from other cultures (using the left side of the brain rather than the right side). *Nihonjinron* reasoning is behind the beliefs held by many Japanese that their language is simply too difficult for foreigners to learn and that Japan has a homogeneous culture ('we Japanese think that . . .'). The darker side to this type of thinking is cultural superiority, which is linked to insensitivity to other cultures and, indeed, racism. It is a disturbing facet of Japanese society, and one which some of Japan's neighbours are quick to point out. Such views were, however, mostly a product of the 1980s economic boom and have waned along with the decline in Japan's economy.

Much of the writing on Japan over the past decades was naturally concerned with explaining the country's 'miracle' economic growth even in the face of adversity (such as the oil shocks of the 1970s). Since the early 1990s, however, there has been a shift to a more balanced analysis. Japan is a country with a number of unique characteristics that both provide advantages and yet present difficulties. The economic downturn of the 1990s has, in this respect, been positive. Japan is not as different as we thought.

What is apparent is that Japan is on the edge of a number of substantial shifts in the way in which its society is organised. In the immediate postwar era its citizens were concerned with avoiding starvation, and then with coping with foreign occupation. The 1950s saw tremendous social upheaval as competing groups vied for power and bargains were struck between business, employees and government. The 1960s were a time of supergrowth, and the 1970s and 1980s saw an expansion as well as consolidation of Japanese wealth and its movement around the globe.

So where does Japan go from here? It is clear that the structures which have served it so well are now approaching their 'use-by' dates. Government is not sufficiently transparent or responsive. The educational system is arguably becoming dysfunctional. Women's talent is largely wasted (in spite of a recent increase in women's workforce participation after marriage) and a severe labour shortage is looming as a massive number of people approach retirement age. Young people wonder why they must sacrifice their lives to the economy and are increasingly concerned with quality-of-life issues. Those who guided Japan so well during the period of rapid economic growth demonstrated a high level of incompetence in the late 1980s and 1990s. They allowed a bubble economy to develop, which turned into a recession, and they seem at a loss as to how to fix the problem. Thus it appears that substantial change must take place before many more years pass.

Examining Japan's past is an essential key to understanding its complex present, for the past is where Japan's fundamental characteristics originated and developed over time. There are clear threads that run through the centuries and explain much of contemporary social practice. This book seeks to identify the origins of the characteristics that explain Japanese society today.

One must recognise that there are many Japans that could be examined. The problem of core versus periphery in the country naturally raises the issue of which Japan we are talking about. Major events usually involve the central government, large cities, areas of important economic activity and so on. While events in these areas are relatively well-recorded, a bias naturally enters into the reporting of history, and one should not forget that any society has variations, whether along geographical lines or those of wealth and power. While the remote, poor or weak are often not noticed, we should not forget their presence.

In terms of broad themes in Japanese history, a number of ideas provide the focus of this book. First, Japan is an island nation, thus isolated and not subject to the same pressures as it would be were it landlocked or surrounded by other peoples. This has led to unique cultural developments despite the population's diverse origins. Second, when new ideas were taken on they were modified to suit existing cultural characteristics. The concept of the Japanese as 'borrowers' tends to obscure the fact that those ideas or items borrowed have also been adapted. Periods of strong borrowing have often been followed by periods of nationalism, a reaction to challenges to basic cultural practices. Third, isolation has led to the self-perception that Japanese are very different from other nationalities, an attitude that still endures today, though younger people are much more internationalised than older generations. Fourth, and modifying the previous point, Japan was as strongly influenced by China in the early development of its civilisation as were other countries in the region, such as Vietnam, Thailand, Korea and others, and thus these cultures share many basic characteristics. Fifth, the fundamental culture of Japan emphasises mutual respect and cooperation, especially working together, in a country where survival is relatively difficult and there are few natural resources and frequent natural disasters. This is linked to cultural practices that avoid social conflict. Sixth, the provinces were historically very powerful in Japan. Much of the country's early political and social development was conditioned by the struggle for power between the political centre and the provinces, and this has had a significant influence on contemporary culture. Seventh, Japanese society has tended to be strongly hierarchical throughout its history and this endures today, in spite of a recent veneer of democracy having been added. This has many implications, one of which is that the elites tend to manipulate the people. Finally, there are different sides to Japanese culture. American anthropologist Ruth Benedict set out the idea as the dichotomy between the chrysanthemum and the sword (in a book written to explain the behaviour of Japanese troops during the Pacific War)—or it could perhaps be thought of as the dichotomy between 'soft' and 'hard' culture. As in many other societies, Japan has both a substantial martial tradition and one of refined and gentle artistic accomplishments.

Above all, Japan is a fascinating country. It is not an easy place to understand, but trying to do so is both challenging and good fun, and an appropriate place to start is at the beginning.

2
IN THE BEGINNING

The geographical setting

Japan is an island nation that derives its identity through isolation from, yet proximity to, the Asian mainland. It is separated from Korea by the Straits of Tsushima, a distance of about 200 kilometres. This was clearly a major barrier to foreign contact in Japan's early history—compare it to the roughly 30 kilometres separating the UK from the European mainland.

This isolation has meant that cultural borrowing from the mainland occurred at a relatively even pace and foreign ideas were modified to suit local cultural practices. This is not to say that there were no periods of dramatic change, but there was never a military conquest by people from the mainland that might have fundamentally altered the path of Japanese civilisation. There was nothing like the Norman invasion of the British Isles. The readiness with which foreign ideas have been adopted has led to a widespread perception that Japan is simply a nation of borrowers. While this is partly true, Japanese culture also strongly reflects domestic characteristics.

Japan is not a particularly small country, being similar in size to Germany and one and a half times larger than the UK.

It comprises four main islands—Hokkaido, Honshu, Shikoku and Kyushu—and some 7000 smaller ones. They stretch about 3000 kilometres from north to south, with corresponding climatic differences. Because of its proximity to Siberia, Hokkaido has cold winters and heavy snowfalls, while the Ryūkyū islands in the south reach almost to Taiwan and are subtropical.

Topographically, Japan is very rugged, with favourable ecological niches which can sustain relatively large populations. The Kanto Plain, location of present-day Tokyo, is the largest of these. It is some ten times larger than either the Nobi Plain (Nagoya area) or the Kansai Plain (Osaka, Kyoto and Nara area), the other two major regions favourable to agriculture. More than half of the country is mountainous, reflecting its volcanic origins. Indeed, one of the best known symbols of Japan is the cone of Mt Fuji (inactive since 1707), the summit of which is about 3800 metres. The central Hida Range has many peaks above 2000 metres, so the interior of Japan contains a substantial natural barrier. Only about 14 per cent of the land is used for agriculture, the rest being covered with forests and fields, roads, water and cities.

Although we often think of Japan as being crowded, this is mostly because the population is crammed into less than 5 per cent of the total land area. In the face of the dramatic images that the media present of crowded urban conditions, we should remember that the high level of urbanisation is a phenomenon of the late nineteenth century and especially of the past 50 years. Finally, it is worth noting that the population of Japan is far from small. With about 126 million inhabitants, Japan has the seventh largest population in the world.

The landscape has naturally affected the way in which Japan was settled and how its culture developed. A rugged landscape, where people are separated by mountain ranges, rivers or bodies of water, leads to cultural diversity. It is not surprising that even today there remain significant regional dialects and variations in customs, as in the UK or Germany. Indeed, a theme running through Japanese history is the extent to which a central government has had problems keeping the provinces under control. The development of powerful central institutions, which attempted to regulate even the minute details of people's lives, was a response to fear of regional autonomy and rebellion.

Japanese mythology

Every country has fictions as part of its nationalist baggage, whether it is the Wild West, forthright and hardy heroes of the revolution—or wise and stately kings. Japan is no different. The mythological origins of the Japanese state are complicated, convoluted, vague and full of differing interpretations, reflecting the different ethnic groups which eventually became the Japanese people.

In one brief version of Japanese folklore the world was a 'chaotic mass like an egg', and there was no division between heaven and earth. Gradually the purer part separated into heaven and the heavier, impure part became the earth. Between heaven and earth divine beings emerged. After a time an object resembling a reed shoot emerged between heaven and earth, which turned into a god. Seven more followed, the most important of whom were Izanagi and Izanami (Male Who Invites and Female Who Invites). They stood on the floating bridge of heaven and thrust a jewelled spear (clearly a phallic symbol, in keeping with early ideas of creation) down into the ocean. As they raised the spear some water dripped from it and congealed into an island, to which they descended. After a time they decided to become husband and wife and in due course Izanami gave birth to islands, seas, rivers, plants and trees. Izanagi himself gave birth to Amaterasu, the sun goddess, while purifying himself (washing one of his eyes). She was so strikingly beautiful that he decided to send her up the ladder to heaven to forever illuminate the earth. Again while purifying himself Izanagi gave birth to the moon god, Tsukiyomi. He was also sent to heaven, but had a disagreement with Amaterasu. She refused to look at Tsukiyomi, and so they were separated by day and night.

The next child was Susanō-Wo (the ocean, or storm god), who was cruel and had a violent temper. After having a terrible fight with him over his bad behaviour Amaterasu hid herself in a cave, plunging the world into darkness. The other gods were understandably upset by this turn of events, and so brought a sacred tree and set it up outside the cave. In its branches they placed a bronze mirror and a jewel. When Amaterasu still did not appear, one goddess performed a lewd dance; the laughter of the others made Amaterasu curious and enticed her out of the cave, whereby the world was again filled with light. For his part in this affair Susanō-Wo was eventually expelled from heaven (the world of the gods). After this he had many adventures, during one of which he killed an eight-headed serpent (after getting it drunk) which had a sword hidden inside its tail, and this he gave to Amaterasu as a symbol of contrition.

So what does this sliver of Japanese mythology mean? One telling point is that the mythological beginnings were written down relatively recently compared to other civilisations, coming from the *Kojiki* (*Records of Ancient Matters*) and the *Nihon Shoki* (*Chronicles of Japan*). These are among the oldest records of Japan, from AD 712 and 720 respectively. They were written at a time when the emperor was trying to consolidate his power—having divine origins was obviously useful. Indeed, the conflict between Susanō-Wo and Amaterasu appears to be an analogy for several groups competing for power at the time (there were a number of regional powers). In any event, the works are full of scholarly inconsistencies and are clearly partly fabricated.

The use of myths for political purposes shows up periodically in Japanese history, and especially during the Meiji period in the nineteenth century. In recent times they were perhaps most obviously manipulated in the years preceding the Pacific War to bind the Japanese together in a spirit of ultranationalism. Generally speaking, it is politically advantageous to have an emperor as the titular head of the Japanese people and the myths legitimise his power. The current emperor is said to be the 125th direct descendant of Amaterasu

Fox kami, Shintō shrine, Kamakura.

(the counting, too, is clearly inaccurate). Such symbols are obviously important, and the mirror, jewel and sword are sacred symbols that continue to be revered by many in Japan today.

The worship of the sun also hearkens back to a time at the dawn of civilisation. One version of Japanese history has it that the early inhabitants were sun-worshippers, and the mythology is connected with rites at the time of the winter solstice to encourage the sun to return, a practice not so different from Western Christmas festivities. Indeed, the names Nihon, Nippon and Japan may be corrupted forms of the Chinese word *Jih-pen*, which means 'the place where the sun comes from', hence 'the Land of the Rising Sun'.

The myths also help explain the existence of various gods, or spirits (*kami*), which are at the core of the indigenous religion of Japan, Shintō ('the way of the gods'). This religion is fundamentally one of nature-worship, an animistic belief system that helped explain changes in the natural environment to a primitive people. A notable characteristic of Japanese

Shintō gate, Izu Peninsula.

mythology is the absence of good and evil. Rather, gods tend to be hot-tempered, or calm, and so on. There is also a complex examination of gender roles and male–female relationships, and the nature of life and death running through these early myths.

There are a few other ideas which emerge from the myths, one of them being the divine origins of the islands, a point reinforced from time to time during Japanese history. There are also explanations for disasters and conflict, and for the divisions between the present world, the world of dead people and the world of the gods. There is also a strong female presence, similar to that seen in the origins of many societies (with a later shift from matriarchy to patriarchy); indeed, some of the early leaders were empresses.

One cannot say that such ideas or belief systems are positive or negative—they are both, like any form of national identity. In the Japanese case, however, they seem to reinforce the perception many Japanese have that they are different from others, a notion much more prevalent in older people, particularly those who were educated before or during the Pacific War. While this may stimulate national pride and identity, the downside is arrogance and xenophobia. This phenomenon finds its way into the present day in a number of forms, particularly in *nihonjinron* writings (which reached their zenith in the late 1980s). In trade discussions, for example, statements such as 'our stomachs are different from yours so we can't digest the food you want to sell us' dumbfounded foreign negotiators in the 1980s.

The archaeological record

Just how different are the Japanese? What does the archaeological record show about their origins? Although the research is still controversial, it appears that people first came to Japan from Korea, China and the Pacific islands perhaps 200 000 years ago, although some put this figure at 600 000 years. The last glaciers receded about 15 000 years ago, and until that time a number of land bridges intermittently connected Japan to the mainland in the north, west and south. Archaeological evidence clearly shows that waves of migration to the islands occurred some 30 000 years ago, forming the Palaeolithic (old stone age) basis of the Japanese people. DNA analysis today shows that the first wave of migrants originated from Southeast Asia, and subsequent ones from the Asian mainland.

The first substantial Neolithic (later stone age) civilisation of hunters and gatherers in Japan is called the Jōmon (roughly 10 000 to 300 BC), named after the cord pattern of their pottery—indeed one of the first examples of pottery in the world. These people were from different genetic backgrounds, depending on whether they came from the Pacific islands, the southeastern part of Asia or the eastern and northern parts of the mainland. There was naturally some mixing between groups but some, such as the Ainu, which are believed to have come from northern China or eastern Siberia, remained relatively isolated on Hokkaido (as well as, perhaps, on the

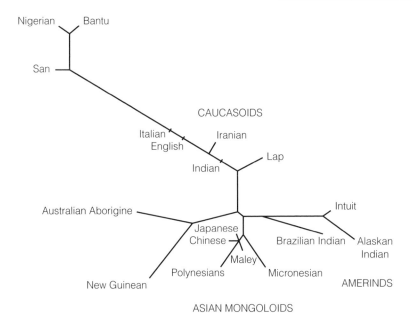

The Japanese people are genetically close to the peoples of both Southeast Asia and the Asian mainland.

Kurile Islands and Sakhalin Island). Originally known as the Ezo (the old name for Hokkaido), they were renamed Ainu about the time of the Meiji period. They are regarded, though only officially since 1997, as the only remaining truly indigenous Japanese people.

The Jōmon period, although the inhabitants remained primarily hunter-gatherers, saw the beginning of a number of changes. Because people tended to remain in particular areas more complex social behaviour appears to have developed and, connected with this, small bands of nomads began to combine into larger communities (up to, perhaps, 500 individuals). Religious rituals became more complex. Very early farming practices may also have emerged; in Kyushu a form of dry rice was harvested from about 1000 BC, a practice which subsequently spread to other regions. Shellfish in particular provided sustenance, and some 2000 shell mounds have been discovered on the Kanto Plain. The population during this time probably varied between 20 000 and ten times that number, depending on changes in the physical environment.

Around 300 BC a group of newcomers from the mainland arrived in (or invaded) Japan by boat, eventually displacing the Jōmon, a process which took hundreds of years. The new group brought bronze and iron technology, and the period has been named Yayoi after an excavation site in Tokyo. Their knowledge reflects their North-east Asian origins, as do arte-facts of the time, such as mirrors, weapons, bells and coins from the mainland. The Yayoi period lasted from approxi-mately 300 BC to AD 300.

Wet rice agriculture was introduced during this time, an innovation which led to a massive impact on Japanese society, and was one of the first examples of borrowing ideas from abroad. It provided the inhabitants with a relatively high level of food production, which led in turn to an increase in population and a consequent settlement of new areas. One can speculate (since these people left no written records) as to the social and political impacts of this form of agriculture that, at its base, requires a high level of social cooperation (building rice paddies, an irrigation system, planting and harvesting). It may be that the strong communal aspect of Japanese society has its origins in this period. In any event, from a practical point of view, it is clear that the emphasis on rice as a staple, along with a dependency on fishing, established the basic diet that exists in Japan today.

The new inhabitants settled first in the western part of the island of Kyushu (the part of Japan closest to the mainland) and then spread northeast to the Kanto Plain. They mixed to some extent with the Jōmon inhabitants but the Jōmon were largely displaced to the fringe areas of northern Honshu and Hokkaido, southern Kyushu and the Ryūkyū Islands, since more people and wet rice agriculture meant the need for more land. Although generally the Yayoi people and their culture spread peacefully, some of the Jōmon resisted domination by the newcomers and eventually were given the name of *Emishi*, meaning 'barbarians'. They were in periodic conflict with the people of central Japan until well into the Edo period. Thus from very early times the Japanese were a mixture of ethnic (cultural practices) and racial (physical characteristics) groups, which stands in contrast to the claim frequently made by Japanese today that they are ethnically and racially homogeneous.

Around this time Japan begins to show up in Chinese records, one of the first contacts being recorded in AD 57, when a Japanese mission travelled to China. There were a number of subsequent visits, in both directions, over the ensuing five centuries. The chiefs of different clans were already competing, and made contact with the Chinese to obtain trade goods and especially new technology. The *History of Wei*, completed by Chinese scholars in AD 297, is the most thorough description of Japanese society in this period. It notes that Japan was occupied by a number of independent tribal units, headed by both men and women, who combined secular power with some degree of religious authority, and that people survived mostly through fishing and agriculture.

The Chinese remarked especially on the clear class distinctions within Japanese society, presumably the result of the relatively permanent settlement associated with wet rice cultivation. In such a culture an interdependent, stable population would be more easily controlled by social elites. War-like competition between tribes was common, and would have led to some becoming more powerful than others. Within tribes the status of warriors naturally grew, a system of slavery emerged, and the complex social hierarchy that developed was noted by the Chinese visitors.

The Chinese description also mentions *Yamatai*, the agglomeration of about 30 Japanese settlements or 'kingdoms' at the time under the shaman-queen Himiko, which paid tribute to the Chinese emperor. Some scholars believe that Yamatai is the present-day Yamato, in central-eastern Japan (in the vicinity of Nara), while others argue that it was in northern Kyushu, the eventual site of the first Japanese state; the archaeological evidence is not clear.

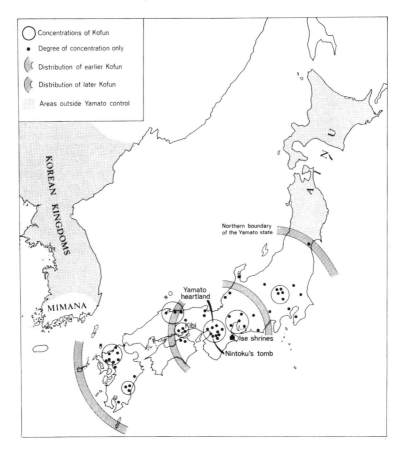

The Yamato state, 3rd to 6th century.

From about AD 300 the Yayoi inhabitants began burying their leaders in large earthen mounds, suggesting a strong hierarchical power structure similar to, for example, that which led to the building of the pyramids of Egypt. The mounds also indicate a strong Korean influence, with similar structures evident in Kyongju, South Korea, today. They are known in Japanese as *kofun*, which has given its name to the period of Japanese history following the Yayoi, about AD 300 to 700, though there is no exact agreement on these dates.

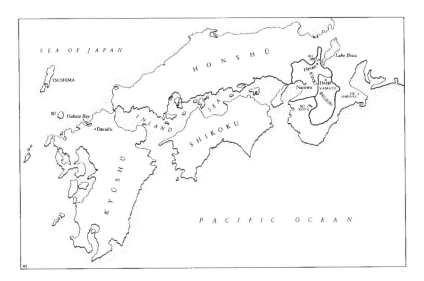

West Japan in ancient times.

More than 10 000 such burial mounds dating from this time have been discovered. Some of them are both large and elaborate, and the carved figures (*haniwa* pottery) decorating them suggest a number of developments in Japanese society. The social system, for example, was clearly very hierarchical, with the elite wealthy enough to secure the labour to work on the mounds. The carvings on the tombs suggest sophisticated building techniques, and a relatively complex religious system.

The Yamato Court—the first Japanese state

The version of events set out mainly in the *Nihon Shoki* has it that the first emperor of Japan was Jimmu, who founded the Japanese state in 660 BC. Although this is accepted officially[1] it is clearly fictitious. The scholars of the eighth century skilfully blended myth and reality to justify the imperial line of the time, so dates are impossible to determine

27

accurately. Most Japanese authorities agree that the first emperor was named Suijin and died in AD 318 (though the *Nihon Shoki* puts Suijin as emperor number ten). About this time a clan emerged as the leader in the Nara area through, it appears, mostly negotiation along with occasional warfare with other clans. The result was the Yamato Court, a political union of kingdoms with *kofun* culture as its base. The head of this court was known as the O'*kimi* ('great king'). The process took some time, however, and it was not until the early part of the sixth century that this clan can be seen as evolving into the imperial family.

Japanese society at this time (in central/southern Honshu) appears to have been divided into three major groupings. The *uji*, loosely translated as 'clan', were families bound together through loyalty to, and intermarriage with, the main family (polygamy was commonly practised). This is a very important characteristic since it played a critical role in how the culture developed through to (at least) the nineteenth century. Below the *uji*, who were the ruling elites, were artisans, organised into communities called *be* whose members had the same occupation, such as weavers, potters, armourers, builders, and temple servants, and whose positions were hereditary. At the bottom of the social hierarchy were household slaves.

Japanese society at this point began to be transformed through its contact with Korea and China. The influence of the latter was particularly powerful, especially from the beginning of the influential T'ang dynasty in AD 618, which lasted for nearly 300 years. The impact on Japan continued for several hundred years, only waning in the eighth century, dramatically changing the culture. Specific dates are, naturally, only approximations used to anchor the period. Some sources give the dates of AD 552 (introduction of Buddhism) to 784 (end of the Nara period) as the period of the greatest Chinese cultural impact.

In the fifth century Japan had a significant presence (sometimes erroneously called a colony or proto-colony) in the southeast part of Korea, around the present-day city of Pusan. At the time Korea contained several major kingdoms but in

Kannon Buddhist temple, Tokyo.

this area, called Kaya, there were a number of smaller independent 'principalities'. Japanese took advantage of the lack
of a central power in the region to make frequent contact, and
for more than a century this allowed for a substantial flow of
Chinese and Korean ideas and trade goods (especially iron)
through to Japan. Japan also provided soldiers in the fights
between Kaya and the larger Korean kingdoms. In the seventh
century, numbers of Japanese envoys (sometimes several hundred people at a time) were sent to China, often staying for
many years, even decades, studying Chinese society, and bringing Chinese ideas back to Japan.

A very important development for Japan was the arrival
of Buddhism from China through the Korean connection. The
main factor entrenching Buddhism was the support of Shōtoku
Taishi (Crown Prince Shōtoku) who ruled as regent 593–622).
One may speculate on the reason for his advocacy; perhaps it
was respect for China and a desire to appear 'civilised',
admiration of the structure of Buddhism (as opposed to the

Cherry blossoms,
Shinjuku Gyōen,
Tokyo.

relatively primitive structure of Shintō), or philosophical appreciation. Buddhism was certainly supported by a number of subsequent emperors, underscoring the point that major social changes in Japan usually occurred from the top down rather than as grassroots movements.

Buddhism had other impacts too, giving rise to the theme of the transience of life that runs through Japanese art and literature and underlies the near reverence placed on, for example, cherry blossoms. Lafcadio Hearn, an expatriate American living in Japan in the late nineteenth century, reflected this mood when he spoke of their 'melancholy brevity'. In practical terms Buddhism was responsible for strictures against eating meat, and the shift to cremation from entombing the dead, signalling the end of the *kofun* period (though this practice was common only among the elites at the time). Architecturally Buddhism has made a substantial impact on the Japanese landscape, not only in terms of statues and temples, but in structures where its ideals of harmony and balance predominate, such as in formal gardens. The type of Buddhism which arrived in Japan was called Mahayana, or 'Greater Vehicle', which developed as it moved across China from India. The essential difference between this type and Theravada Buddhism (or 'Lesser Vehicle', found in, for example, Thailand, Burma and Sri Lanka) is that the former holds that anyone can achieve eventual enlightenment through proper behaviour, and the emphasis is on accepting that followers will have varying degrees of understanding of life depending on their effort and karmic level. It puts more emphasis on the behaviour of individuals than on the role of the Buddhist clergy. In its journey across China, Mahayana Buddhism also picked up a range of Chinese characteristics and by the time it arrived in Japan it had a heaven and hell, numerous deities, and alternative interpretations of Buddhist teachings and ways to achieve enlightenment. These differing views led to the emergence of multiple sects, which have had varying historical impacts.

Buddhism brought an element of structure to Japanese religion. In spite of early secular frictions, reflecting the power of rival clans and other groups with vested interests, Shintō and Buddhism fitted together with relative ease, the two belief systems broadly complementing each other as they dealt with essentially different aspects of a person's life. Indeed, in later years it became common practice to build Buddhist temples on the grounds of Shintō shrines, and policies were worked out to allow the two religions to function together in philosophical terms. Philosophically, from the Buddhist point of view, the various Shintō spirits (*kami*) could be seen as *bodhisattvas* (sometimes loosely translated as 'saints'): those who had achieved enlightenment but who had chosen to stay on earth as guides to nirvana for others. Structurally, Buddhism was primarily concerned with moral behaviour, through the eightfold path to enlightenment (basically, rules to live by), and with death (one example in Japan today is the Buddhist festival of *Bon*, a type of All Souls' Day).

Shintō, with its pantheon of gods (collectively referred to as *yaoyorozu no kami*, literally 'eight million deities', meaning too many to count) is concerned with day-to-day matters, mostly keeping various spirits onside and out of mischief. It is fundamentally an animistic religion, and there is no substantial ethical code implied, though it is grounded in the close relationship with the natural environment and the early communal life of Japanese. It is also concerned with natural disasters and seasonal cycles. Shintō shrines are often located on the tops of hills and mountains, in beautiful natural surroundings—places which are emotionally or spiritually stimulating. The connection with nature is also apparent in the fertility festivals and phallic cults associated with Shintōism. Purification rituals also play a large role, and this may be at least partly related to health issues, that is, to preventing the spread of disease. Certainly the daily bath plays a prominent role in the lives of Japanese people—there may be a connection here. The emperor is the titular head (or chief priest) of the Shintō religion and still performs ceremonies symbolic of planting and harvesting; it is partly his place within Shintōism that has accorded him sacred status throughout most of Japan's history.

It is generally accepted that Confucian ideas came to Japan early in the fifth century. It is a philosophy of moral behaviour and social stability, and would have found fertile soil in a society that already had a well-established hierarchical social order (it remained most powerful among the elites, however, until the advent of feudalism). It rarely came into conflict with Japanese Buddhism. Confucianism focuses on the duties of care, obedience and respect in relationships between ruler and subject, father and son, husband and wife and so on, where the former must take proper care of the latter in return for obedience. In Japan it is usually said that the aspect of obedience, or loyalty, was emphasised more than care, or benevolence—a philosophical reinterpretation called Neo-Confucianism. In other words, respect for and loyalty to

Chinese character	安	以	加	多	奴	保
Original meaning	peace	take	add	many	slave	protect
Chinese pronunciation	an	i	chia	to	nu	pao
Katakana			カ	タ	ヌ	ホ
Hiragana	あ	い	か		ぬ	ほ
Phonetic value in Japanese	a	i	ka	ta	nu	ho

Examples of the derivation of Kana.

superiors was paramount. This philosophy has had an enormous impact on the way in which Japanese society is structured, from the family to the government to the workplace. The system of *senpai/kōhai* or senior/junior relationships, where the former are responsible for nurturing the latter, who in turn are obligated to learn and obey, as found in Japanese companies, appears to have its origins here. The same may be said of the value Japanese place on service. Confucianism is a theme which runs through Japanese society in many different ways, and has had an impact on the social system from early state development to feudal times through to the present.

Politically, Japanese leaders accepted the Chinese concept of a centralised state, though the Japanese emperor rarely enjoyed the power accorded his Chinese counterpart. The complex Chinese bureaucratic system was also adopted to reinforce the power of the centre. Borrowed, too, was an intricate system of court ranks. The two together meant that one's rank in the bureaucracy was often determined by inherited position rather than individual ability, though a limited system of entry by examination was also used, adapted from the Chinese model. Japanese bureaucracy thus stood in opposition to the Chinese bureaucracy, where individual ability was paramount. Chinese laws were also taken on board. These were adopted first by Prince Shōtoku, at least partly to limit the power of the clans while building up that of the imperial family, and were written down in a set of seventeen principles—somewhat akin to an early constitution—in AD 604. Other threads running through the laws of the seventh century are an emphasis on social hierarchy, obedience and responsibility. By the beginning of the eighth century Japanese society was thus characterised by a very complex system of codified rules and regulations underpinning a strongly hierarchical social order.

Japan also adopted and adapted the Chinese writing system. While the Korean and Japanese languages may have a common root in an Altaic language from central-northern Eurasia (some linguistic connection with both Hungarian and Finnish is apparent, perhaps through these tribes splitting up and moving in different directions), there is no linguistic connection with Chinese. The Japanese language seems to have first appeared between 5000 and 3500 BC on the island of Kyushu, and spread out from there.

Chinese characters, though, were readily accepted, some time in the fourth or fifth century. Before this there was no written language in Japan. Japanese scholars, however, were faced with a formidable task in adopting a writing system which is inherently different from the spoken language, and it took many centuries for it to evolve and to move out from the educated elites. The fundamental problem was that the existing Japanese word for a particular item and the Chinese pronunciation of the Chinese character for that item were different. This eventually led to multiple pronunciations (and sometimes multiple meanings) for many of the Chinese characters used in Japanese. In spite of this, there remained a gap between the way in which Japanese was spoken and how it was written in the new characters (*kanji*). The problem was solved between the seventh and eleventh centuries by taking about 100 Chinese characters, removing their Chinese meanings completely, and giving them Japanese sounds only. The result was today's phonetic Japanese alphabets, *katakana* and *hiragana*. Hence, modern Japanese is a mixture of early spoken Japanese, Chinese characters and two phonetic alphabets (Chinese in shape but Japanese in sound), along with numerous other foreign words. The Japanese language, like other languages, is a product of diverse origins.

Large numbers of Chinese and Koreans settled in Japan in this period, including artisans skilled in metalwork, weaving and writing. These skilled immigrants were held in high regard, unlike immigrants in the twentieth century, and were assimilated into the Japanese mainstream over time. Indeed, in the family register of 815 about one-third of Japanese aristocratic families stated they had either Chinese or Korean ancestors.

In spite of the massive changes resulting from their influence, the Japanese selectively borrowed from China and Korea. The Japanese elites did this partly to reinforce their own standing, but the selectivity also occurred because of the different stem onto which foreign practices had to be grafted. The distance between the mainland and Japan also meant that Chinese and Korean ideas became altered over time in particularly Japanese ways.

The mid seventh century was a time of both change and consolidation. In 645 a coup d'etat was carried out against the ruling Soga clan, which at the time held power in Japan. It was planned by a prince who later became Emperor Tenchi (r. 661–71) and led by a man named Fujiwara no Kamatari[2] (614–69), who established the Fujiwara family as a substantial power, a situation which was to endure until the eleventh century. This was a consolidation of an earlier trend of influential individuals or families (sometimes though not always) wielding power while emperors remained figureheads.

Fujiwara no Kamatari used the Chinese form of government as the basis for a number of political changes in Japan, which taken together are known as the *Taika* ('Great Change') Reform of 645. Enhancing the power of the central government was a key feature, with the result being that a very small number of people (about 400) could run the country. The other major change was the abolition of private ownership of land. Although it progressed in stages and was never fully carried out, this policy meant that farmers began to work for the state rather than individuals, and land was controlled and parcelled out by the government.

In addition to the control of land, which clearly increased the government's power, there were other measures designed to reinforce the authority of the centre. One of these was the first census, taken in 670. For the first time an attempt was made to determine who owned what, which naturally allowed for more vigorous social control as well as a more efficient taxation system. As we know all too well today, the latter also increased the government's power.

By the time this first Japanese state ended a number of characteristics were apparent. The status of the imperial family had been set firmly in place, and the mythology written within the next few years accorded it divine status. An attempt to count the Japanese people was undertaken (the population was estimated at about five million), and occupational categories were recorded that would allow them to be more efficiently taxed and controlled. The structured system of religion generally reinforced the status quo. For the first time Japan had a codified system of criminal and civil law statutes (*ritsuryō*), though the emphasis was on the latter function of government structure rather than on the criminal system. Japan had become a highly stratified society, underpinned by a range of social conventions.

The Nara period (710–784)

Along with a centralised state came a capital city. Nara was the first 'permanent' capital, built between 708 and 712 to a design imitating the rectangular grid pattern of the imperial Chinese city of Ch'ang-an (Sian). The beauty of its design and architecture, and especially its temples, reflects the increasing

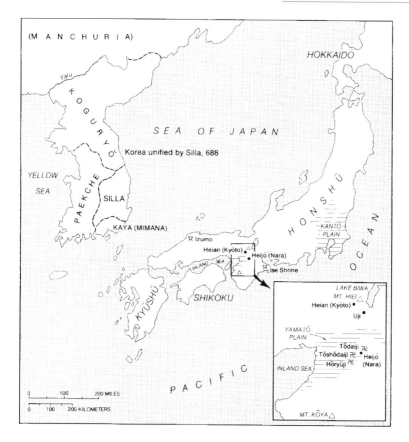

Korea and Japan.

refinement of the time, dominated by the influence of China, but with other influences coming from as far away as India, and even Greece and Italy. Buddhism in particular was the focus of a wave of artistic expression coming from the Japanese elites expressed in architecture, sculpture, drawing and music. The great Buddhist statue in Nara—the Daibutsu of the Tōdaiji temple—was completed in 749. It stands about 16 metres tall and weighs 560 000 kilograms, an impressive example of religious art that even today attracts visitors from throughout Japan and around the world.

The Nara period may be seen as a bridge between the establishment of the Japanese state, which set in place a number of the fundamental characteristics of Japanese society, and the sophistication of the Heian period (784–1185), a time of flourishing Japanese culture which preceded control of the country by military elites. Nara was an initial attempt at permanency, to provide a lasting physical centre for the new state, and reflects the shift from the very beginning of a state to a relatively sophisticated one over a short period of about 300 years.

Generally speaking, Japan's governing system of the time was highly conservative. Essentially, the country's isolation from the continent allowed elites to resist change which would have been forced on them had they had hostile groups on their borders. This ability to slow social change is a broad theme that runs through the country's history. In spite of massive Chinese influence, the institutions that developed in Japan had distinctly Japanese characteristics. The Japanese system, for example, did not allow for upward mobility through a civil service examination system like that developed in China. In Japan positions in the civil service were primarily allocated on the basis of birth rather than ability and court rank was also hereditary. Indeed, the aristocracy was set firmly in place during this period, evolving from blood connections with the emperor's family. To consolidate their position further the aristocracy did not adopt the Chinese idea of 'mandate of heaven', where an emperor (or, periodically an empress) could be legitimately removed through revolution if he or she failed to provide good government.

Buddhist philosophies also began to permeate the lives of upper class Japanese, with a number of different sects becoming active. In addition to material manifestations, such as temples and statues, the underlying beliefs began making themselves felt. Execution became much less common, being gradually replaced by exile. Cremation rather than burial became the norm. The idea of earning merit through good deeds began to take hold, linked to the idea of improving one's karma, so the practice of charity became more widespread.

Buddhist influence in a Japanese cemetery, Tokyo.

Buddhism also provided hope and comfort to those in need. Kannon, for example, came to be a key figure of worship. This is the same deity as the Chinese Kuan Yin, the goddess of mercy (originally the Indian Avalokitesuara).

The move of the court away from Nara seems to have been associated with competition for power between rival groups, though the growing political power of the Buddhist clergy also appears to have played a role. In any event, Emperor Kanmu (r. 781–806) moved the capital to nearby Nagaoka in 784. Because of intrigue, murder and alleged evil spirits, it was moved again in 794, this time to Heiankyo, meaning 'Capital of Eternal Tranquillity'. Like Nara, Heiankyo was set out in a grid pattern modelled on the Chinese city of Ch'ang-an. This is present-day Kyoto, a magnificent example of urban design, which remained the home of the Japanese court (though not necessarily of political power) for more than a millennium, until the nineteenth century move to Tokyo.

The Heian period (794–1185)

The Heian period has come to be seen as a golden time in Japanese history. While Europe was just coming out of the Dark Ages and China was going through the turbulence of dynastic change, Japan's culture was blossoming and developing in uniquely Japanese ways. This was a time of courtly elegance in which the arts flourished in an aesthetic, cultivated and highly ceremonial atmosphere—some say effeminate and over-refined. It was also a time of decay that saw power slowly slip away from the emperor. A unique system of government evolved, where the emperor became essentially a figurehead while powerful families ruled from behind the scenes (though this had already occurred periodically), a system that was to prevail for most of Japan's subsequent history. This period also set the foundations for feudalism in Japan, a system which was to endure for almost 700 years.

Historians usually divide the Heian period into at least two subperiods—the Early and the Late Heian. The first century of the Heian was effectively a continuation of the trends associated with the previous Nara period, where China remained the dominant influence. The Late Heian was a time of relative isolation, of 300 years of slow decline to the point where the rulers became vulnerable to rival forces.

In the early Heian period the country was governed for nearly 30 years by Emperor Kanmu, one of the most powerful rulers Japan has seen. The Chinese style of powerful central government was in place, and the shifting of the capital to Kyoto is one example of the authority of the emperor. Various policies adopted around this time reinforced the power of the centre, even after the departure of Emperor Kanmu. In 810, for example, the *kurōdo-dokoro*, or household treasury office, was created, where a few close advisers worked with the emperor to control the government. A new metropolitan police force emerged and spread its authority to the provinces where developments were watched closely. By the ninth century Japan was a highly centralised and unified state. This is not to say it was despotic, however. On the contrary, it is known for its humanistic and relatively benign rule.

An important date, signalling the beginning of the Late Heian, was 894, the year that Japanese rulers decided to stop sending official missions to China, which for hundreds of years had provided a steady flow of information and ideas and influenced Japanese political and social development.[3] Primarily because of the decline of the T'ang dynasty, both China and the Korean peninsula had become very destabilised, and Japanese rulers were afraid that this social upheaval would spread to Japan. Civil problems in China also retarded the country's dynamism, so there were relatively few new developments to interest the Japanese. By the end of the tenth century contacts were reestablished in commerce, as well as in the areas of religion and art, but official government linkages were not. This lack of political contact with China was to endure for some 400 years. During this period the Japanese government reworked some early Chinese ideas and developed institutions that had a distinctly Japanese flavour.

Political changes of the time had far-reaching implications. One of the most important developments was the growing strength of the Fujiwara family. Effectively the Fujiwaras started acting as regents (*sesshō*) for emperors who were too young to rule, encouraging them to abdicate before reaching adulthood. Various forms of manipulation included marriage to Fujiwara women, which meant that subsequent emperors had Fujiwara mothers. Eventually the Fujiwara clan came to rule in place of the imperial family, despite ongoing friction with abdicated emperors who tried to control their younger replacements. The height of Fujiwara power came with the rule of Fujiwara no Michinaga (r. 995–1027) who saw several emperors come and go. Many Fujiwara leaders during this period also assumed the title of *kanpaku*, or 'civil dictator'. Fujiwara practice set in place a system of government which effectively continued up to the Meiji restoration of 1868, and even then the power of the emperor was limited in practical terms because of his need to rely on trusted and capable advisers.

Simplicity of style in architecture, Kyoto.

It is perhaps not surprising that this shift in power occurred without causing a major stir. In some respects it is a very sensible system. The emperor was thought (at least officially) to be divine. As we know, daily involvement in politics can reduce the perceived 'holiness' of a country's leader, so by removing the emperor from effective power the imperial institution was protected. This has allowed the imperial family to endure for many centuries, and has given support to the system of separating the head of state from the government, found in Japan through most of its subsequent history.

The literature of the period highlights the fact that the court had lost its power of government by the end of the millennium. Given the intrigue and struggles for power taking place within the court, it is no surprise that the government had become divided and weak. Nobles who had no governing role generally spent their time playing games, writing poetry, practising calligraphy (a true mark of a person's level of refinement), painting, dreaming of love and distracting themselves with other pleasurable pursuits—not so different, perhaps, from the lives of the idle rich today. Linked to this sense of an age coming to an end was a melancholy, reflected in the term *aware*, meaning 'the sadness of things'. It is the feeling that life is wonderful but over too soon, an aesthetic sense reinforced by the Buddhist perception that life is like a dream, a notable characteristic of Japanese arts of the period.

We are familiar with the activities of the nobility principally because of several literary works of the time, written by maids of the emperor's wives. Murasaki Skikibu wrote *Genji Monogatari* (*The Tale of Genji*) around 1003, a story of court life of the preceding century.[4] Her contemporary was Sei Shōnagon, whose *Makura no Soshi* (*Pillow Book*) is a description of daily life in the capital at the time. These books highlight the point that the Heian period has left Japan with a tremendous legacy of artistic creativity, attention to refined detail (such as emphasis on the visual presentation of food or gifts) and a respect for education that is still evident today.

The Heian period came to an end, as dynasties often do, for a variety of reasons. One is the old story of the struggle for power between the central government and the periphery, where traditions of local identity and the rough topography of Japan made control of outlying regions difficult, which was reinforced as the power of the central government began to fade. Another element was the practice in which members of aristocratic families were periodically awarded estates from government-owned land (often tax-free) as a reward or, perhaps, to remove mischief-makers from the capital. Eventually many began to identify with their new homes rather than Kyoto.

A second reason had to do with land, the basic unit of wealth and therefore of power. It was the problem of land scarcity that led to a return to it being privately owned. The population at the time was increasing and there was a consequent need to bring more land under cultivation. To encourage this the government allowed newly cultivated land to be tax-free for three generations. Because of the already heavy demands on peasants, however, those best able to take advantage of this new policy were farmers (especially clan leaders) who already had substantial landholdings (and who, if they possessed business acumen, bought land from poorer peasants in these new areas), aristocrats and bureaucrats governing in the countryside, and those looking after larger shrines and temples. They often used slave labour (i.e. indentured labour or criminals) or landless peasants for the work on the new fields. Many of the latter had fled their villages when the demands on them became too much, and negotiated with those opening up new areas to work in the fields while avoiding *corvée* labour and military service.

This new land formed the basis of the private estate, or *shōen*, system. Private ownership provided tremendous incentive for various groups to enlarge their estates as much as possible, leading to the emergence of new regional centres of wealth and power. Generally speaking there were two different kinds of *shōen*. The first were owned by aristocrats or bureaucrats sent out from the political centre. The second were owned by farmers who had, over time, built up sizeable holdings. The latter were constantly fearful of losing their tax-free status to a government that needed revenue. In order to protect themselves, they often gave up the formal title of their lands to a local aristocrat or bureaucrat, or a clergyman from a shrine or temple. The latter protected them from government pressure, in exchange receiving a portion of the rice cultivated on the land.

The *shōen* spread throughout Japan from the eighth century onwards. By the twelfth century about half of the agricultural land in Japan fell under such estates, with the other half belonging to the government under the old land-allocation system. Ultimately, this new development reinforced the decentralisation of power away from the Chinese model of a centralised state, and strengthened the earlier Japanese structure of relatively powerful provincial leaders. The loyalty/

obligation system that formed between farmers and those to whom they looked for protection of their tax-free status also contributed to the early development of feudalism.

Another locus of power was Buddhism, which continued to flourish through the Heian period, and became even more syncretically connected to Shintō. Over time a number of sects amassed substantial wealth, and developed armies to protect it. In this way Buddhism became more than just a religious force; rather it was a force with a measure of political and military power—not so different from Christian groups such as the Knights Templar in the West. Various Buddhist sects also evolved with variations in doctrine and leadership (Tendai and Shingon were the largest) and periodically they came to blows as well.

In the late Heian period a warrior class also emerged, a response to the abolition of military conscription in 792, with several points of origin. In the urban areas, especially Kyoto, the guards who served as protectors of aristocratic families, and as police, evolved into warriors. The second group, the *kondei*, or 'stalwart youths', were given legal authority by the central government to protect their landholdings in outlying areas, and to protect the borders from 'barbarians'. The third group was connected to the *shōen*. Local elites (provincial clan leaders, aristocrats/bureaucrats and clergy) had to protect their estates, sometimes from bandits and at other times from officials of the central government (as well as each other), so warriors also emerged there. Some families focused particularly on developing their military prowess and over time became powerful regional forces. These groups, taken together, formed the basis of the early *samurai*. Those who came from aristocratic families carried proud names. Two of the great warrior families of the time were the Taira and Minamoto.

Eventually the weakened central government came to depend more and more on the military power of these families, partly to control unruly elements in the countryside, and partly to help settle disputes over succession within the imperial family. The power of the Fujiwara clan declined from the late eleventh century, with subsequent disputes over who would become the next emperor. Direct military intervention by regional clans in a political dispute (called in to back rival claimants to the throne) first occurred in 1156, and from that time the warrior families played a central role in governing Japan. By 1160 the government was controlled by the Taira clan but eventually, after much intrigue and fierce fighting on both land and sea, a Minamoto rival, Minamoto no Yoritomo, took power. Many of his Taira opponents were put to death, the first time this had been officially done to political rivals in more than 300 years. It was a sign of the growing ascendancy of the military.

The shift of leadership to warrior clans heralded the effective start of feudalism, even though its seeds had been planted centuries earlier with the growth of regional centres of wealth and power. While for most of the ensuing four centuries political power (and the imperial family) remained in Kyoto, the first of the military-dominated governments fixed its headquarters at Kamakura, on the southeast edge of present-day Tokyo, and the next chapter in Japan's history begins there.

3
CHAOS TO UNITY: FEUDALISM IN JAPAN

IN THE WEST, IT is widely recognised that feudalism long-dominated Japanese society, but this is frequently a distorted understanding, based on clichéd images drawn from popular Western films and novels. They have given us images of sword-wielding *samurai* in winged helmets fiercely battling stalwart foes, of warrior heroes who, faced with dishonour, might disembowel themselves in ritual suicide or *seppuku*. Added to this mix is frustrated love, always a popular topic. Given the rigid social structures of the 700-year feudal period there was plenty of opportunity for this, as well as displays of pride, honour, duty and glory. Men and women stoically endured the unendurable. This era is also a favourite among Japanese, a period bursting with images of strength and power—vibrant with masculinity, in contrast to the effete Heian period which was likely to present an image of a young man crying with his lover over a particularly touching poem (not a picture that appealed to everyone).

What, then, were the key developments in Japan's feudal period? What type of political and social structures emerged and why? How has this era shaped the Japan we know today? This period is characterised by civil conflict and ended with Japan shutting itself off from the rest of the world for more than 200 years, appearing reluctantly on the world stage in the middle of the nineteenth century, the result of which was a dramatic change in the world's twentieth-century history.

The rise of the military—the Kamakura bakufu (1185–1333)[1]

The Kamakura period signals a shift in Japanese society, as anthropologist Ruth Benedict might have put it, from the chrysanthemum to the sword. The rather confused days of court bureaucrats trying to manage a complicated administrative structure while power steadily slipped from their hands was largely over. The more vigorous, focused power of the military took its place. The *samurai* were also innovators. They were not bound by the old formalities of the Japanese court, but developed their own very practical culture that attempted to restructure Japanese society. Attitudes to commoners became more flexible, and culture spread from the elites into the mainstream of Japanese society. At the same time, the upheavals in China caused many refugees from the mainland elites to flee to Japan, bringing their own particular values and ideas. The threat posed by the Mongols also led to a greater sense of unity among Japanese, as they resisted foreign domination.

There are several key aspects to the way in which the government was structured at this time, one being the use of the earlier practice of leaving the imperial family intact as the symbol of ultimate authority in the land while real power was exercised behind the scenes. This was, perhaps, especially appealing to Minamoto no Yoritomo, who reportedly held the imperial court in high regard. The imperial family remained sacrosanct. Indeed, it was necessary to pay it due respect to gain proper legitimacy. Hence, Yoritomo asked the emperor to grant him the title of *shōgun*, the abbreviated form of *seii tai-shōgun* ('barbarian-suppressing supreme general'), first accorded to Sakanoue no Tamuramaro in 797 for his part in subduing restive *Emishi*. Yoritomo received the title in 1192.

Yoritomo's government was known as the *bakufu*, meaning 'tent headquarters', a reflection of its military origins. It was not located in Kyoto (which remained the official capital) but in the then small town of Kamakura, near present-day Tokyo. This was near Yoritomo's power base of Izu, and he probably felt safer there (away from the rival Taira power in Kyoto), not to mention relief at being away from the interference of court officials. It also bordered the rich agricultural area of the Kanto Plain, an important source of revenue.

Feudalism matured slowly in Japan. It did not spring forth fully developed in 1185, having already been evolving for several hundred years. Even before he received the title of *shōgun*, and while still fighting the Taira clan in some provinces, Yoritomo was reinforcing feudal structures. In 1185 he 'requested' permission from the court to appoint military governors (or 'protectors') for the provinces, known as *shugo*, and under them *jitō*, or land stewards. The former held regional political power while the latter were primarily responsible for collecting taxes on behalf of the *bakufu*. In this way Yoritomo was able to govern (and spread his power throughout Japan) without completely replacing the administration set up during the Heian period, which would have meant massive social upheaval.

Once peace returned to Japan Yoritomo continued to use this administrative structure, as well as his (often very personal) connections with his vassals, to preserve his authority as well as the peace in the countryside. This built on the well-established system of loyalty to a leader that hearkened back to the time of the early family clans, though in the early part of this period connections were also based on formal contracts, where a vassal was financially rewarded for his services. The vassals were known as *gokenin* ('housemen') and the mounted warriors who served them were called *saburahi*, from an old word meaning 'to serve', which eventually evolved into the well-known term *samurai*. The principal duty of the *saburahi* was to serve their lords rather than the emperor, thus diminishing the emperor's importance—he became simply a symbol without real power. The code of behaviour that eventually developed among the *samurai* came to be known as *bushidō*, 'the way of the warrior', and contained elements of Confucianism, Buddhism and Shintō. Training in the martial arts was central to their lives, and from here we eventually see the refinement of Japanese swordsmanship, archery and horseback riding.

The *shugo-jitō* system worked well, not only to control the countryside and raise revenue for the *bakufu* but, in combination with the idea of vassalage, it formed an early explicit structure of loyalty and financial reward. Vassals received land and the right to keep private soldiers. This reciprocal obligation (loyalty/benevolence), underpinned by Confucianism, over time became an established pattern of vassalage, the hallmark of feudalism. This is not to say that all vassals or lords were trustworthy, and there are numerous examples of broken promises, treachery, double-dealing and opportunism, but a rough form of ideal behaviour was laid down at this time.

In these early years the *shugo-jitō* system lay rather thinly on top of the old, not yet being strong enough to ensure complete control, and many aspects of the old administration persisted for some decades. The *shōgun* continued to derive his power, at least in principle, from the emperor, and the *bakufu* could be seen as the imperial government's military force. The *shōen* estate system also continued to exist, in spite of many estates being confiscated by Yoritomo from his defeated rivals and redistributed.

The nascent feudal structure was not without problems. Yoritomo in particular was highly suspicious of those who might challenge his authority. This led to his liberal use of violence to control others, including murdering his brother Yoshitsune and his family. As in many other countries, an enduring theme in Japan is the desire of its leaders to hold onto power and a fear of other powerful forces, which often leads to ruthless and violent acts as well as policies to limit potential threats. This was to reach an apex centuries later under the Tokugawa shōgunate.

The Hōjō regency

An ongoing theme in Japanese history is government characterised by a difference between official authority and real power. The imperial family had experienced this for centuries by the time of the Kamakura *bakufu* and Yoritomo continued the practice. After Yoritomo died in 1199, the Hōjō family came to act as regents for his successors, an ironic twist given that the Hōjōs were descendants of the Taira family, Yoritomo's early enemies. For various reasons Yoritomo's heirs were not strong enough to exercise the power of the shōgunate in those chaotic times. Hence, there developed a situation where there was real power (the Hōjō regent) behind official power (the *shōgun*) behind imperial authority (the emperor). Family relationships muddied the waters further, with the Hōjō regent Yoshitoki (1162–1224) being the brother of Masako (1156–1225) who was the widow of Yoritomo. It is generally accepted that Masako was the real power in the *bakufu*, so one could add a fourth behind-the-scenes power at this point. She had become a nun (*ama*) after Yoritomo's death, and was widely known as the *ama-shōgun*.[2] Government at this time was astonishingly complicated, and it is a reflection of the ability of the regents and the personal loyalty that they commanded that it worked as well as it did. The governing system also points to the phenomenon of *kuromaku* ('black curtain'), referring to the power-brokers that operate invisibly behind the scenes, a practice well-established early in Japanese history and which continues today.

In spite of Yoshitoki's questionable hold on power, in 1221 the Emperor Go-Toba (1180–1239) targeted him in a bid to regain imperial power. At issue in this first major challenge to the authority of the *bakufu* was the right to allocate land, which was at the heart of the reciprocity aspect of feudalism. The resulting Jōkyū War (1221) saw the banishment of Go-Toba to the Oki Islands in the Sea of Japan and the cementing of the feudal system. Some 3000 *shōen* were confiscated from the losing side and distributed to faithful vassals of the *bakufu*, thereby reinforcing its authority, especially in the (often rebellious) central and western provinces. The conflict also meant that the imperial court came to be very closely watched and regulated by the *bakufu*.

Overall the next half century was a relatively peaceful one,

Dai Butsu, Kamakura.

in spite of ongoing intrigues among the elites. The Hōjō regents continued to rule well. A notable development was the first legal code of 1232 (the Joei Code), which set out practical rules for the behaviour of vassals, as well as regulations governing such things as land tenure and punishments for various crimes. This code was so well-constructed that it was incorporated into the legal system that endured until the end of feudalism in the late 1900s. These rules were for vassals only, however—the rest of the population continued to be governed either by customary law or remnants of the older, more general legal system (the Taihō Code).

The thirteenth century is also known for the beauty of its court poetry, and the *Shinkokinshū* (*New Collection of Poems Ancient and Modern*), published in 1205, is the outstanding example. Interestingly, Go-Toba did much of the editing and contributed 33 poems to the anthology.

Buddhism flourished, perhaps because of the widespread suffering of the people through civil disruptions as well as a number of natural disasters. The weakening of the court system also led to the more rapid spread of Buddhism to the common people. Its increasing importance is reflected in the creation of the huge bronze statue of Amida Buddha in Kamakura (the *Dai Butsu*), cast in 1252. The Kamakura period also saw the beginning of several new Buddhist groups, including the *Jōdo* ('Pure Land') and *Nichiren* sects. While these had widespread public appeal, given their relative simplicity and pragmatic characteristics, the refined Zen Buddhism that came to be practised primarily by samurai emphasised discipline and austerity, which closely fitted the warrior code.

A range of social practices that we identify with modern Japan have their origins in this period. The bath, for example, came into vogue then, and was often associated with treatment for illnesses. The tea ceremony was introduced, strongly influenced by the philosophy of Zen Buddhism. Along with tea from China came porcelain and Japan began to manufacture its own, of very high quality. Sword-making reached high levels of sophistication and formed a principal export to China. Overall this was a time of significant cultural advancement, and art and literature enjoyed the support of the feudal warriors, even though many had come from humble backgrounds and had little education.

This period is also famous for the Japanese resistance of the Mongols, who tried twice to invade the Japanese islands in the late 1200s. China had come under the sway of its northern tribes around the middle of the thirteenth century, and in 1268 Kublai Khan (grandson of the founder of the Mongol empire, Genghis Khan) sent the first of half a dozen envoys to Japan, demanding a show of submission. The *bakufu* chose to ignore the messages and/or beheaded the messengers, and in 1274 and again in 1281 Mongol invasion fleets arrived off the northwest coast of Kyushu. Both times Japanese defences held, though the fighting lasted for nearly two months in 1281, the Mongols showing up with a massive force of some 4400 ships and 140 000 troops. Both times, too, storms scattered the Mongol fleets, the second one being particularly severe—a typhoon. The Japanese called it a 'divine wind', or *kamikaze*, a term which called up the perceived divinity of the Japanese islands, and which was to resurface in the mid 1940s with the suicide pilots during the closing months of the Pacific War. Despite having saved Japan from the Mongol invasions, the Kamakura *bakufu* only lasted another half century. The major problem, strangely, related to the victories in the two battles, where costs had been high but there were no spoils of war with which faithful warriors could be compensated, and this led to grumbling in the ranks. Costs continued to mount because of the expenditure on defences in preparation for a third Mongol invasion (which never materialised). Added to this was a lack of leadership under the later Hōjō regents. Finally, the emperor of the early 1300s, Go-Daigo (1288–1339), attempted to wrest power from the *bakufu*, convincing several leading families to withdraw their support for the government. In 1333 a battle took place which saw the Ashikaga family (along with a few other powerful clans) switch sides from the *bakufu* to Go-Daigo at a critical juncture, leading to the defeat of the government. The last Hōjō regent, his family and some 800 retainers, were killed or committed suicide. The Kamakura period was at an end.

The Muromachi period (1336–1467)

The battle of 1333 had been fought, presumably, to restore the emperor to power but Go-Daigo's reign lasted less than three years. He tried to consolidate his postion by reintroducing the system under which all land belonged to the imperial family. By this time, however, the power of the *samurai* had grown too strong. The head of the Ashikaga family, Takauji (1305–58), defeated the emperor's forces in 1336, and set himself up as *shōgun* in 1338. His successors eventually established their administrative headquarters in an area of Kyoto called Muromachi, which gives its name to this period. Go-Daigo fled to the mountains near Kyoto and set up a rival government that contributed to the instability of the next half century.

Garden of the Ginkakuji (Silver Pavilion), Kyoto.

Loyalty at the time existed principally between each regional lord and his retainers rather than to the shōgunate, so power became increasingly diffused. This change was reinforced by the taxation system, with regional leaders keeping an increasingly large share. This naturally reduced the power of the central government and enhanced the capacity of regional lords to reward followers. The lack of income to the centre struck particularly hard at the old imperial court and a number of old aristocratic families slowly faded away. Even emperors were at risk of becoming impoverished, and there is a well-known story of one emperor having to sell samples of his calligraphy to pay his bills.

At the other end of the social scale the peasants, too, were becoming restive. The early 1400s saw both famine and plague. The peasants suffered under heavy tax and debt burdens, with commodities other than rice (e.g. sake) being subject to tax for the first time, along with services such as transportation. In 1428 the first armed peasant uprising took place.

Kyoto itself was attacked in 1443. These events indicate both the difficult circumstances under which the majority of Japanese lived and the increasing weakness of the *bakufu*. At the same time, it is important to remember that the peasants of the time were usually free—not the serfs of the Heian period. They often grouped together for protection and this gave them cooperative strength, a factor that was also evident in the insurrections.

The stresses of the time did not preclude advancement in cultural pursuits. The third *shōgun* of the Muromachi period, Yoshimitsu, was a strong patron of the arts, as were a number of his successors. An enduring example of 'high' art, as well as an indication of the affluence of the elites, is the *Kinkakuji* (Golden Pavilion) that Yoshimitsu had built on his estate near Kyoto. This building remains today as an example (though now a replica) of the creativity of the age. The *Ginkakuji* (Silver Pavilion), which is actually made of wood, was built nearly a century later on the other side of the city and illustrates the delicate, subtle and more austere taste of the Muromachi period, a characteristic that remains evident in Japanese culture today.

Nō theatre, which aims to create a sense of mystery in the telling of a story through abstract drama, also developed into a refined form, and most of the 240 classical plays now performed date from the fifteenth century. It remains today an element of Japanese 'high' culture. Added to this art form were landscape painting, refinements of the tea ceremony and flower arranging, and linked-verse poetry which hearkened back to the days of courtly sensitivity. Gardening, too, was raised to new heights, and included the creation of the famous *Ryōanji* ('Rock Garden') of Kyoto. Many gardens of this period were strongly influenced in their design by Zen Buddhist philosophy.

In 1467 tensions came to a head between two feudal lords in Kyoto, and Japan disintegrated into civil war. The *O'nin* War of 1467–77, over the succession of the *shōgun*, began what is known as the *Sengoku-Jidai*, the Age of Warring States, a century of conflict reminiscent of feudal Europe. The Ashikaga family became progressively weaker, with the last

*Daimyō's castle, Izu
Peninsula*

shōgun of this line stepping down in 1573. Japan became a
stronger feudal state, based on powerful lord–vassal relationships in the provinces.

The Sengoku period—the Age of Warring States (1467–1568)

The Sengoku period was a chaotic time of struggles for power
within and between feudal families. Relatively small cohesive
units emerged within the larger ones controlled earlier by the
shugo (though sometimes these new units were similar in size
to the old provinces), and it was the leaders of these areas
who became the feudal lords, or *daimyō*, of the next four
centuries. Some were from old families while others were from

lower ranks who had managed to overthrow the failing *shugo*. *Samurai* swore allegiance to a particular *daimyō* and in return were granted fiefs, in which each samurai had control over both land and people. The old *shōen* system of estates disappeared, along with many other remnants of the centralised Japanese state.

Many *daimyō* built castles around which grew up commercial activities, similar to urban developments in mediaeval Europe, which facilitated economic activity. These castle-towns were regulated by new 'house laws' which set out the rights and responsibilities of those who served the *daimyō*, the emphasis remaining on a highly personal connection between lord and retainer, with vassal loyalty at the centre. Not all vassals were loyal, however, and betrayal was commonplace in struggles for power. To counter this to some degree, the old practice of a family or village having mutual responsibility for its members was reinforced.

Given the loyalties within each feudal unit, and the anarchic character of the times, it is not surprising that fierce fighting between rival *daimyō* was endemic. At the same time Buddhist monasteries and their lands came to be protected by warrior-monks, so we see the emergence of an additional type of regional authority. It was an age when success or failure depended on one's military power, and this also gave rise to much larger armies of which foot soldiers were the mainstay rather than (relatively expensive) mounted warriors.

There was significant growth in the economy despite the chaos of the time. Indeed, because survival depended on military power, which in turn relied on income, there was great incentive to promote economic expansion. New types of rice, double-cropping and improvements in agricultural techniques led to much higher output. More land was brought under cultivation. Markets flourished and a rudimentary money economy developed. Both domestic commerce and trade with China and Korea grew (though so did Japanese piracy along the mainland coast). Japan exported such items as swords, copper and sulphur, which created some modest industries. Ports developed to handle the cargo—especially notable here

Christianity has left its mark on the Japanese landscape.

was the growth of the town of Sakai (present-day Osaka) as a type of free city (not under the control of a particular *daimyō*) run by merchants. Its strong commercial character is still evident today.

To protect themselves from civil strife and the often arbitrary taxes of different *daimyō*, merchants combined to form *za*. These were an early form of guild based on economic activity (carpentry, sake-brewing and the like), and merchants paid dues in return for protection by powerful *daimyō*, shrines or temples. Ultimately the *daimyō* came to control the *za*; the tendency for government to closely regulate economic activity, and to use it for political ends, has remained characteristic of Japan.

Essentially the Muromachi period was one of transition, from the old centralised system to a system of feudalism in which power was regionally based. Elements of both systems were apparent throughout the period, but progressively Japan moved towards a comprehensive feudal state.

The Momoyama period (1573–1603)[3]

The century of conflict, or the Age of Warring States, was terribly wasteful of money and lives, and it left Japan broken up into numerous, mostly small, principalities. A divided country is fundamentally a weak one, and into this scene stepped the first of three great leaders, Oda Nobunaga (1534–82). He was followed by his contemporaries Toyotomi Hideyoshi (1536–98) and Tokugawa Ieyasu (1542–1616). Each brought to bear different characteristics and talents, and the end result was the unification of Japan under strong feudal leadership.

There are numerous stories and sayings about these three famous men. One saying has it that Nobunaga mixed the dough, Hideyoshi baked the cake and Ieyasu ate it, indicating the sequential roles they played.[4] Another story has the three men confronted by a bird which would not sing. Nobunaga is supposed to have responded by saying, 'I'll kill it if it doesn't sing.' Hideyoshi said, 'I'll persuade it to sing', and Ieyasu added, 'I'll wait until it sings.' This vignette is said to demonstrate their different characters—impulsive, self-confident and patient.

The story of this period is one of careful planning, hidden deals, self-interest, bold action and, of course, massive bloodshed. Nobunaga, a particularly capable and ambitious *daimyō* from central Japan, was a brilliant tactician and a ruthless adversary. In a cruel age he was particularly merciless, murdering family members, burning thousands of defeated enemies and their families alive and butchering troublesome Buddhist priests. His rather pointed and appropriate motto was 'Rule the Empire by Force'.

Two foreign imports in this period were to have an enormous impact on the way in which Japan developed. One was Christianity, the other modern weapons. Western contact had begun in 1543, when three Portuguese traders were blown ashore by a storm onto an island in southern Kyushu. Christianity and weapons were closely connected, since trade occurred primarily where Christianity was allowed to be practised. The *daimyō* were very competitive, and some accepted Christianity simply to secure trade, especially in weapons. Muskets were adopted quickly, and several *daimyō* began to manufacture them. By 1575 Nobunaga was able to field musketeers carrying smooth-bore weapons at the Battle of Okehazama (near Nagoya), where they gave him a crucial edge.

Nobunaga had taken the first step in unifying Japan. He followed up with a number of administrative changes. Trade between different *daimyō*-controlled areas, for example, was made easier through the abolition of customs duties. More roads were built. Christianity was encouraged to balance the power of the Buddhist sects. Weapons were confiscated from the peasants. Finally, a land survey was undertaken to determine the contents of Nobunaga's domain. Despite Nobunaga's brilliance, however, less than half of Japan's provinces were under his control by 1582, with powerful *daimyō* remaining in the outer provinces. In that year, at age 49, he was murdered by one of his officers and Hideyoshi became embroiled in the struggle for succession between other officers and Nobunaga's sons. When he emerged victorious he carried Nobunaga's plans forward.

Hideyoshi, like Nobunaga, had personal characteristics that allowed him to flourish in difficult times. Reportedly very small and ugly (Nobunaga called him 'Monkey'), he was a self-made man, a peasant foot-soldier's son who rose through the ranks to become one of Nobunaga's most capable generals. Perhaps most importantly, Hideyoshi was known as a brilliant leader, able to win friends and forge alliances to avoid needless bloodshed, yet he could fight ruthlessly when necessary, and the story of his life is principally one of conflict. He continued the old policy of redistributing the fiefs of defeated enemies to faithful followers, in part so they could keep an eye on potential rivals. This was necessary given the perennial problem of controlling both the regional *daimyō* and the powerful ones close by, like Tokugawa Ieyasu. Sending troublesome vassals to remote areas cut them off from their original bases of power, and they were less likely to scheme against Hideyoshi. The technique became so commonplace it was given the name *kunigae*, or 'province-changing'.

Hideyoshi also began a number of practices (or continued those of Nobunaga) that were later used by Tokugawa Ieyasu to consolidate his power. One was to confiscate swords so only *samurai* had access to them. This move helped substantially to reduce peasant uprisings. At the other end of the social spectrum Hideyoshi made use of the hostage system, whereby regional *daimyō* had to leave family members under his 'protection' while they were away visiting their fiefs. He also made social mobility difficult—it was easier to control people when they could not change their vocations or places of residence. A rigid class system was put into place which was to severely curtail upward mobility until the late nineteenth century. Added to this was a continuation of the policy of collective responsibility to reduce the possibility of rebellion. A comprehensive land survey was carried out. All of these measures were further amplified under Ieyasu's rule, and to this day have left a strong cultural imprint on Japanese society.

By 1591 Hideyoshi finally had all of feudal Japan under his nominal control, the first time Japan had been at peace in more than a century. He never sought the title *shōgun*, partly because he had left alive the last of the Ashikaga shōguns, Yoshiaki, and partly because of his humble beginnings. Instead he took the title *kanpaku* ('civil dictator') and later *taikō* ('retired regent'). He continued the policy of governing through the authority of the emperor, administratively consolidating his gains and building a number of strategically located castles, the most impressive of which is in Osaka.

Hideyoshi needed revenue for his vassals and to support his army. He therefore placed key trading cities, such as Osaka and Nagasaki, under his direct control. He encouraged international trade, securing substantial income from this as well as through control of gold and silver mines. He strengthened government control over economic activity begun in the Age of Warring States.

Hideyoshi used his wealth to send armies to invade China and Korea in the 1590s. The reasons for this remain a point of debate among historians. He may have wanted to extend his power, or to realise a dream of humbling an arrogant China. Some scholars argue that he wanted to kill off the soldiers of troublesome *daimyō*. Others believe that he needed more land to distribute to faithful followers. In any event, the result was the weakening of the government of China and substantial destruction of parts of Korea, but the attempt at empire ultimately failed. It also poisoned relations between Korea and Japan, accounting in part for the enmity that exists between the two countries today.[5]

Of concern to Hideyoshi was the growing popularity of Christianity, first spread by Jesuits under the leadership of Francis Xavier, who arrived in Japan in 1549, and later by Franciscan and Dominican friars. It is difficult to accurately estimate the number of converts, but some put the figure at 300 000 out of a population of 15–20 million. If this is reasonably accurate it would make the proportion of Christians about 2 per cent, compared to less than 1 per cent today. Hideyoshi's initial response was to follow Nobunaga's policy of welcoming Christianity (with the practical agenda of increasing trade—it was apparent that Nobunaga was a strong opponent of organised religion), but he distrusted the power of a religion that was not closely connected to Japanese tradition and hence threatened his legitimacy. Christianity was also the religion of technologically advanced foreigners, and he must have been concerned with the possibility of pros-elytisation being followed by colonisation. At the same time, missionaries did provide a window on the outside world, and were connected to trade with China as well as Europe—and the weapons trade was especially important. Since a number of Hideyoshi's generals were Christians, to appear to welcome Christianity was also a useful technique for avoiding the formation of a cabal that might oppose him. Christianity was a useful counterweight, too, against the power of the Buddhist clergy. These pros and cons are reflected in Hideyoshi's erratic policy towards Christianity, at times harsh (torturing and killing of Christians and friars) followed by periods when tough new edicts were promulgated but not enforced.

This early contact with the West had other implications. Pumpkins and corn, potatoes and sweet potatoes were introduced. Tobacco was first planted in 1600, beginning a blight that still plagues Japan today. Cotton, too, arrived. Portuguese words connected to these consumables made their way into the Japanese lexicon as well, including *pan* for bread and *tenpura*, a popular dish of battered and fried vegetables and seafood.

Hideyoshi became a father very late in life when one of his concubines bore him a son he named Hideyori. Worried that his heir would be eliminated (which was partly the reason behind the severe policies of his later rule), he created a five-member Council of Regents. His plan was to have the council govern until Hideyori came of age, on the assumption that the opposing forces within the council would preclude any one member taking over.[6]

Given the tradition of centuries of scheming and treachery among leaders vying for power, however, it comes as no surprise that the structure Hideyoshi left in place did not last long after his death in 1598. In October 1600 Ieyasu Tokugawa was victorious in a battle at Sekigahara against a coalition led by Ishida Mitsunari, another member of the Council of Regents (which generally supported Hideyoshi's heir). Although the battle was decisive in the struggle, and Ieyasu secured the title of *shōgun* in 1603, the conflict only completely ended in 1615 with the deaths of Hideyori and other family members, and the establishment of the Tokugawa shōgunate in Edo, present-day Tokyo, on a site dominating the rich Kanto Plain.

The Tokugawa shōgunate (1603–1868)

Ieyasu Tokugawa was of the Minamoto family, a descendant of the founder of the Kamakura *bakufu*, Minamoto no

Yoritomo, and thus had the lineage required to take the title *shōgun*.[7] He abdicated two years later, however, and was replaced by his 26-year-old son, Hidetada (r. 1605–23), but continued to formulate policies behind the scenes, and to strengthen the family's hold on power. The practice of leaving the imperial family intact but politically powerless was continued, and theoretically the *shōgun* ruled at the pleasure of the emperor. In reality the emperor was primarily occupied with symbolic ceremonies and spiritual issues, and had no active part in running the country.

Ieyasu and his successors, especially Hidetada and the next *shōgun*, Iemitsu (r. 1623–51), were to set in place policies that have left an indelible mark on Japanese society. The guiding principle of the Tokugawa leaders was maintaining control, a reaction to a century of civil war and their own tenuous hold on power. Their policies were implemented out of fear—fear of provincial lords, unruly peasants, organised religion, foreigners and, naturally, each other.

Ieyasu initially used the 'province-changing' technique to remove unreliable *daimyō* from their home bases and also placed loyal followers on fiefs located between his former opponents. Added to this he instituted the *buke-sho-hatto* ('laws for military houses') which set out a variety of rules for the *daimyō*, from the need to report on castle repairs to the right of the *shōgun* to approve their marriages. A well-developed network of informants was established and government officials frequently inspected fiefs. Everyone was watched. The number of *samurai* that the *daimyō* were allowed to have was fixed. The *sankin-kōtai* (literally 'alternate attendance'), or hostage system, continued to be used to control provincial *daimyō*. The usual practice was for their families to remain permanently in Edo while the *daimyō* themselves had to spend four months every year or every second year in the capital. Linked to this practice, since a poor person is easier to control than one with money, the *daimyō* were also forced to maintain a second (frequently elaborate) residence in Edo, which often proved to be very expensive.

Shintō shrine, Nikko, burial place of Ieyasu Tokugawa.

Curiously, regular taxation was not used, though special levies were made from time to time.

Daimyō were divided into groups, depending on their closeness to the Tokugawa line and their previous loyalty to Ieyasu. The *shinpan*, or 'collateral *daimyō*', were related to the Tokugawa family, and provided shōguns when the main family line was unable to do so. *Bakufu* officials were mostly drawn from the *fudai*, or 'house *daimyō*'—those from families who had been vassals of Ieyasu prior to 1600—while the offspring of Ieyasu's opponents (*tozama*, or 'outside houses') were barred from government posts. Of the 250–300 *daimyō* of the early seventeenth century, about 90 were *tozama*.

The government that developed was a composite type, sometimes referred to as 'centralised feudalism', or *baku-han*. *Baku* came from *bakufu* and *han* ('domain') from the houses (landholdings) of the *daimyō*. In other words, it recognised the fact that there were multiple centres of power in the country and yet tried to manage and control them. As each *han* generally functioned as an independent unit, few bureau-cratic mechanisms evolved at the national level, but instead did so within each *han*. This was reinforced by the system of land distribution, where the Tokugawa family and loyal vassals held about 60 per cent of the land in the country while *tozama* houses, mostly located in Tohoku, Shikoku and Kyushu, jointly held about 40 per cent. Ieyasu was apparently very cautious in his dealings with these powerful regional families, including the well-known Shimazu clan in Satsuma (present-day Kagoshima prefecture), the Chōshū *han* (western Honshu), the Hizen *han* (Nagasaki area) and the Tosa *han* (Shikoku Island), though he killed the Tosa leaders. Generally speaking, Ieyasu did not want to cause the *tozama* such offence that they would create long-term problems, and this was especially the case in the early years of his leadership when his position was not yet secure. The outer regions were difficult to control, and leaving the existing power structure in place (with its web of formal and informal linkages), while controlling the leaders, was a sensible solution to a difficult problem.

Japan came to have the characteristics of a police state, begun by Ieyasu and, after his death by illness in 1616, consolidated by his successors. Fear drove the Tokugawa leadership to ever greater regulatory heights. Travel was con-strained with the need to secure permits, and roads had numerous checkpoints. Minute details of people's lives were regulated, including the clothing they could wear, appropriate gifts, the food people of different classes could eat, and even housing design. A limit was set on the size of ships that could be built. A curfew system was put in place. Most bridges were destroyed so that the movement of people could be controlled.

Punishments for criminal activities, though more clearly set out, regulated and consistently applied than previously, were often severe. Torture and execution were common, even for relatively minor offences such as petty theft (though heavy punishments were also the norm in the West at this time). Mutual (group) responsibility also meant that family and friends might be killed along with the offender. This is un-doubtedly one source of the high level of social responsibility (including a very low crime rate) that continues in Japan today. Some scholars also point to this period as being important in the development of the concepts of *honne* and *tatamae*, literally 'inner reality' and 'outward appearance'. Under the system of mutual responsibility it was important for groups (such as villages) to preserve the appearance of harmony at all costs, even if there were problems beneath the surface. This behaviour eventually developed into a type of etiquette in which conflict is avoided by never being blunt or direct, and this remains a marked characteristic of Japanese society.

Social mobility was highly restricted as another means of social control. A caste-like class system developed, comprising the four classes of *daimyō/samurai*, peasants, artisans and merchants (in descending order of importance). There was little movement between classes though it did occur occasionally. There were also 'outcast' groups, the *eta* (those who worked with dead animals and made leather goods) and the *hinin* ('non-people', outcasts through occupation, including beggars, guards in jails, executioners, police informants and road cleaners). These groups are today called *burakumin* and continue to fight for equal treatment.

It was primarily fear on the part of the Tokugawa leadership that led to the closing of Japan to the outside world (*sakoku*, or 'national seclusion'), similar to the path followed by Korea at the time. In part this was done to stop regional *daimyō* from becoming too powerful through international trade. Indeed, Japan had well-established trading networks by this time, with Western countries as well as Asia. Some 100 000 Japanese living abroad, mostly in Southeast Asia, formed networks similar to those fashioned by the overseas Chinese today. A second reason for closing Japan was religion—a reaction to the machinations of foreign priests and the concern first voiced by Hideyoshi that Christians (especially priests from Spain and Portugal) would undermine the existing power structure and perhaps pave the way for foreign control of parts of Japan. A number of powerful *daimyō* had become Christians, a further source of concern. A series of edicts against Christians was set out in the early seventeenth century. Then, in 1637, there was a revolt at

Shimabara (east of Nagasaki) by some 37 000 peasants, most of whom were Christians. Although the primary reason for the revolt was the peasants' dismal economic circumstances, the uniting force of Christianity worried the *shōgun*, and ultimately nearly all who took part in the revolt were killed. Thereafter Christianity was effectively banned. In a sense the reaction to this religion was symbolic of the reasoning behind closing Japan—all foreign influences were dangerous, and could be used by anti-Tokugawa forces to create civil disruption. Control meant isolation.

The result was that foreigners were permanently ejected from Japan, and the Japanese themselves were not allowed in or out of the country, on pain of death. The building of ocean-going ships was prohibited. Trade with Europe, however, continued, albeit limited to annual contact with the Dutch on Dejima Island in Nagasaki Harbour. Much greater trade continued with China, with about 26 ships arriving in Nagasaki each year, compared with the single Dutch ship. There was also a good political relationship with Korea, though this was not important commercially. Thus, while Japan was officially closed, contact with the outside world did continue to a degree.

For the most part the two centuries following the closing of Japan were peaceful ones. As had happened during previous periods of relative isolation, such as the late Heian period, particular Japanese cultural characteristics came to the fore. From this time we see even greater emphasis put on group identification, respect for authority and a strong sense of loyalty. Confucianism (especially Neo-Confucianism) became a very powerful philosophy—indeed the ideology underlying the Japanese state. A greater sense of national identity emerged. Many schools were established for the debate of various philosophies, however, and the principles of science and technology (including those of Robert Boyle and Isaac Newton) filtered through from the foreign contacts in Nagasaki. In the early eighteenth century the ban was lifted on foreign books, provided they were not concerned with Christianity.

So, although Japan was closed this meant neither cultural stagnation nor complete isolation. During this period of peace, strangely enough, the virtues of the *samurai* came to be polished, and this has left a legacy of appreciation of characteristics such as duty, loyalty, discipline and sacrifice. The 'way of the warrior', or *bushidō*, came to be seen as a philosophy of moral behaviour. Loyalty to one's lord was the centrepoint, based on Neo-Confucian ethics. A famous story which exemplifies *bushidō* virtues is 'The Forty-Seven *Rōnin*', which tells of the 'masterless *samurai*' who took revenge on an official who had been responsible for the death of their master. Their actions and subsequent deaths are still seen in Japan as a reflection of traditional *samurai* values.

The earlier part of the Tokugawa period was not only peaceful but a time of substantial economic expansion. In part this was because the burdens of expenditure placed on the *daimyō* to keep them relatively malleable generated economic activity in the urban centres. This in turn led to pressure on the agricultural system upon which the *daimyō* depended for their wealth, and the result was a significant jump in agricultural output through improved agricultural practices, the use of better technology and the eventual doubling of the area of land under cultivation. The introduction of a money economy, initially necessary for the *daimyō* to convert agricultural produce to currency to support their Edo residences, also made the agricultural system much more efficient.

The population remained reasonably stable (at about 30 million by the end of the period), partly because of periodic famines in the countryside and partly because, according to *bakufu* law, only the first son could marry and have children (unless a younger son married the first daughter of a family without sons, thereby becoming part of a different family and taking a new name). This reduced conflict over rights to land, as did the law that land could not be bought or sold, and slowed population growth.

A relatively small population combined with economic growth led to a general rise in the standard of living, though mostly in urban areas. Edo had a population of more than a

Maiko—trainee geisha, Gion district of Kyoto.

million by the nineteenth century—probably the largest city in the world at the time. Educational levels were perhaps the highest in the world, with a literacy rate of about 30 per cent (45 per cent for men and 15 per cent for women), a result of the expansion of both private and religious (temple) schools.

The merchant class also grew. The upper class looked down on trade, so usually did not become involved in it, though some *samurai* families became merchants (such as the family behind Mitsubishi). As commercial activities were perceived as unimportant, they were not taxed heavily; consequently, some urban merchants amassed great fortunes through activities such as sake-brewing, pawnbroking, shipping and selling dry goods. The Mitsui family, for example, started off selling kimono cloth in Ise in the early seventeenth century, and today is one of the world's leading commercial firms. In the late 1600s the Sumitomo family began mining copper and silver. Some merchants also went into money-lending (Mitsui is one example). Indeed, through this activity they often became the creditors (and, therefore, sometimes the controllers) of the *samurai*, since the latter remained on fixed incomes. This led eventually to a serious imbalance in the power structure.

One famous result of the growth of the affluent urban merchant class was the creation of pleasure quarters in the cities, the so-called 'floating world' where men of various classes could shed their worldly cares. The best known was probably the Yoshiwara district of Edo. It was often in adjoining areas that new types of art, theatre, music and literature developed.[8] The woodblock print has its origins during the Tokugawa period, and the *ukiyo-e*, or 'pictures of the floating world' (often sexually explicit), are especially well known. *Kabuki* theatre, too, started at this time. It was seen as being a corrupting influence on women (most of the female actors were prostitutes) and so the *bakufu* banned them from participation, the result being that even today all *kabuki* actors are men. It was during this time that *geisha*, or female entertainers, made their debut, a reflection of the overt sexuality of the period. The poet Matsuo Bashō (1644–94) became famous for the type of short poem known as *haiku*. All these artistic developments reflect the stresses between a dynamic commercial class and a traditional, culture-bound leadership.

Over time the rigid structure that the Tokugawas had put in place began to crack, for a number of reasons. Through the eighteenth and nineteenth centuries, the introduction of a money economy at the village level, as well as the increase in cash crops (e.g. cotton, tea, sugarcane, tobacco), meant that some peasants prospered more than others. Headmen in particular tended to accumulate wealth. In time they began to lend money to poorer peasants to tide them over difficult times, and this led to the development of a class called *jinushi*, or 'usurer-landlords'. They were able to invest their profits in various commercial activities, such as textile-making and the processing of foodstuffs, which further increased their wealth. This naturally exacerbated inequalities at the village level, and ultimately led to conflict in the countryside.

It is difficult for a country to remain economically viable in isolation. The same argument put forward by the proponents of globalisation in the twenty-first century can be applied to Japan in the Tokugawa period. Isolation inhibits the development of effective production systems and the generation of wealth through the production of specialised goods. For a while the *sankin-kōtai* system forced a type of wealth generation and redistribution but over time it was not enough to sustain economic development. Economic problems were at the core of the Tokugawa government's eventual collapse. The feudal system's stress on stability led ultimately to a lack of vitality, and could not be sustained. The economic and political systems had become seriously out of step, with many wealthy citizens now in the bottom, merchant class. The system where elites' income was tied to agricultural production meant that when agricultural output fell (due to both periodic famines and frequent riots in the countryside) so too did the incomes of the *daimyō* and the *samurai*, and this income fluctuation meant that many *samurai* in particular found themselves in dire financial straits. These financial problems led to a growing discontent with the leadership of the country. At the same time the *samurai*, who comprised a relatively large 5–7 per cent of the population, and who staffed the bloated and overly complex *han* bureaucracies, were on balance a burden on the economy. Bureaucratic positions became hereditary, talent being replaced by lineage.

The *bakufu* had its own economic problems, running a deficit from around the beginning of the nineteenth century. Attempts to deal with the problems included forced loans, a reduction in the number of officials employed by the *bakufu* and currency depreciation, which occurred on nineteen occasions between 1819 and 1837. Fundamentally, however, the rigid political economy of the seventeenth century had become largely irrelevant. Economic problems led to political ones, and the government became progressively weaker in the early nineteenth century.

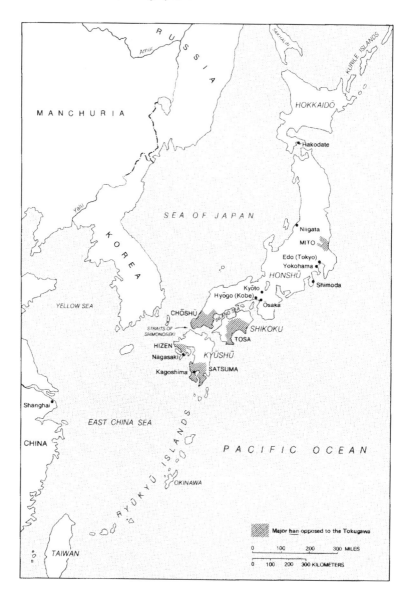

Japan on the eve of the Meiji Restoration.

Into this scene in 1853 sailed Commodore Matthew C. Perry of the United States Navy. He was not the first foreigner to arrive in Japan in the nineteenth century—the Russians and the British had been there before—nor even the first American, but his visit coincided with domestic problems coming to a head. He was sent by President Fillmore to establish proper treatment for shipwrecked American sailors, ensure supplies for visiting vessels (especially whaling ships) and open ports to trade. With steam engines coming into production coal was needed, and Japan was a convenient refuelling stop on the San Francisco to Shanghai route. The Industrial Revolution in the West was also creating a need for new markets, and a closed Japan was not a country where profits could be made.

Perry's 'black ships' created quite a stir in Edo Bay—both for their steampower and their weaponry. His visit brought home dramatically to the Japanese that they were at the mercy of the technologically more advanced countries of the West, particularly when Perry defied the *shōgun* and his guns and sailed directly into the bay. The striking power of the foreigner even led to a call in Japan for temple bells to be melted down to make guns. Perry sailed away after presenting his letter of demand, making it clear that he expected a positive response when he returned in a year. Thus, in 1854, the Treaty of Kanagawa was signed, which gave in to the principal American demands; this was followed by commercial treaties with Britain, France, Holland and Russia. Gunboat diplomacy had carried the day.

Reaction in Japan to the foreign incursion was, naturally, mixed. Some favoured closer contact with the West while the views of others were encapsulated in the slogan *sonnō-jōi*, meaning 'honour the emperor—expel the barbarians'. In between were more cautious yet nationalistic groups, their attitude exemplified by a slogan meaning 'open the country to expel the barbarians'. These groups advocated learning as much as possible about Western science and especially military technology, and were instrumental in the opening in 1857 of the 'Institute for Investigation of Barbarian Books'. The need to know more about modern weapons was driven home to

Japan opens to the West.

the leaders of the Satsuma and Chōshū *han* in particular, when both lost in battles with the British.

Various groups in Japan would either profit from, or be disadvantaged by, closer contact with the outside world, so there was naturally significant self-interest in positions taken at the time. Also, although trade opportunities hinted at the possibilities of greater wealth, events in China must have worried Japanese leaders as various European countries carved off pieces of that country. Britain in particular was engaging in the opium trade that not only spread drug addiction in China but also led to the humiliating treaties that awarded it Hong Kong and associated territories. Indeed, for a time the UK supported the Satsuma and Chōshū *han* (which formed close relationships with the British after their losses in battle) while the French backed the *bakufu*. The divide-and-rule approach of the Western powers brought Japan close to suffering the same fate as China. Adding to this turbulent time was the arrival of numerous Western traders who tended to look down upon the 'backward' Japanese. Foreigners also enjoyed the right of extra-territoriality, that is, when they broke the law they were tried by their own consuls under their own laws rather than by Japanese authorities. Not only did this damage the prestige of the Japanese government, it also carried with it an aura of condescension—that Japanese were in some way uncivilised. The reaction to this was the addition of Japanese nationalism, including the extremist variety, to the emotional mixture.

Foreign trade caused other problems. The *bakufu*'s monetary system worked reasonably well in isolation but not as part of an international trading system, since the Japanese currency was not sufficiently backed by gold reserves. This problem, coupled with the rapid increase in demand for foreign goods, led to a dramatic rise in inflation. The price of rice, for example, increased fourfold between 1853 and 1869, causing substantial hardship. Worse, the *bakufu* seemed incapable of implementing policies which would resolve the economic problems it faced.

The period 1853–68 was a time of confusion and instability. Both Japanese leaders and foreigners were assassinated as the conflict between the various groups escalated. Alliances shifted, and different Western countries backed different groups. The Satsuma and Chōshū clans, traditional enemies of the Tokugawas, were principals in the fray. The *bakufu* tried different policies but was unable to navigate the shifting currents. There are many details of political manoeuvring during this time, but the end result was that the fifteenth Tokugawa *shōgun*, Yoshinobu (1837–1913), resigned and was banished to his lands at Mito, northeast of Tokyo. He had put the unity of Japan before his own personal position, as did most of the other principal leaders of the time. After some skirmishes and outright battles between his followers and their rivals, the Tokugawa period, and along with it some 700 years of *shōgun* rule, came to an end. Japan was about to enter the modern world.

4
MODERNISATION AND IMPERIALISM

THE PERIOD 1868 TO 1937, with the exception of the years of the Pacific War, is perhaps the most tumultuous era in Japan's history. In the span of one person's lifetime virtually every aspect of society underwent profound change—government, legal codes, class and economic structures, education, foreign relations and dress—as part of the shift from feudal authoritarianism to a form of constitutional democracy, from isolation to one of the most powerful countries in the world. The changes also unleashed a fierce nationalism, which in turn fed the fires of imperialism. Ultimately this led to war—with China, Russia and eventually the Western Allies. From the end of isolation to consolidation as a world power took less than 70 years.

The Meiji restoration (1868–1912)

Japan was faced with enormous difficulties in 1868. The government of some 250 years had been overthrown. Having been forced to open up by foreign powers, it was apparent to the Japanese elites that the country was technologically backward and militarily weak—vulnerable to the same forces of colonisation that had already infected much of Asia. Japan had little industry, poor defence capability and in feudalism a seriously outmoded system of social organisation. Added to this were enormous divisions between clans, classes and geographical regions, in attitudes towards foreigners and the ideas about the course the country should now chart.

The immediate goal was to make Japan strong, in order to resist foreign pressure. The rallying cry was *fukoku-kyōhei* ('rich country, strong army'). Ironically, while fear of internal rivals had driven the policies of the Tokugawas, it was fear of foreigners, even xenophobia, that now drove the country to unite. This is understandable, given that for more than two centuries distrust and rejection of foreigners was a key government policy. Descent into anarchy would most likely have meant direct foreign involvement in the government of Japan, and the overriding goal of the Japanese leadership was to maintain independence and, indeed, to have the country take its rightful place with other leading powers as quickly as possible. The last Tokugawa *shōgun* therefore stood down with grace and an appeal to national unity. To achieve this a rallying point for the disparate groups was needed, and found in the 'restoration' of the authority of the emperor, an authority not enjoyed for a thousand years. The person on whom this burden fell was Mutsuhito (1852–1912), who chose the period name Meiji, meaning 'Enlightened Rule'. The main feature of the Meiji restoration was a return to centralised rule from a diffuse feudal state, and a consequent growth in national identity as a mechanism for holding the country together during a time of massive social and economic change.

The main supporters of the emperor were primarily middle and lower ranking *samurai* who had helped overthrow the Tokugawa *bakufu*. Those from the Satsuma and Chōshū *han* in particular gained substantial power. They had for years understood the need for change, while seeing their own position steadily erode, but had been frustrated in their attempts at reform by the conservative forces at the top levels of government. No one asked the peasants what they thought, even though they made up about 90 per cent of the population

Emperor's palace, Tokyo.

of the time. It was clear they had a poor deal, with very hard work expected, high levels of taxation and little personal freedom, and they often rebelled against changes that worked to their disadvantage. The new policies were again implemented from the top down, one of the enduring themes of Japanese history.

In June 1868 a new government was established. It was based on the American model, with a separation of powers (to placate those who were calling for democratic reform), but with a more highly centralised focus. The emperor (a youth of just sixteen) was advised and aided by a Council of State (*Dajōkan*). The bureaucracy was staffed at the upper levels by *daimyō* and members of the imperial family, but many positions were occupied by young *samurai* who came to have considerable power in shaping the new Japan. Change was also signalled by the move the following year of the emperor and imperial house to Edo. The city was renamed Tokyo ('Eastern Capital'), and the emperor installed himself in the former castle of the *shōgun*, now the Imperial Palace.

Once the new government had been set up changes came quickly. One of the first was a decision on land ownership, whereby the major clans, followed by others, voluntarily gave their lands (and control of people) to the emperor, a dramatic gesture that underlined acceptance of the end of feudalism. Wealthier farmers were able to gain ownership of land, and to buy and sell rice, while poorer farmers often came to work for them. Although the change was by no means universally accepted at the time, by 1871 the Minister of Finance was able to announce that all fiefs had been abolished. In their place prefectures were established with governors (sometimes former *daimyō*) appointed by the government. State stipends replaced han revenue—the *daimyō* received 10 per cent of former revenues as personal income while *samurai* allowances were cut by half. These were, in 1876, changed to lump-sum payments and government bonds, which helped reduce the government's ongoing deficit at a time when the spending priority was on modernising the country's society and economy.

The *samurai*, too, had to surrender their individual rights for the greater good. In 1871 the government urged them to quit wearing their hair in topknots, reducing their visibly special status. Trousers replaced *hakama*, the skirt-like traditional pants worn by the male elites. In 1876 the *samurai* were forbidden to wear swords. Their martial role was also undercut by a move to a conscript army in 1873, following the disbanding the year before of *han*-based military forces. All Japanese citizens could be called up for three years of military duty followed by four years of reserve service.

With the initial reduction and eventual loss of their stipends, the nearly two million *samurai* also had to find jobs. Some continued in the bureaucracy where they had been a long-time presence. Others became entrepreneurs, occasionally enjoying outstanding success with the application of their martial ethics to the business scene, though most failed dismally. Still others became teachers, journalists and farmers, or found careers in the police force or the new military. Many others were unable to adjust and suffered poverty and humiliation at their loss of status.

In terms of foreign relations, associations with Western countries were mixed. Reformers soon came to realise that they needed Western help in order to industrialise rapidly, and one of the new mottos became 'catch up, overtake'. This did not preclude some radicals from periodically murdering foreign merchants and officials, but generally speaking the shift was from vehemently anti- to pro-foreigner in the early years of the restoration. Necessity, it seems, was at the heart of this policy.

Young Japanese were sent abroad in droves, particularly to the technologically advanced countries of the West. As early as the 1860s many of the more powerful *daimyō* had sent people overseas to learn about the outside world. The Iwakura Mission, for example, comprising nearly a hundred people and including a number of future Japanese leaders, spent the period 1871–73 in the USA and Europe. The mission included five women, who stayed abroad for more than a decade, substantially contributing to the development of women's education on their return. Foreign influences began to pervade Japan's social structure.

Education in particular was a focus for the reformers, given that it was the primary mechanism for facilitating nationalism. It was also a necessary underpinning for the new technology arriving in the country. In 1871 a new Ministry of Education was established, and in 1872 compulsory education was introduced. At first it was only for sixteen months, but by 1907 it was for six years, by which time attendance was near universal, putting Japan far in advance of many countries in the West at the time. The educational system was initially based on the French model and later incorporated American practices. German ideas emphasising duty to the state were added to the amalgam, all of this resting on a basis of traditional Japanese Confucianist beliefs. The latter was especially apparent in the 1890 'Imperial Rescript on Education', which set out the ideological basis of the new educational system. Its emphasis on such values as loyalty, duty, respect and obedience reflected the influence of former *samurai* in the Ministry of Education. This, coupled with the use of symbols such as the Japanese

Beer vending machines, a common sight in Japan today.

flag and patriotic songs, was effective in promoting national identity and, at its core, a respect for the emperor.

Universities, too, were created at a rapid rate. In 1877 Tokyo Imperial University (*Tōdai*) was established from an amalgamation of educational institutions from the Edo era, and many others followed in the late nineteenth century, including Kyoto, Waseda and Hitotsubashi. Fukuzawa Yukichi (1835–1901), the founder of Japan's first private university, the eminent Keio University in Tokyo, was particularly interested in the way in which foreign societies were organised and he even wrote best-sellers on the topic. Not for a thousand years had Japan been so massively exposed to foreign ideas and Japanese leaders had no qualms about utilising an early form of the contemporary 'world best practice' approach in their drive to modernise the country.

Western customs were taken on wholesale by ordinary Japanese citizens. Western-style clothes made significant inroads. Men's suits were called *sebiro*, the Japanese pronunciation of London's famed street of tailors, Savile Row, and bureaucrats were the first to wear them to the office. Women donned Western dresses complete with bustles. Western-style haircuts came into vogue. Western uniforms were adopted by schools and universities, and they are still visible on the streets of Japanese cities today.

Western literature made inroads, including works by Jules Verne and Daniel Defoe's *Robinson Crusoe*. Books which gave advice about how to cope with the widespread changes in the country were especially popular, such as Samuel Smiles' 1859 publication *Self-Help*. Associated with the flood of Western literature came an interest in learning Western languages. New medical practices were imported, principally from Germany, and even today many Japanese medical terms are of German origin. The Western calendar replaced the lunar one in 1873. A new transportation device, the *jinrikisha* ('human-powered vehicle'—later known in English as the rickshaw) made its debut in 1869 and subsequently spread throughout Asia. The electric grid was extended substantially under a joint venture with American Western Electric, the origin of today's Nippon Electric Company (NEC). The Tokyo Shibaura Electric company, which later became Toshiba, also came to the fore at this time, again connected with electrical generation. Baseball was introduced in 1873.

In the artistic world the scene was similar. In the early years of the Meiji restoration Western influence was a dominant factor in art, music and literature. At the same time, it should be noted, the West developed a fascination with Japanese art and architecture, so influence flowed in both directions. Even the Japanese diet began to change, with beer being produced for the first time in the 1870s and beef consumption growing significantly. Today's popular dish *sukiyaki* (similar to beef fondue) dates from this period. Some of the fascination with Western practices bordered on the absurd, however. There was some discussion among Japanese elites,

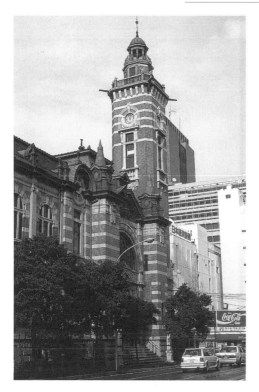

*Meiji-era Western
architecture, port of
Yokohama.*

for example, of replacing rice with bread as the staple carbo-
hydrate. The period was characterised by the impact of
Western practices throughout Japanese society, though urban
dwellers and the relatively wealthy had much greater exposure,
and a substantial cultural gap grew up between the cities and
the countryside.

As a result of both international influence and domestic
imperatives, the life style of many Japanese changed at breakneck pace. By 1882, for example, when the Bank of Japan
came into being, there were already more than 150 banks in
the country, often based on the American model. Banking
through the post office (another innovation) was also made
possible in order to utilise people's savings for national economic development; this has played a major role in Japan's
growth through to the present day.

The tremendous upsurge in transportation and communication technology, including the introduction of the railway and telegraph, had far-reaching implications not only for economic development but also for the daily life of Japanese citizens. Commuting came into being, and the problems of overcrowded transport associated with Japan today were already evident by the turn of the century. There was a virtual explosion in newspapers. The first English-language newspaper appeared in 1861 and ten years later the first Japanese daily, the *Yokohama Mainichi Shimbun*, went into circulation. These were often the vehicles of criticism of the government, and consequently the first laws controlling the press were enacted in 1875. By that time there were more than a hundred newspapers in circulation.

The class system of the Tokugawa period was altered, though a basic nobles-and-*samurai*/commoners division persisted. The *eta* and *hinin* 'outcast' categories were formally abolished and subsumed into the commoners class. Commoners were also legally allowed to take surnames from 1870. Restrictions on changing one's place of residence and occupation were lifted, a significant social shift from the Edo era.

It is not surprising that such massive change met with stiff resistance in some quarters. Even today, relatively minor policy shifts cause the government to come under severe criticism, and the country then was undergoing wholesale change. This resulted in a number of regional rebellions in the early 1870s. Opposition came to a head in 1877, however, with the Satsuma rebellion, when more than 40 000 troops battled the Japanese government. The rebellion was led by Saigō Takamori (1827–77), who had played a key role in the overthrow of the Tokugawa shōgunate and enjoyed a lofty reputation in Japan at the time. Such resistance was doomed, however, and government forces overcame the rebels later that year. This last civil conflict in Japan ended with the suicide of Saigō and a widespread acceptance of the inevitability of the new Japan.

Japan's transformation, however, did not mean a complete break from the past—a near impossibility in any case. The country's symbolic core remained the emperor, as the embodiment of Japanese tradition. In a deliberate move to foster a connection between the bulk of the population and the emperor, he was removed from his previously secluded existence and brought into contact with elites around the country. It was important to the stability of the government and its modernisation program that there was seen to be imperial support for the new social and economic policies. The leadership also wished to retain 'the spirit of the old Japan'. The rallying call was 'Japanese spirit, Western learning', indicating a desire to maintain fundamental cultural characteristics such as duty, obedience, loyalty and discipline, though it may be argued that these ideals reflected the wishes of the upper class rather than the bulk of the population. In any event, they were characteristics which met the needs of the reformers admirably. Despite the popularity of their ideas, Westerners were often kept at some distance. As early as 1873, for example, a law prohibiting foreign ownership of land was passed.

Political parties emerged at this time, a development that must have seemed outlandish to many Japanese. They represented a radical departure from the tradition of authoritarian rule, which had been particularly harsh in the preceding two centuries. Along with other things Western came philosophies of representative government. The works of the English political scientist and philosopher, John Stuart Mill, and the French writer and philosopher, Jean-Jacques Rousseau, were particularly in vogue, and their ideas spread rapidly, in step with the dramatic increase in literacy levels under the new mass education system.

The early Meiji leaders recognised the need for a legitimate outlet for the new ideas circulating at the time, even though their primary goal was to harness and control the populace during the drive to modernise. In the early stages, however, the call for democracy came from the relatively small middle class. Groups with different interests naturally gravitated toward each other, and the two earliest parties reflected this division. The *Jiyūtō* (Liberal Party) represented the centre-left, taking many of its ideas from French liberal doctrines. It gained support from some samurai and journalists but mostly from wealthier farmers in the countryside. The *Kaishintō* (Progressive Party) appealed to the centre-right, its beliefs loosely based on British ideas of constitutional democracy. Support came mainly from new capitalists, academics, merchants and small landowners. The *Teiseitō* (Imperial Government Party) was further to the right, and found support among religious leaders, those with strong Confucianist principles and the military. Not surprisingly, there was substantial conflict between these groups, as well as factional rifts within each.

A landmark political development of the period was the Meiji Constitution of 1889, which established the first representative government in Asia.[1] This marked a significant change in the course of Japanese history, the beginning of a shift away from authoritarianism. The constitution contained elements of both the old Japan and the new, reflecting the disparate positions of different groups and the tensions between tradition and change. Indeed, one should not forget that these reformers were products of the Tokugawa era and its authoritarian government. Finding the best model available was again the approach taken by the leadership. Itō Hirobumi (1841–1909),[2] the individual who figured most prominently in the development of the constitution, had gone to Europe in 1882 to study constitutional forms. The upshot was a constitution that tended towards the German (Prussian) system which, while limiting the authority of the emperor, accorded greater power to the higher mechanisms of government and the bureaucracy, and was more strongly centralised than the systems of other countries such as Britain.

The Meiji Constitution set out the rights and responsibilities of citizens. Freedoms included speech and assembly, religion and the sanctity of the home. Responsibilities were essentially limited to paying taxes and military service. An important rider, however, is found throughout the constitution in the phrases 'except in the cases provided for by law' and 'within limits not prejudicial to peace and order' which effectively made a citizen's rights conditional rather than absolute. The tradition of authoritarianism in Japan was not dead.

The constitution also provided a venue in which the new politicians could argue. The upper house, or House of Peers, was reserved for the elites. They were drawn from a hereditary peerage established in 1884, and included former *daimyō*, court nobles, Meiji leaders and senior military officers. The lower house, or House of Representatives, was an elected body, but the right to vote was limited to the relatively wealthy, then about 1 per cent of the population. Together they formed the Diet, the new government of Japan; curiously, members of the powerful Cabinet did not have to belong to this body, but could be outside appointees.

We can trace a number of prominent aspects of contemporary Japanese society to this time. The bureaucracy, for example, is immensely powerful. The pre-eminent position of Tokyo Imperial University was consolidated then, and its law school became the premier path (as it is now) to high-level positions in the civil service. The competitive examination system, which in turn is the path to Tokyo and other elite universities, came into being at this time as well. A departure from the earlier system of inherited positions, it was a major factor in releasing the talents and energies of the general population.

New policies focused in particular on industrialisation since this was the key, along with the requisite socioeconomic underpinnings, to a strong country. A Ministry of Industry was established as early as 1870 and the government often took the lead in the early years in establishing new enterprises, where the private sector was unable or unwilling to invest. It must be said that it was often difficult to find investors, since Japan's industrial structure in the early years of the Meiji restoration was primitive and its manufactured products were inferior to those of the West. As economic growth was the linchpin of Japan's emergence as a national power, the government felt it must direct and control industrial development, and thus very close links were established with the business sector. From the 1870s, therefore, the government became heavily involved in such industries as coal-mining and ship-building, and in the production of textiles, machine tools, cement and bricks.

At the same time foreign experts were brought to Japan, as advisers on railway construction and operation, ship-building, agricultural innovations, military organisation, educational systems, mining practices and so on. Not for the Japanese the Chinese disdain of foreign knowledge—they could not learn fast enough, an enduring characteristic.

The first railway track was formally opened in 1872 (Yokohama–Shinbashi in Tokyo) and the length of track increased from about 120 kilometres in 1881 to 3300 in 1895 and 5000 by the turn of the century. Britain provided a loan for the first track between Yokohama and Tokyo in 1870 as well as engineers and train drivers. British experts also supervised construction of the first telegraph line.

As was later the case in a number of other Asian countries, notably China, income from agriculture was used to support industry. In 1880 about 80 per cent of tax revenue came from the agricultural sector and was ploughed into industrial development. Agricultural output also grew substantially, especially from this time through to the early twentieth century. Partly this was because of the new farmland opened up following the settlement of Hokkaido by people from other parts of Japan, and partly it had to do with the use of new types of seeds and better farming practices.[3]

A land tax implemented in 1873 meant that farmers were now taxed a fixed amount on the value of their land rather than on a proportion of their harvest. As output varies from year to year depending on growing conditions, however, many farmers eventually found themselves in financial straits. They had to borrow from money-lenders at high interest rates during the lean years, which eventually had the result of land becoming concentrated in the hands of fewer and fewer individuals. Not surprisingly, many people in the countryside came to resent the Meiji government, and the period is characterised by violent protests in rural areas.

The government was perhaps visionary in its realisation that the private sector was more efficient than the public in

the day-to-day operation of businesses, and once new industries were up and running they were often sold. As in modern
times, the sales of these assets also helped to balance the
government's budget. From the late 1880s onwards such enterprises were often sold to individuals closely connected to
government officials, and it is during this period that we see
the emergence of some of the great family-owned industrial
combines known as the *zaibatsu*.[4]

Mitsubishi was founded by a former low-ranked *samurai*
of the Tosa clan, Iwasaki Yatarō (1834–85). He purchased the
government shipyards in Nagasaki, and was given thirteen
ships (used for the military expedition to Taiwan in 1874,
mentioned below) by the government which allowed him to
start what eventually became the *Nihon Yūsen Gaisha*, Japan's
first shipping line (which incidentally broke the foreign mon-
opoly on shipping). These two enterprises laid the foundation
for his family's industrial empire. The four industrial groups
of Mitsubishi, Mitsui, Sumitomo and Yasuda emerged during
this period as part of the country's military–industrial complex.
Their owners all had close personal ties as well as strong
political links with politicians and bureaucrats, and their view
of business as being a patriotic enterprise in addition to a
profit-making venture made working for their concerns socially
acceptable to the *samurai* class.

The bureaucrats supervising this handover of assets were
mostly still of *samurai* descent, and were not hesitant in
exercising their personal and professional authority. The substantial influence of the bureaucracy in the economic affairs
of modern Japan can be traced from this time, in particular
the contemporary Ministry of Finance (MOF) and the Ministry
of International Trade and Industry (MITI). Hence we can say
that, in addition to some members of the old merchant class,
Japan's industrialisation was powered by the government and
the new group of entrepreneurial *samurai*.

Along with the sweeping changes in other areas, the military was substantially reorganised. Officers were sent abroad
to study modern methods and by the mid 1870s Japan had a
new army of about 9000 based on the French model.

Conscription dated from the Conscription Ordinance of 1873. In 1878 the structure was again altered to include a general staff organisation based on the German system. The driving force was a Chōshū *samurai* named Yamagata Aritomo (1838–1922). Interestingly, most troops were recruited from the former *tozama han*, especially Satsuma, Chōshū and Tosa. The Satsuma clan dominated the new Japanese Navy, which was based on that of Britain—indeed, the British Navy played a significant role in its organisation.

An ongoing irritant to the country's leadership was the form of the treaties under which Japan interacted with Western powers, which constantly reminded them of their second-class status in the community of nations. The treaties, dating from 1858, were particularly objectionable on the issues of extra-territoriality and the restrictions placed on the government over the setting of tariffs (which meant effective Western domination of Japan's foreign trade). The former issue was tackled through legal reforms between 1872 and 1898, and both criminal and civil laws were revised to bring them into line with Western practice (such as banning the use of torture). The problem of tariffs proved more difficult, however, and it was not until 1911 that Japan gained complete control over its tariff rates. That these two issues took decades to resolve was a potent indicator of the degree of Western self-interest, and served to hinder the development of positive international relations over the period. They were also issues that Japanese nationalists could focus on in their crusade against the over-Westernisation of Japanese society.

Changes in religious structures were also attempted to support the increase in nationalistic sentiment. Shintō, which had become syncretically linked to Buddhism over the centuries, was (at least partly) separated out as a truly Japanese religion. At its core, of course, was worship of the emperor, which tied in nicely with the values being encouraged by the educational system, the government and the military. A formal Shintō office (*jingikan*) was established in 1869 with the goal of bringing Shintō under government control. It was not effective, however, and after two years was closed. Not until the 1930s would Shintō emerge as part of the nationalistic ideology. Christianity, being a foreign religion, continued to be suppressed early in the reformation. The ban was reaffirmed in 1868 but lifted in 1873 following Western protests. The 1889 Meiji Constitution provided for freedom of religion, with the qualification that it must not disturb the harmony of Japanese society.

The increase in Japan's military power went hand in hand with the growth of nationalism. Japan's leaders remained very concerned about the threat of Western colonisation, given the instability of the country early in the restoration. This concern underpinned Saigō's 1873 plan to invade Korea (which remained in isolation—the time of the so-called 'hermit kingdom'). The military thought that a pre-emptive strike in Korea would preclude Western countries from establishing themselves there, which would give them a base for threatening Japan. Saigō was dissuaded, however, by others who felt that the military was not yet strong enough to make such a move. A year later a Japanese force was sent to Taiwan (then Formosa) following the murder of a number of shipwrecked Okinawan sailors by the locals. China eventually paid an indemnity and the Japanese troops withdrew. It was a harbinger of events to come.

In 1894 a rebellion took place in Korea, in the course of which both Chinese and Japanese troops entered the fray. Japan then pressured China to accord it special privileges, which China refused to do. The Japanese Navy (with the tacit support of the UK) then attacked Chinese ships and the Sino–Japanese war broke out. Within a year Japan had defeated the Chinese on both land and sea, and the 1895 Treaty of Shimonoseki gave it, among other things, Taiwan, Port Arthur and the Liaotung (Liaodong) Peninsula, and also removed Korea from Chinese control. Under pressure from Germany, France and Russia, however, who felt their imperial ambitions threatened by the Japanese control of these areas, Japan handed back Port Arthur and the peninsula before ratification of the treaty. The result of this was a tremendous popular nationalist backlash in Japan. It also drove home to Japanese leaders the lesson that the use of force was the deciding factor in international affairs. Another outcome was the growth in prestige of the armed forces, and as a result a legal change in 1890 made it compulsory for the Japanese government to choose the War and Navy ministers from serving officers. This was to have serious implications over the coming decades.

Both the government and the military, for the first two decades of the twentieth century, were dominated by members of the Satsuma and Chōshū clans. Between 1885 and 1918, for example, all but two Japanese prime ministers came from these two clans. They were also overrepresented in the bureaucracy, though their influence was diluted once the competitive examination system was introduced into the educational system (particularly the pathway of the Faculty of Law at Tokyo Imperial University). The clans' dominance of the machinery of government brought them into conflict with the more 'popularly' supported parties in the House of Representatives, and the result was often brutality and violence during elections. A second complicating factor was a degree of division within the two-clan oligarchy. Essentially, some members favoured the long-term prospect of at least some measure of parliamentary democracy while others wished to retain the government's authoritarian characteristics. This was to give rise later to a civil–military division within the government.

The early years of the century were a confusing time in domestic Japanese politics. The shifts in alliances, parties and policies were more a game of musical chairs than the operation of a coherent political system. An event which put a temporary halt to the problems, and brought Japanese together, was yet another external threat, this time from Russia.

The Japanese had been displeased with Russia since being forced to hand back to China the strategically placed Liaotung Peninsula. Russia had subsequently made a grab for it, securing a 25-year lease in 1898 and beginning a military build-up in the region, using the Trans-Siberian Railway and its spur line across Manchuria, the Chinese Eastern Railway. This gave Russia access to ice-free seaports and some of the mineral

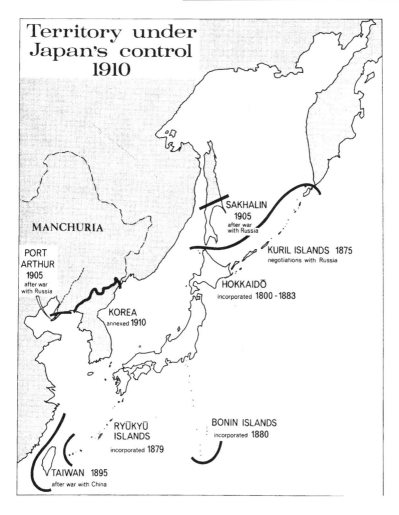

Territory under Japan's control, 1910.

wealth of the region. Both these developments worried Japanese leaders and reinforced their 'might is right' view of international relations, the lesson learned in 1895. The resultant military build-up was reflected in the defence budget, which accounted for 50 per cent of government expenditure after 1897.

Russian ships were attacked by the Japanese Navy on 8 February 1904, and two days later Japan declared war on Russia, a move that enjoyed widespread support on the domestic front. The result, after much bloody fighting, was Japanese victory on the sea and at least a good showing on land, leading to a stalemate. Japan felt its position was strong enough militarily by the middle of 1905 (though it was in dire straits in terms of loss of soldiers and expenditures on the war) to ask US President Theodore Roosevelt to mediate a settlement. The Tsarist government, reeling from the 1905 revolution, also favoured a resolution. The upshot was the Portsmouth Treaty of 1905 which gave Japan the southern half of Sakhalin Island, the Liaotung Peninsula (under lease this time), a section of Russia's South Manchurian Railway and recognition of Japan's 'paramount interests' in Korea (which it subsequently annexed in 1910). The lack of an indemnity from Russia, however, which Japan needed to pay for this costly war, produced an upsurge of nationalism in the country, including riots in Tokyo. Martial law had to be declared before order was restored.

The Japanese victory sent shock waves through the international community, with the realisation that Japan was a power to be reckoned with. It also challenged the idea of white superiority, which in turn galvanised nationalistic movements throughout colonial territories in Asia. At home Japan had the beginning of an empire with its new possessions and Taiwan, and they were used as areas of settlement for the rapidly growing population. The country also came away with a new confidence in its ability to use force on the international stage to secure its interests.

The end of the period came with the death of the Meiji emperor in 1912. His 44-year rule had seen tremendous change, with Japan transformed from an isolated feudal country to a major player on the global stage. The country was rapidly becoming technologically modern as well, though politically there remained strong elements of authoritarianism, and nationalistic sentiment was especially powerful. These trends were to become particularly apparent over the next three decades.

The road to war

During World War I Japan was on the Allied side, declaring war on Germany and attacking German possessions in Shantung (Shandong), China, and their Pacific islands (Mariana, Caroline and Marshall island groups). Japan also sought to extend its influence in China, though the Western powers at first constrained its activities there. The Chinese began to see Japan, rather than the West, as their main threat.

As the European powers became preoccupied with war in the West, Japan seized the opportunity to expand its influence in China. The 'Twenty-One Demands' of 1915 was an attempt to place China under effective Japanese control in the chaotic period following the Chinese Revolution of 1911. Although the demands were far-reaching in a number of areas, the key point was for Japanese advisers to be spread throughout the Chinese bureaucracy. While a watered-down version was eventually forced on the Chinese, the result of the original set of demands was twofold. Popular opinion in China became vehemently anti-Japanese and the USA in particular came to see Japan as a serious competitor for influence in China. It was the beginning of the perception in the USA of Japan as the enemy, and contributed to its later support of Chinese nationalism in the form of Chiang Kai-shek's Kuomintang.

The Peace Treaty of Versailles confirmed Japanese control of Shantung and the former German Pacific islands, and Japan took her place on the Council of the League of Nations, forerunner of the United Nations. It had clearly become a major world power. This did not mean complete acceptance, however. Even at the time the League was formed Japan had sponsored a clause of racial equality which was defeated, partly because of opposition from Australia, the government there fearing that such a clause would undermine its 'White Australia' policy. Racial equality was also a delicate issue in the USA, not only because of restrictions on Asian immigration, but because of laws suppressing its African–American population. The message was that Japan might be respected for its military power but would not be accepted as an equal (with an emphasis on racial differences) among Western nations.

Japan's economy fluctuated considerably in the early twentieth century. Over the course of World War I the economy grew by 50 per cent and exports increased threefold. Heavy industry, including naval ship-building, prospered, despite being highly dependent on imports of iron, steel and petroleum. The *zaibatsu* benefited greatly during this period, though there was a huge difference in both their economic power and their better treatment of labour, compared with smaller companies. By the early 1920s, however, substantial problems were besetting the country. The boom produced by World War I came to an end by 1921, resulting in substantial labour unrest in the industrial sector. The disparity between the rich, especially those who had profited from the war, and the poor, caused popular resentment. The price of rice had also increased dramatically during the war, leading to the Rice Riots of 1918, which spread to almost all of Japan's prefectures. Added to this was the Great Kanto Earthquake of 1923 and the subsequent fires that destroyed Yokohama and half of Tokyo, killing somewhere around 100 000 people and leaving three million homeless. Finally, in 1927 there was a crisis in the banking sector in which 25 per cent of Japan's banks went under.

Following the sweeping changes of the Meiji period, in the 1920s different interest groups sought to find their place, and relative power, within the new Japan of the Taisho era, begun in 1912 and lasting through to 1926. Though the new emperor was physically weak and died at a relatively young age, it was a time of flourishing democracy. More political parties emerged, including the Social Democratic and Communist parties. Labour unions gave workers a voice and there were numerous strikes through the 1920s as they struggled with management. Some liberal ideas took hold, reflected in the granting of universal suffrage for males over the age of 25. Social roles underwent further change. Women began to make up a larger share of the labour force, in factories (where working conditions were often deplorable) and offices, and began to appear more assertive, reflected in the term *moga* ('modern girl'). The male equivalent was *mobo* ('modern boy'). Western books, music and theatre made further inroads. This was reinforced by a substantial rise in urbanisation, which nearly quadrupled between 1895 and 1935, by which time about 45 per cent of Japan's population was living in cities of more than 10 000 people. The mood of the time was summed up by the phrase '*ero, guro, nansensu*', meaning 'eroticism, grotesqueness and nonsense'.

As a counterweight to the modernisation, urbanisation and Westernisation of Japan, the military, the repository of conservative influence, now expanded to include conscripts from relatively poor, backward, mostly rural areas. They were receptive to the nationalistic line being fostered at the time, in part through the basic education they were provided with in the military. At the same time the hawks in the upper echelons of the armed forces were pressing for a greater regional role for Japan, especially in China. Moderates in the military risked assassination by extremist groups.

Domestic politics was characterised by a swing back from democracy to authoritarianism. Various parties vied for power and cabinets were regularly formed and dissolved. A particular problem was the rule that the War and Navy ministers had to be chosen from the active (later, also the inactive) officer list. Given the solidarity of the armed forces, no replacement for these ministers was forthcoming when they resigned, and a cabinet would therefore be forced to dissolve. This inevitably led to a rise in the influence of the military within the government. Additionally, as Japan had never worked out clear democratic conventions, politicians tended to use whatever tools were available to garner support, including bribery, intimidation and violence, which became particularly apparent during elections. The growing move to the right was reflected in the Peace Preservation Law of 1925, which made it illegal for anyone to agitate for fundamental changes to the political system. Linked to this law were stronger powers for the police. Democracy was steadily fading in the face of growing right wing power.

The Great Depression, which began with the stockmarket crash in 1929, hit Japan hard, and there was a subsequent loss of prestige for the centrist parties in the government. Extremists began to emerge as 'champions of the people'. The most difficult period was the early 1930s. By the middle of the decade, however, Japan's economy was on the road to recovery and annual growth through the later 1930s was about 5 per cent, the result of low-cost Japanese goods being in demand during a time of global recession. This naturally caused friction with manufacturers in competitor countries and ultimately led to restrictions on Japanese imports in a number of Western countries, causing resentment in Japan.

The instability of the political system, as different groups competed for power, led to the emperor becoming a much stronger symbol. In part this was the result of cynical manipulation of his position by some members of the elites (as had often been seen before), and in part it was a way of reassuring people caught up in a time of great change. The new emperor, Hirohito, who acceded to the throne in 1926, gave his reign the title *Shōwa*, or 'Enlightened Peace', and remained a symbol of stability and continuity. Emperor worship reached its theoretical apex in the book *Kokutai-no-Hongi (Cardinal Principles of the Nation)*, published in 1937 by the Ministry of Education. This document pushed the line that the head of state was divine and the life goal of every Japanese should be utter devotion to, and self-sacrifice for, the nation. Education was thus used as a key mechanism in strengthening a form of nationalism centred on the emperor as a figurehead. This was reinforced by state sponsorship of Shintō, which in turn reinforced the idea of the divinity of the Japanese islands as well as that of the emperor. In short, the nationalism of the time had a religious, or perhaps crusading, flavour to it.

The economic improvements, however, did not benefit everyone equally. Those most disadvantaged were naturally at the lowest levels of society, principally small farmers and factory workers, and they suffered grievously. Some starved. Others were forced to sell their daughters into prostitution. The fact that much of the conscript army was drawn from

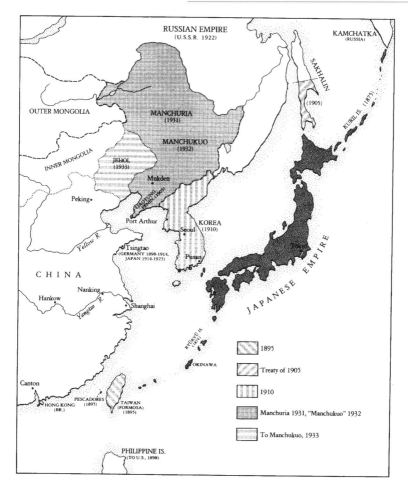

The growth of Japan's empire.

rural areas led to a demand within the military that it take steps to solve Japan's problems, which further fed the fires of ultra-nationalism and imperialism.

In September 1931 troops of the Japanese Kwangtung Army (troops assembled for use in China), in an unauthorised response to a (possibly faked) attack by Chinese bandits, assaulted Chinese troops in the Manchurian city of Mukden—

the so-called 'Manchurian Incident'. By early 1932 the puppet state of Manchūkuo had been established, the titular head of which from 1934 was Pu Yi, the last emperor of China. A Chinese bureaucracy was put in place to run the state under Japanese control. Japan continued to expand its influence in northeast China and Inner Mongolia.

The League of Nations condemned the Japanese actions and Japan left the organisation in March 1933. Japan in turn produced the concept of the 'Greater East Asian Co-Prosperity Sphere' (*Dai Tōa Kyōei-Ken*), which would unite Asians, with Japan as leader, to resist the power of the Western countries. The prized mineral resources of Manchuria were quickly exploited. Coal mines, iron and steel factories and railways were opened or expanded. The *zaibatsu* of Mitsui and Mitsubishi benefited in particular, even more so than Sumitomo and Yasuda; to balance their power the government promoted newer companies such as Nissan and Toyota, which rapidly became common names.

On the domestic front the government moved steadily to the right. The emperor remained publicly silent on the military's activities in Manchuria, partly because he was perhaps not fully informed, and partly because he chose to make his reservations known only in private. The public generally accepted that this meant his tacit approval. Those agitating for a more moderate course, including some scholars and members of left-wing parties and labour unions, were often assassinated, arrested or jailed. Media came under stricter censorship. The army was particularly right wing, the navy less so, but the presence of active officers in the cabinet made it difficult for moderates to advance their positions. An attempted overthrow of the government was mounted by right-wing junior army officers in February 1936, at which time both the Diet and Army Ministry buildings were occupied and several ministers murdered (the most serious among numerous attacks on government in the early 1930s). Though unsuccessful, this attack signalled the growing power of the radical right.

Imperialism was accepted as a doctrine in the military—seeking first to occupy China, then Southeast Asia and India. The Japanese government sought security by signing an anti-communist agreement with Germany in 1936. In Manchuria the Japanese army began practising manoeuvres which brought it into conflict with Chinese troops at the Marco Polo Bridge near Peking. The scene was set for the Pacific War.

5
WAR AND PEACE

APAN TODAY STILL SHOWS the scars of the Pacific
War in its constitution, armed forces, international
relations, economic structures and internal social divisions. No
other event in the country's history has had such a traumatic
impact and so changed its historical course. The Pacific War
was a confusing time. In the years leading up to it Japan simply
played the international relations game as it had been taught
by other major participants: When diplomacy fails, use threats.
When threats do not work try gunboat diplomacy. Be prepared
to go to war if necessary—audacity and tenacity often pay off.

Japan's teachers were the British, the Americans, the
Russians and the French—the major colonial powers of the
day—and they too were ruthless in their pursuit of raw
materials and markets. Hence, while one cannot condone the
inhumane behaviour of Japanese troops during the war, it is
also unfair to portray the country as some kind of 'Evil
Empire', along the lines of the propaganda generated in the
West at the time. This chapter looks at Japan's road to war,
its attempt to carve out an Asia-Pacific empire, its failure and
resurrection. The period covered is a mere fifteen years—
starting with war in China in 1937 and finishing with the

formal end of the Allied Occupation in 1952—but it changed Japan and the world forever.

Prelude to war (1937–41)

In the last chapter we saw Japan emerge from self-imposed isolation in the middle of the nineteenth century. There followed a remarkable period of extremely rapid change throughout its society and economy, in good part a response to the threat of colonisation by the dominant Western powers. During this tumultuous period a unifying force was needed to prevent social disintegration, and the Meiji leaders found it in the ancient symbol of the emperor. A powerful nationalism was encouraged with worship of the emperor, both secular and sacred in nature, at its core. The advantage was social cohesion at a time when it was desperately needed. The disadvantage was a wariness, even hostility, towards foreigners. These elements came together as Japan sought to increase its economic strength. Given the relative poverty of its home islands, the country had to secure raw materials from outside its borders, and this eventually brought it into armed conflict with China and then Russia. With victories in both wars, Japan sought further expansion into China, a desirable hinterland of natural resources given its proximity to Japan and existing Japanese control of parts of Manchuria and Korea. Such was the scene in 1937, with troops poised to push further into Chinese territory.

There is no clear picture of Japanese plans at this time, partly because of the conflicts between the (mostly) civilian government and the military (and competing factions within each), with the government having only partial control over the latter. It appears that even the military was reluctant to engage in a full-scale war with China, recognising the limited resources available for engaging in a long-term conflict, but the ultra-nationalists carried the day. At the same time it seemed almost inevitable that, with Japanese troops stationed in Peking and Shanghai as well as in parts of northeast China, open conflict would eventually occur. This took place on 7 July 1937, at the Marco Polo Bridge just outside Peking (Beijing), and marks the effective beginning of the Pacific War. Within three months Japan had 200 000 troops stationed in China—the new North China Army. Peking and Tientsin (Tianjin) fell quickly and the army continued on to Nanking (Nanjing), the headquarters of Chiang Kai-shek's Kuomintang (Guomindang) government. One of the worst atrocities of this ugly war occurred in Nanking, where approximately 42 000 civilians, primarily women and children, were massacred, and there were perhaps 20 000 cases of rape. Some 100 000 military and civilian 'prisoners of war' were also killed. These figures come from the Tokyo War Crimes Trials of the late 1940s, and would seem to be relatively accurate. Today, however, there are counter-claims, with the Chinese putting the figure as high as 340 000 killed and the Japanese insisting on one as low as 30 000. Matsui Iwane (1878–1948), the commander of the Japanese troops in the city, was hanged in 1948 for his role in the massacre. This incident remains a stumbling block in relations between China and Japan today, partly because of Japanese reluctance to admit fault. One argument put forward in rebuttal of the charges is that many of the atrocities were perpetrated by communist Chinese, who saw that in the chaos they could settle old scores with their Kuomintang enemies. More publicly, some Japanese leaders continue to deny either that the event ever occurred, or that Japanese troops were responsible for the carnage.

The Japanese atrocities in Nanking produced concern in the West, but not enough to bring Western countries into open conflict with the aggressor. Their attention was on events in Europe. The same response had been forthcoming earlier, when Japanese troops encountered Westerners (including British and American naval ships, which they sank) in their push up the Yangtze River to Nanking, and later when they occupied Chinese ports such as Shanghai, Hangchow (Hangzhou) and Canton (Guangzhou), damaging British and American commercial interests in particular.

Japan set up a puppet government in 1940 with co-opted

Chinese nationalist Wang Ching-wei (Wang Jinwei) as its head. In spite of this structure and their domination of a number of cities and ports the Japanese were never able to achieve full control of China. As happened in the later conflict in Vietnam between the French (then the Americans) and Vietnamese nationalists/communists, the Japanese were able to control the main roads, railway lines, rivers and cities, but not the countryside. Guerilla forces, especially those organised by the communist Chinese, harried the Japanese throughout the war. The main Chinese armies (both nationalist and communist), poorly equipped and fighting in appalling conditions, set up bases in the western part of the country, where they formed a temporary truce. Supplies for the Chinese troops came principally from the USA and Britain, first overland from Burma and later via aircraft from India over the 'hump' of the Himalayas, and through to the mid 1940s Japanese troops had to regularly engage Chinese forces.

Neither did Japan do well against the Soviet Union at the time. In 1938 and 1939 there were border conflicts between Soviet and Japanese troops, first in the area where Korea, Manchuria and Russia meet and later at Nomonhan, on the border between Outer Mongolia and northwestern Manchuria. Soviet mechanised forces stopped the Japanese advances. By this time, however, the USSR had to contend with the build-up to, and then the outbreak of, war in Europe, and a cease-fire was signed with the Japanese in September of 1939.

Partly to reduce the Soviet threat and partly to send a warning to the USA to maintain its neutrality, Japanese leaders had earlier signed an anti-communist pact with Germany, in 1936. By September 1940, following the German occupation of France, the pro-German Vichy Government allowed Japanese troops into French Indo-China. The Japanese left the French administration largely in place while taking over effective control of the colony. Japan's empire was growing.

On the home front, the political scene was characterised by a steady move to the right, with suppression of both left-wing and liberal politicians. There were waves of arrests, imprisonments and some executions. Assassinations continued to be carried out, especially by extreme nationalists, and the voices of moderation were pressured into silence. Military budgets were increased. Prime ministers changed regularly, with ten men holding the post between 1935 and 1945. (Prince Konoe Fumimaro was, for example, three times Prime Minister during this period.) Eventually, in an attempt to reduce this instability, a coalition called the Imperial Rule Assistance Association was created in 1940, into which all political parties as well as lobby groups (such as labour unions) were subsumed. Key government decisions came to be made by a body entitled the Liaison Council (between the government and military), composed of the Prime Minister, Foreign Minister, War and Navy ministers and the chiefs of staff of the branches of the military. This concentration of power moved Japan closer to a totalitarian state, though there was never a dictator similar to Hitler in Germany. General Tōjō Hideki took over as Prime Minister in October 1941, and general mobilisation for war began.

The government had, over several years, passed a number of laws designed to give it more direct control over the country. It was largely able to control savings levels, wages and prices, and some key industries under the National General Mobilization Law of 1938. For the exploitation of resources in Manchuria the Manchurian Industrial Development Corporation was established in 1938, followed in 1940 by the North China Development Corporation.

Japan steadily built up its military strength, stockpiling strategic material, including a two-year supply of oil. In the key area of naval shipping, an agreement had been reached in 1930 (the London Disarmament Conference) to limit the size of the navies of Britain, the USA and Japan to a ratio of 5:5:3. This eventually became unacceptable to Japan and it withdrew from the agreement in the middle of the decade, beginning a massive build-up of its navy and by 1940 feeling confident in the strength of its Pacific fleet.

At the same time, with the German–Soviet non-aggression pact of 1939, Japan suddenly found itself once again under potential threat. Germany, Japan felt, had betrayed it, underlining the weakness of a marriage of convenience between partners who fundamentally neither liked nor trusted each other. Japan therefore tried to shore up relations with the USA to limit the problems it might have to deal with. The USA was unwilling, however, to enter into any agreement while Japan's army continued to'advance into China. This had the effect of pushing Japan in the opposite direction, and in September 1940 the government signed a defence agreement with Germany and Italy (the Tripartite Axis Pact). Germany must have looked like a good bet at the time, given its spectacular military successes (the *blitzkrieg*) in Europe.

In the convoluted realm of international relations there were additional benefits for Japan. Since Germany and the USSR had a non-aggression pact, and Japan had a defence agreement with Germany, it followed that Japan and the USSR could come to some arrangement. Hence, in April 1941 the two countries signed a neutrality pact, thereby relieving pressure to Japan's northeast. Only two months later, however, in June 1941, Germany turned on the USSR. Japan's foreign relations were again thrown into confusion, but its leaders resolved not to meet its defence obligations to Germany until it was clear who would be victorious (and by September 1941 German forces had bogged down before taking Moscow). It suited the Japanese to have the USSR preoccupied in the West, thereby removing the Soviet threat from Japan's flank.

The USA at the time was still dominated by a policy of non-intervention, in spite of war in both Europe and China. Its response to Japanese aggression in China was to impose economic sanctions, a familiar reaction today. Japanese leaders were outraged by limits on the sale of raw materials to their country, including aviation petrol, scrap iron and steel—all matériel necessary for waging war. Then, with the Japanese move into Indo-China (now Vietnam, Cambodia and Laos) in 1941, at least partly to get closer to the oil supplies in the Dutch East Indies (now Indonesia), the USA, along with Britain and Holland, completely cut exports to Japan. The reduction in oil supplies was particularly serious as approximately 75 per cent of Japan's oil came from the USA (and a further

15 per cent from other foreign sources). Indeed, it is surprising that the USA continued to trade with Japan as long as it did. One explanation is that the USA welcomed the anti-communist activities of the Japanese government and was thus willing to continue its support until Japan's military activities made this position untenable. Some of the black humour later circulating among American troops in the Pacific had to do with their own iron and steel being fired back at them, a situation that was to be repeated in coming years, indeed as recently as the Gulf War (where American weaponry provided to Iraq during the Iran–Iraq war of the 1980s was subsequently used against American troops).

The embargo has been a point of debate ever since. Did it in fact force Japan to go to war with the USA? Leaving aside moral positions, the situation could be seen as a continuation of geopolitics, the struggle for supremacy among the major powers of the day. Each was attempting to maximise its self-interest, though to be fair to Japan, the situation was complicated by the refusal of the Western powers to accept the country as an equal, a situation that had caused resentment for many years. Conflict appears to have been nearly inevitable. Japan entered China in large part for access to raw materials. To guard its flanks it made agreements with Germany and the USSR. Both threatened the USA, which responded by trying to force Japan to back down through starving it of the materials it needed to continue its industrial build-up and wage war, especially petroleum. This left the Japanese leadership with a fundamental choice: give in to American demands and accept second-rate status in the global power structure, or go to war with the USA in a calculated gamble that it could win before its supplies ran out (or it could secure new sources in Southeast Asia). Japan did not have enough time, given its limited reserves of oil, to enter into long negotiations over the issue. As we know, driven by its military successes over the preceding half century, its military-dominated government and the nationalism Japanese leaders had encouraged for a century, Japan chose war.

The Pacific War (1941–45)

Japan's military leaders appeared to hope that with one massive attack they could destroy US naval power to such an extent that the Americans would agree to a peace treaty. Few (except, perhaps, those in the highly nationalistic army) thought that Japan could win a drawn-out war, but based on their experiences with China and Russia a decisive defeat should force their opponents to the bargaining table. Japanese naval strategists estimated that Japan could not maintain a war effort for more than a year and a half without new sources of raw materials.

The well-known Japanese bombing of Pearl Harbor took place on 7 December 1941. In just two hours approximately 350 Japanese bombers attacked, resulting in the loss of four American battleships, three destroyers and 180 aeroplanes; three aircraft carriers were at sea and thus were spared. Nearly 3400 personnel were killed and more than 1000 wounded. The American public was outraged, particularly at what it saw as an unfair move—Japan had attacked before it declared war. While this ploy had worked against Russia at the beginning of the century, it galvanised America into action. The attack was a serious miscalculation of American attitudes, and resulted in the resolve to destroy Japan.

For most of the past half century conventional wisdom has had it that the attack came as a complete surprise. Indeed, Admiral Nomura Kichisaburō, who was in the USA at the time trying to persuade the Americans to lift their oil embargo, was reputedly deeply offended at not having been told of the plan. Alternative versions of the truth have been suggested over the years, however. For example, a recent book by Robert Stinnet, entitled *Day of Deceit: The Truth About FDR and Pearl Harbor*, contends that the American President and his advisers knew the attack was coming (the US military having broken Japanese diplomatic and naval codes and received other intelligence that suggested a Japanese attack was imminent). It was allowed to go ahead in order to swing American public opinion away from isolationism (the policy of not getting involved in the problems of other countries). The truth perhaps lies somewhere in between, with America at the very least not taking the Japanese threat seriously. The result, however, was unambiguous—the USA entered the war against Japan and Germany.

At about the same time as the bombing of Pearl Harbor the Japanese military launched attacks against Malaya, Hong Kong and the Philippines. It seemed for some months that the Japanese forces were unstoppable. In the early days American aircraft in the Philippines were destroyed while still on the ground. The British ships *Prince of Wales* and *Repulse* were sunk off the coast of Malaya on 10 December 1941. Hong Kong was taken in late December and Manila in early January 1942. Thailand negotiated an 'accommodation' without fighting and Japanese forces occupied it in short order. The Malayan states, starting with Kelantan in the northeast, were overrun one by one. February saw the fall of Singapore, in spite of 70 000 British and Australian troops being stationed there, double the number of the Japanese forces attacking it. The Japanese launched their attacks from the Malayan Peninsula to the north while Singapore's major defences faced south. On 6 March Batavia (Jakarta) was taken by Japanese troops and two days later Rangoon (Yangon) fell.

Why were the Japanese so successful? One reason is that the Western powers were principally concerned with the war in Europe and thus were not paying sufficient attention to Japan's activities, nor did they have the resources at the time to fight on both sides of the world. Another is the audacity of the Japanese attacks, by troops who were highly motivated, courageous and imbued with nationalistic fervour and fighting spirit. Western arrogance seems also to have played a role, in part due to a colonially inspired belief in white superiority. Indeed, in a number of colonies the local inhabitants initially welcomed the Japanese as liberators. The framework for 'co-operation' had been set out years before in the Japanese concept of the 'Greater East Asian Co-Prosperity Sphere'. The motto used by Japanese leaders at the time of the Pacific War was 'Asia for the Asians', though there was a certain arrogance in assuming Japan would play the leadership role in such a movement. Disillusionment with the Japanese set in quickly in the overrun countries—one colonial master had merely been substituted for another. The fighting spirit of the Japanese forces produced problems, however. Officers had tremendously high expectations of their troops and discipline was often harsh. The army mentality retained vestiges of older civil conflicts in Japan where those defeated neither expected nor received mercy. Soldiers who allowed themselves to be taken prisoner were despised, and this attitude extended to the Allied troops who fell into their hands. Few Japanese soldiers allowed themselves to be taken prisoner, preferring to die fighting or to commit suicide. Army troops were often recruited from the lower classes of Japanese society, most from poor farming backgrounds—they were used to a hard life and severe discipline from their superiors. When they had control over prisoners they treated them as they themselves had been treated, or worse. Korean soldiers were also recruited into the Japanese Army; often used for lowly jobs, such as guarding prisoners, they too handed out to prisoners of war (POWs) the kind of treatment that they themselves received. This hierarchical problem was compounded by different customs and the language barrier. Western prisoners may not have shown their captors what was expected in terms of due respect, a failing exacerbated by the problem of communication. Frictions arising from these problems often led to even harsher treatment of prisoners. While it is well known that POWs suffered severely from lack of food, it must also be remembered that the Japanese troops themselves suffered from a lack of supplies, thus even less was set aside for the despised prisoners. Once the Allied blockade of Japan began to take effect, even Japanese living in the home islands experienced severe food shortages. Finally, there were frictions between commanders in the field and the generals in Japan. The Geneva Convention was usually unknown or disregarded in the field in spite of the Ministry of War issuing directives about the proper treatment of prisoners. This behaviour contrasted sharply with Japan's relatively good treatment

Bridge over the River Kwai, Kanchanaburi district, Thailand.

of Russian prisoners in 1904–05 and of German prisoners during World War I.

The maltreatment of prisoners of war has to this day left lingering hostility towards the Japanese throughout the world—the conditions of the POW camps such as Changi in Singapore, of the forced marches such as the 'Bataan death march' in the Philippines and the use of forced labour where tens of thousands perished in appalling conditions (not to mention the recent publicity over the Japanese army's use of women from Korea and other countries as sex slaves—the so-called 'comfort women'), means that even now there is a clear anti-Japanese sentiment throughout Southeast Asia and the West. Perhaps the worst case of forced labour was the building of the 'death railway' between Bangkok and Rangoon in 1942–43 by Asian and Allied prisoners, made famous (or infamous) by Hollywood in the film *Bridge Over the River Kwai*.

While POWs have received much attention from Western

historians, the exploitation of native labour has often been overlooked. Throughout the region local people were often treated with disregard, and those resisting Japanese rule were dealt with harshly. In the building of the Thai–Burma railway mentioned above, for example, many more Asians died than Allied prisoners. Reliable estimates are difficult to find, but one figure is 63 000 total deaths, of which only 16 000 were Australian, British and Dutch prisoners. Japanese military archives discovered in the early 1990s have detailed experiments by Imperial Army Unit 731 (Biological Warfare), in which thousands of Chinese and Koreans died after being deliberately infected with plague bacteria (as well as cholera, anthrax, typhoid and haemorrhagic fever). The military police (*kempeitai*) were particularly feared and hated (often by the Japanese themselves as well as by the people in occupied territories). Ethnic groups were often pitted against each other in the colonies, such as Malays and Indians against the Chinese, in the old divide-and-rule approach. The ethnic Chinese in particular suffered; there was widespread killing of Chinese in the Malay Peninsula and Singapore. This often resulted in a move towards communism, especially among the Chinese, a legacy that later proved difficult to remove in many places.

On the other hand, the Japanese did encourage self-determination when it suited their ends. Throughout the war hundreds of offspring of the elite families of conquered countries in Southeast Asia were brought to Japan to be indoctrinated in the spirit of Japanese imperialism (and, ironically, anti-colonialism), though a less subtle purpose was to use them as hostages to make sure their parents supported Japanese actions in the occupied territories. These endeavours were aided by the fact that an Asian country had so decisively defeated the forces of the Western colonial rulers, thus destroying the notion of white supremacy. Hence, nationalist movements in Malaya, the Dutch East Indies and Burma, among others, were assisted by the Japanese (mostly in the final days of occupation), with the end result of hastening decolonisation.

The antipathy towards Japan remains strong in Australia (especially among older Australians), partly because of the many Australian POWs who died in Japanese camps, and partly because the country narrowly escaped invasion. Darwin was bombed repeatedly from February 1942 to November 1943. The Battle of the Coral Sea in May 1942 may have prevented the Japanese invasion of Australia via airbases in southern New Guinea; subsequent overland movements were stopped by Australian troops along the Kokoda Trail. The next month saw the Battle of Midway, where the US Navy destroyed four Japanese aircraft carriers, significantly affecting Japan's ability to use air power, and hence their capacity to invade other countries. Some historians view this early battle as the turning point of the Pacific War.

For a while Japan was able to maintain war production through tremendous efforts on the part of domestic industry and the people. However, in spite of new sources of raw materials now being available in Southeast Asia, ensuring steady supplies proved impossible. Heavy-handedness on the part of Japanese managers alienated local workforces, and transportation of materials to Japan proved increasingly difficult once the Americans had organised their Pacific submarine force. Japanese shipping losses during the war, the most significant factor in disabling the economy, were estimated at between 75 and 90 per cent, and about 60 per cent of this was due to American submarines.

The war had clearly turned against Japan by the middle of 1943. On all sides Japanese troops had been stopped or pushed back—in China, Burma and the Pacific islands. By July 1944 Saipan had been captured and Japan's cities came within range of American bombers. General Tōjō was replaced as Prime Minister. A year later, after ten weeks' intense fighting and terrible loss of life on both sides, Okinawa fell. Major Japanese cities were levelled by bombing. Only Kyoto, because of its historic significance, was spared. In a single air raid in March 1945, more than 100 000 people died in the incendiary bombing of Tokyo. The famed *kamikaze* ('divine wind') pilots could mount only a heroic, not a significant, defence of their home islands.

On 6 August the *Enola Gay*, an American Superfortress bomber, dropped the first atomic bomb used in warfare on Hiroshima. On 8 August the Soviet Union declared war against Japan, and invaded Manchuria. A second atomic bomb was dropped on Nagasaki the next day. Approximately 340 000 people died in these two cities. Japanese leaders continued to debate whether or not the country should surrender and, if so, what form surrender should take. (In July 1945, at Potsdam in Germany, the Allies had called for unconditional surrender. The argument was mostly over the issue of the postwar position of the Imperial House, even though Hirohito himself supported a complete surrender. On 13 August a major air raid on Tokyo took place, involving some 1500 Allied aircraft. The next day Emperor Hirohito recorded his message of surrender, to be broadcast throughout Japan. After the suppression of an eleventh-hour attempted coup, it was broadcast on 15 August, the emperor asking Japan's citizens to 'endure the unendurable and suffer what is unsufferable'. The formal surrender was signed on board the USS *Missouri*, anchored in Tokyo Bay, on 2 September 1945. The Pacific War had come to an end.

There continues today a debate over whether it was necessary to use atomic bombs on Japan. Conventional wisdom has it that Japanese forces, entrenched as they were in many parts of Southeast Asia and China, would have been difficult to remove without such a horrific incentive. (Indeed, until recently Japanese soldiers were occasionally being discovered in isolated parts of Southeast Asia and the Pacific.) Any invasion of the major Japanese islands (based on Allied experience in taking Okinawa) would have been very costly for the Allies in both men and matériel, which was also why the Soviet Union was asked, at the Yalta Conference in February 1945, to enter the war against Japan. Opponents of the bombing argue that an atomic bomb could have been dropped on an unpopulated area, that a second bomb was unnecessary, and that the USA primarily wanted to test its new weapon.

Occupation and resurrection (1945–52)

Japan was destitute at the end of the war. The country had lost massive numbers of its people—some say 2.5 million soldiers and nearly one million civilians died. Many of its cities and much of its infrastructure had been destroyed. A quarter of its industrial base lay in ruins. The population, bewildered and tired, was on the edge of starvation. Adequate shelter and medicines were in short supply. The problems were exacerbated by high levels of unemployment, made worse by vast numbers of demobilised soldiers. Its empire gone, Japan had now to face the prospect of the relative poverty of its home islands.

Initially many were terrified at the prospect of occupation, the first in Japan's long history. They had little idea of what to expect. The occupying Allied troops were a mixed lot. Enlisted troops often behaved poorly, with rape being a particular problem, and women left the cities in droves to avoid assault. Those in authority, however, especially the officer corps, on the whole acted responsibly. On the Japanese side, the emperor's call for surrender was almost universally obeyed, underlining the entrenched authority of this institution. This set the stage for broad support for the changes that were to be made during the Occupation.

The main administrative body for the Occupation was technically the Far Eastern Commission, headquartered in Washington and made up of representatives of the thirteen nations who had fought Japan. In Tokyo the Allied Council (representing the USA, USSR, Britain and China) was to oversee policy implementation but unsurprisingly, the variety of competing ideologies within the group meant that it was rarely able to be effective. Real power rested with the USA, especially the Supreme Allied Commander of the Pacific, General Douglas MacArthur, who was given the responsibility of supervising the dismantling of the Japanese war machine and its socioeconomic underpinnings. His new title was Supreme Commander for the Allied Powers (SCAP) and the American-dominated Occupation administration came to be known by

Top:
Coming of Age, Tokyo.
Bottom right:
Yasukuni-jinja, a Shintō shrine dedicated to Japan's war dead.
Bottom left:
Fox god (*kami*), Niigata.

Top left:
Buddhist monk, Tokyo.
Bottom left:
Japanese garden.
Top right:
Shinjuku's central business district.
Bottom right:
The Dai Butsu of Kamakura, cast in 1252.

Top:
Gate of a Shintō shrine, Niigata.
Bottom left:
Asakusa Kannon temple, Tokyo.
Bottom right:
Sakura (cherry blossom) party, Tokyo.

this name. Curiously, he ruled from an office in the heart of Tokyo, never travelling around the country. Some historians view this as American arrogance (or the arrogance of MacArthur himself), while others believe that this *shōgun*-like rule was understood and welcomed by Japanese citizens who at the time desired clear authority and stability.

It is often argued that Japan is the way it is today because of policy decisions made during the Occupation. This view places the Japanese as the receivers of American policies rather than effective participants in the rebuilding process, seeing Japan today as simply the 'step-child' of American foreign policy. Another view holds that the Japanese were provided with the potential for change and they themselves were responsible for the outcome; because the Occupation authorities had to work through the Japanese bureaucracy (since there were few Allied administrators who were competent in the Japanese language or understood Japan's system of government), the latter had substantial influence over how policies were implemented and therefore over their eventual form. A spin-off argument here is that the bureaucrats have considerable power today partly because they were given it then.

The initial concern of the Allied Occupation was to keep people from starving, and to this end 500 000 tons of rice set aside for the use of the Australian military in Japan was used. American food aid was also critical until 1949. At the same time the military itself was demobilised. Nearly seven million people (the figure varies substantially) had to be brought home from occupied territories, half of them soldiers. Unemployment soared. One can only imagine their disillusionment at returning to such a devastated country. Added to this group, later on, were Japanese who had been in Korea and China where they were used as forced labour by the Chinese and Soviet governments. Many, perhaps most, of these troops however, died before they could return home.

The Allies immediately set out to dismantle Japan's war industries. Military hardware was destroyed and the industries which had made it dismantled. The *zaibatsu* in particular were targeted. They had made huge profits during the war, being

heavily involved in the production of war matériel. The Zero
fighter, for example, had been manufactured by Mitsubishi. At
war's end these companies were of immense size, and intimately connected with the wartime government. It was felt
that if they were allowed to continue to operate they would
interfere with the American plan for a wider distribution of
income in Japan, which was expected to underpin democratic
reforms. The big four *zaibatsu* were special targets and 83 of
their holding companies were broken up. Approximately 3000
senior businessmen were removed from their jobs. The smaller
subsidiary companies were separated from the core businesses,
and their ability to work together was limited by tax reform
and laws against collusion (such as the Anti-Monopoly Law
of 1947). At the same time harsh measures to restore balance
in the economy were put in place by Joseph Dodge (1890–
1964), a banker from Detroit. Although his plan caused
short-term suffering, it had put Japan on a solid economic
footing by 1950.

Once this economic restructuring was well under way
MacArthur and the Allied Occupation forces set out to change
the nature of the Japanese state, to turn it into a peaceful,
pro-Western, democratic country. Japan's aggressive tendencies
were to be stopped by law. The new American-designed constitution, written in under a week by SCAP employees, was
based on the British model, which was closer to Japan's
pre-war system than America's. It came into effect on 3 May
1947, re-creating the Diet with two houses, and a cabinet
responsible to both. It also provided for universal suffrage,
entrenched fundamental human rights, and made the judiciary
relatively independent of the executive. Finally, the constitution
contained the well-known Article 9, in which Japan renounced
war and the creation of matériel for waging war.

MacArthur's mandate stated that he was not to rebuild
Japan's economy except insofar as it was necessary to make
sure the people could survive and that there was a 'wide
distribution of income and ownership of the means of production and trade'. In this regard a key policy was the break-up
of large private landholdings in the countryside. Under the

plan no rural family was allowed to own more than ten acres of land; the land taken from the large estates (about four million acres) was purchased by the state and sold to tenant farmers at low rates of interest. In spite of some lingering inequities, this had several beneficial effects. It encouraged rapid agricultural production at a time when Japan badly needed food, created a substantial body of small capitalists (about three million), and (importantly in US eyes) reduced the power of the Communist Party. By 1946 approximately 90 per cent of Japan's farmland was owned by the farmers themselves.

Social changes, too, were far-reaching, helped perhaps by the purge of more than 200 000 wartime politicians and bureaucrats, which effectively removed the 'old guard' and made changes easier to effect (though many remained 'purged' for only a few years). Shintō was removed from state control. The secret police were broken up and political prisoners released. Trade unions were encouraged as a bulwark against the power of large companies. Women were given the vote. Education was made compulsory to age fifteen (up from twelve years of age previously) and textbooks changed to emphasise the values of democracy over authoritarianism. More than 100 000 teachers were fired, and the new curriculum used the American model as its basis. The number of universities was increased substantially to improve access to higher education for lower income groups, and from this time we see the emergence of the contemporary form of the university entrance examination system so prominent in the country today. Reaction within the field of education against the previous fascist regime was particularly strong, and the teachers' union (*Nihon Kyōshokuin* Kumiai, usually shortened to *Nikkyōso*) continues to be a left-wing organisation.

The Military Tribunal for the Far East was convened in Tokyo between 1946 and 1948 to punish those who had been instrumental in moving Japan into war. Interestingly, there was considerable public anger towards the leaders who had engineered a police state and brought the country to ruin, and therefore no great resistance to the war crimes trials. Of approximately 6000 people charged with war crimes, 920 were executed. Of the military and political leaders, 28 were charged with major (Class A) war crimes and seven executed. Among these was General Tōjō who, in his defence, was unrepentant; indeed, he publicly accepted responsibility for Japan's role in the war. His argument was that Japan was poor and needed colonies for resources, a telling point that highlighted a level of hypocrisy among the Western powers (and reinforced the idea of 'victor's justice').

Some Japanese believed that Tōjō was executed in place of the emperor. In any event, Hirohito was not punished, though in 1946 he was forced to publicly renounce his divinity. The theoretical implications were significant. The nationalism fomented during the Meiji period, connected with Shintō, was rejected, and the emperor set off touring the country as a sign of the new Japan. He remained, however, as throughout Japanese history, the symbol of the country. Indeed, Article 1 of the new constitution stated that the emperor was the 'symbol of the state'. The continuity of the institution was particularly needed during the struggle of the Japanese to survive following the war, in the face of the social dislocation caused by exposure to the new ideas of the Occupation authorities.

In terms of the domestic political scene the Japanese government became, not surprisingly after its wartime adventurism, very conservative. The Liberal and Democratic parties dominated, though about a quarter of the seats in the first parliament went to the Socialist Party. The first Prime Minister of note was Yoshida Shigeru (1878–1967), a pre-war diplomat who supported the Anglo-American group during the war and had been jailed by the government for a short time in 1945. Appointed Prime Minister in 1946, his goal was to restore the fundamental characteristics of Japanese society as quickly as possible, while maintaining the values of the Meiji restoration—a strong government and a regulated society. To this end he was a tenacious adversary of the Occupation authorities, often stating that the Pacific War was Japan's 'historic stumble' and that proposed socioeconomic changes would produce 'anarchy, chaos and confusion'.

An early sign that Yoshida was right in his assessment was the abrupt rise in union activity. The Allies initially supported trade unions as a counterweight to the large Japanese corporations, and by 1948 there were nearly 34 000 unions in the country. Very quickly, however, they proved to be a significant impediment to economic recovery, particularly as they tended to be ideologically based and closely connected to the Socialist and Communist parties. On May Day 1946, for example, more than 1.5 million unionists came out to demonstrate against Japanese companies and government policies. This caused alarm in both Japan and the USA, and when in 1947 a general strike was called, MacArthur forced it to be called off. This was the end of early union power, though they were not to be truly curbed until the 1960s.

The reaction to unionism was a reflection of the change in geopolitics at the time, which forced a rethink of domestic policies in Japan and its role in Asia. The Cold War had a number of starting points, and some argue that it had begun even before World War II had ended. The term itself dates from 1947, and in March that year the Truman Doctrine, which committed the USA to the fight against world communism, was announced. Communism was seen to threaten American interests in Asia as early as 1948, when Communist Chinese forces overran Manchuria. In October 1949 the People's Republic of China (PRC) was declared. The reaction to this and other advances by communism in the region and around the globe resulted in the rise of strong anti-communist sentiment in the USA.

The Cold War had the immediate effect of changing Allied economic policies in Japan. In March 1948, US Undersecretary of the Army William S. Draper was sent to Japan. Known as the 'Wall-Street General', he recommended a build-up of industry and trade that would make Japan the bulwark against communism in Asia. George Kennan, of the US State Department, also sent to Japan to review its economic growth and potential Cold War role, came to a similar conclusion. Indeed, by this time the USA would have liked to remove its Occupation forces and sign a peace treaty, giving Japan free rein to rebuild. This was proposed in the late 1940s, but the Russians refused to support such a move and the Occupation dragged on for another five years.

It is often said that the Occupation was put into reverse by late 1947 and this direction was even more apparent in 1948. Japan was given aid to build up its infrastructure and industrial base (the 1947 American aid budget for the country was approximately US$400 million[1]). Japan was to be the engine of growth for regional economies, which would provide raw materials and markets for finished products, ironically not so different from the economic plans Japan had envisaged during the war. As part of these new developments, the planned continuance of the purge of the *zaibatsu*, involving the break-up of a further 1200 companies, was shelved. Instead, a modified form of the *zaibatsu*, called the *keiretsu kigyo* ('aligned companies', usually shortened to *keiretsu*), emerged. They were similar in structure to their predecessors though more loosely linked and no longer family-owned. They did, however, retain their original appellations, so once again the names Mitsui, Mitsubishi, Yasuda and Sumitomo became commonplace in Japan.

In the late 1940s the Allied plan was for Japan to produce relatively low-level manufactures, with sophisticated products being the purview of Western countries, especially the USA. Japan was to be 'the workshop of Asia'. This would protect America's technological superiority and ensure that Japan remained a receiver of American goods rather than becoming a competitor (though few people thought of Japan in these terms at the time). The disadvantage of such a plan was clear to Prime Minister Yoshida and his government. He bluntly stated that Japan did not want to 'trade with beggars'. He would have preferred access to the rich markets of the West, but this was not part of the American vision.

The event that dramatically changed the structure of Japan's economy was the outbreak of the Korean War in June 1950. While the Cold War was slowly settling into place, this conflict was a clear indication to the USA of the power of world communism. It was apparent that communism was a major threat and that American power had to be brought to bear to halt it. Indeed, the USA had been caught unprepared and was very nearly defeated early in the Korean War. The American military, which became part of a larger UN force, had to secure a massive supply of war matériel very quickly to stop the sudden invasion of South Korea by the North. The result was $4 billion in orders for Japanese companies for so-called 'special procurements' (*tokuju*), consisting primarily of motor vehicles, textiles and communications equipment; this provided the basis for the subsequent development of Japan's automobile, clothing and electronics industries. One could argue that were it not for the Korean War, Japan today (and the global trading system) would be very different.

Prime Minister Yoshida called the Korean War a 'gift from the gods' and officials at the Bank of Japan called American orders for war matériel 'divine aid'. Industry took off. To ensure adequate quality and speed of production, American manufacturing specialists were sent to Japan to teach mass production techniques and methods of quality control. The result was the rapid production of world-class products. When the first Toyota trucks began coming off the assembly line Toyota's chairman claimed his feeling was one of 'tingling joy'.

In September 1951 the San Francisco Peace Treaty was signed, to come into effect on 28 April 1952. Only six years had passed since the end of a devastating war, yet Japanese industry was surging ahead and Japan was now welcomed as an ally of the USA. Japanese incomes had almost returned to pre-war levels. The sudden change in fortune and in Japan's position in the world was nothing short of miraculous— a unique combination of Japanese cultural characteristics, good decisions, geopolitics and luck—the exact proportions of which remain a point of debate today.

With the end of the Occupation in 1952 the machinery of government was formally returned to Japanese control, although in reality the country had been managing most of its affairs for several years. While the USSR and China (and a few less prominent countries) boycotted the conference where the peace treaty was signed, Japan and the USA also signed a

Mutual Security Treaty which placed Japan under the US nuclear 'umbrella' and allowed the US to retain military bases in Japan. These were part of a circle of American bases in the Pacific, from the Canadian Arctic through the Aleutian Islands down to Japan, Korea, Taiwan (American-supported), Guam, the Philippines and Australia—the front line of defence against communism in Asia. US commentators began referring to the Pacific as the 'American lake'.

The USA would have preferred that Japan also build up its own military as part of the bulwark against communism, US Secretary of State John Foster Dulles pressuring Japan to rearm (only five years after Article 9 had been written into the constitution at American insistence). As early as 1953 US Vice-President Richard Nixon admitted during a visit to Tokyo that Article 9 had been a mistake (from the US point of view). Prime Minister Yoshida, however, refused to rebuild Japan's military forces, rightly seeing that Japan's economic surpluses could be eaten up by military expenditures. At first Yoshida argued that Japan was economically too weak to afford to rearm, and besides, the constitution forbade it. Under continued American pressure, however, and in exchange for signing the security treaty, he did agree to a small defence force (with funding limited to under 1 per cent of GNP), which by 1954 numbered a not insignificant 165 000 personnel and came to be known by the name it has today, the Self Defence Forces (SDF, or *Jieitai*). As the name implies, the force was for defence only—it could not be used outside Japanese territory, a point that continues to cause friction with Japan's allies today.

The years from 1937 to 1952 covered arguably one of the most dramatic periods in Japanese history. It began with a country that was strong, dynamic and aggressive. The example of Western colonialism had inspired the Japanese to strengthen their own country through conquest, and the relative economic poverty of their home islands forced them to search outside Japan for the raw materials crucial to their economic development. Unfortunately, the nationalism of the time, and competition with Western powers (along with their rejection of Japan as a major international player) precluded the peaceful development of a trading empire such as we see today. Japan's leaders chose aggression, and in doing so seriously misjudged their country's strength and the reaction of other world powers. The eventual destruction of Japan is not so surprising. What is astonishing is its dramatic recovery. From utter devastation Japan rose like a phoenix, partly of its own volition and partly because of events beyond its control. The result was an almost complete turnaround of its position in only a few years, and in spite of the Occupation there was substantial cultural continuity. By 1952 Japan was once again under Japanese control. It had a solid, if small, industrial base, a coherent government and strong allies. In many ways this could have been accepted as a sufficient victory, but it turned out to be only the starting point. Japan was, amazingly, about to take off.

6
THE MIRACLE ECONOMY

ONE COULD BE FORGIVEN for being pessimistic about Japan's future at the time it regained its independence in 1952. The country was faced with a plethora of problems. In addition to a relatively small economic base there remained considerable social dislocation from the Pacific War. Japan had never before faced defeat nor such widespread devastation, which called into question the way in which the country's political and economic systems had been organised. The changes introduced during the Meiji restoration had some-how led to a nightmare of destruction; there was widespread public support to prevent such a thing ever happening again. The question was, therefore, how was society to be organised to prevent Japan repeating its mistakes? The Allied Occupation authorities had introduced a number of measures to remake Japan into something akin to the USA, but would this fit with Japanese culture? What should be the guiding principles of the new Japan? The response to these questions divided society. On the left were reformers who wanted to see wholesale change in the way in which Japan's social system was organised, and in particular to limit the concentration of power in the hands of a political and economic elite. In the middle were those who desired cultural continuity but were concerned about a return to pre-war problems and also wary of the radical changes proposed by the left. On the right were the powerful, conservative business groups and old-school bureaucrats and politicians who wanted to regain their power. This group was given a tremendous boost in the early 1950s by the Korean War and American efforts to rapidly rebuild Japan's economy.

The 1950s were, therefore, years of struggle between these groups, as the postwar social, political and economic framework settled into place. The centre/right forces eventually carried the day and by the 1960s Japan was beginning to take the shape we know today—conservative, conformist and generally without strong political affiliation. This was reinforced when economic success became Japan's central goal; the human resources of the country were marshalled for this end, and the 1960s became a decade of economic supergrowth.

The 1950s

Only four days after Japan regained its independence, left-wing demonstrations on May Day (mostly by students and primarily over the issue of US bases in Japan) rocked Tokyo. More than 2000 people were injured. The far left, however, lacked substantial support; it was noisy and visible (as was the far right), but the Japanese public by and large had had enough of radical political movements. Social stability and economic recovery were far more important.

Yoshida Shigeru, Prime Minister 1946–47, also held that position from 1948 to 1954 when his government was brought down by a financial scandal (the first of many over the years ahead). His conservative government, characterised by his sentiment that Japan should avoid an 'excess of democracy', emphasised stability, which was welcomed by Japanese citizens anxious about the future. By the mid 1950s the Democratic Party found that it needed the Liberal Party (a combination of the former Progressive Party and members of the moderate right) in order to govern effectively in the face of rising socialist opposition. Combined with pressure from the business sector in particular, the result was their merger in 1955. Except for a brief interlude in the early 1990s, the Liberal Democratic Party (LDP) has remained in power ever since. This re-emphasises the public's desire for stability and continuity, and highlights the complex web of mutual dependency that developed between politicians and other groups (the electorate, lobby groups, business and so on), that over time reinforced the party's hold on power.

The main opposition in the 1950s came from the Japan Socialist Party and, to a lesser extent, the Japan Communist Party. Although not sufficiently powerful to pose a major threat to the LDP, they have at least fulfilled the role of a watchdog on government. The primary opposition to the government is found within the LDP itself, in the form of factionalism, a feature of Japanese politics throughout its history in one form or another. One of the reasons prime ministers regularly come and go in Japan, even though the LDP remains in power, is the relative power of the different factions at different times. They are formally constructed, usually around a key person who has spent a considerable number of years building up networks of support and obligation, so personalities and personal connections often take precedence over ideologies or policies. It also takes substantial experience in the intricacies of politics to put oneself in the running for the top position, and one's rise in the party is linked to seniority, so most Japanese prime ministers are relatively old. At the same time, because a faction leader is responsible to his faction members, and has to balance the interests and power of other factions, a prime minister's position is also relatively weak. Factionalism is also supported by the election system, under which there may be more LDP candidates than seats in a particular electoral district. This has the effect of pitting faction against faction in support of different candidates.

One of the reasons the parties on the left became steadily weaker through the 1950s was that they primarily represented labour, and one of the key developments of the 1950s was the sorting out of the relationship between capital and labour. Japan has a long history of strong control over workers, principally peasants, and it is difficult to change political culture. During the Meiji restoration power rested in the hands of a relatively authoritarian bureaucratic, political and business elite who strictly regulated labour in the lead-up to, and then during, the Pacific War. To a significant extent labour in the postwar period found itself for the first time holding a degree of power, and was initially given a boost by the Occupation authorities as a democratic counterweight to big business. The result was an outpouring of frustration over working conditions that had been pent up for (at least) decades, manifested in widespread strikes and demonstrations in the late 1940s and 1950s and even into the 1960s. Two of the more notable strikes were those at Nissan in 1953 and the Mitsui-owned coal mines at Miike (Kyushu) in 1960. (In both cases capital came out ahead, however.) The end result was that workers tended to organise themselves into 'enterprise unions' which represent workers in a single business organisation (i.e. they are not linked to others); they are therefore relatively powerless.

Management practices tended to remain relatively severe and businesses continued to have a rigid hierarchical structure. The political circumstances of the time reinforced this trend. Domestically the Japanese government became increasingly authoritarian, undoing a number of Occupation reforms in a 'reverse course' program which included policies which weakened the left and recentralised various government functions. The National Police Agency, the Ministry of Education and the Ministry of Home Affairs are examples. Moreover, the far left was not generally viewed in the context of the time as a legitimate alternative to the LDP. The Cold War and Japan's role as an ally of the USA meant that labour unrest came to be seen as a tool of the left, and this could not be tolerated in the political climate of the 1950s. Indeed, a 'Red Purge' in 1950 removed some 10 000 union activists from their jobs and made it difficult for them to find new employment. Even earlier, in 1948, the right to strike was removed from civil servants.

Despite this, there was broad agreement between capital and labour, for both cultural reasons as well as practical business decisions. While radical labour was not acceptable industry recognised that it was necessary to provide adequate working conditions if long-term unrest was to be avoided. Some historians point to the cultural value of Confucianism, and indeed feudalism, to demonstrate that Japanese capitalists inherited a sense of responsibility for workers. Others point to American ideas on human resources in the 1950s, which emphasised the commercial advantages of workers who felt themselves to be an integral part of a company. Labour won concessions such as relatively secure and long-term employment as well as good pay (though this was generally limited to larger companies). In response, company loyalty began to emerge within the employment system. Japanese workers, once they had accepted the new arrangement, proved to be tremendously dedicated and hardworking employees. They were also relatively passive. In the late 1950s some six million work-days were lost to strikes, but this had declined by more than half (with some yearly fluctuations) by the late 1960s.

Japanese manufacturing also grew quickly because of the strength of the *keiretsu*, the economic power that such corporate groups could bring to bear being formidable. Each *keiretsu* has a financial institution to fund the activities of its group, a cluster of companies characterised by both formal and informal linkages and direct and indirect support. Each group also has a trading company (*shōsha*) which buys and sells a range of goods domestically and abroad. In the 1950s they tended to concentrate on the basic industries favoured by the government, such as steel production, mining and shipbuilding, and were aided substantially by orders from the American military for the war in Korea.

The Occupation had also opened the way for the establishment of new companies, which released energies that might otherwise have been stifled by the rigidity of the pre-war system. These newer companies tended to find niche markets where cutting-edge technology and responsiveness to change gave them advantages over their more cumbersome, much larger, competitors. Examples here include Honda and Sony (originally Tokyo Communication Industries).

Smaller companies, however, remained the backbone of the Japanese economy. Even today they are not particularly visible internationally and receive relatively little attention in the Western press, partly because many are just providers of components for larger companies and partly because much of their output is destined for the domestic, not the international, market. However, their employees constitute the bulk of the workforce. As early as 1965, 83 per cent of Japanese workers were employed in businesses with fewer than 1000 employees, and 53 per cent in those employing fewer than 100 people. This trend continues today. These businesses tend to be family-owned and their employees are both paid less (generally about 60 per cent) and enjoy far fewer benefits than employees of large companies. The bulk of the female labour force is found in this category.

Bureaucrats and businessmen both recognised that the old problem of access to resources had to be dealt with. Since imperialism was no longer an option, Japanese companies would have to secure raw materials through trade, and this meant making products that would be in demand in the world market. The result in the early 1950s was an emphasis on relatively low-level, inexpensive products that could be easily sold abroad, initially such things as low-cost clothing, toys, cutlery, pottery and bicycles. Profits from these manufactures were ploughed back into research and development and better production techniques.

Other factors which helped the Japanese economy to grow rapidly included vision. As early as 1957 the government set out its 'New Long-Range Economic Plan' which stated that Japan would aim to compete with the advanced economies of the world. This was backed up by the more concrete activities of the Development Bank, replacing the Occupation's Recon-struction Bank in making low-interest loans available to favoured industries. Economic strategists encouraged the diversification of older (so-called 'sunset') industries into new areas through various incentives while providing other forms of economic encouragement for the new ('sunrise') industries. Industry was also highly protected during this period. While industrial policy was considered anathema in much of the West, Japanese bureaucrats often used it effectively under the heading of 'administrative guidance' (*gyōsei* shido). Ministries such as the Ministry of International Trade and Industry (MITI) were not, of course, omniscient, and sometimes they made poor choices or applied policies in ineffective ways (the Ministry told Honda, for example, to stick with motorcycles and forget car production, and only very reluctantly loaned money to Sony to buy the patent rights to the transistor). Scholars point to the confusion of the time, with such rapid changes occurring in technology, production and delivery systems, trade policies and so on, to make the point that organisations such as MITI could only hope for occasional successes. Moreover, the focus on central government-directed economic development tends to obscure both the role of often energetic and supportive prefectural governments as well as the dynamic entrepreneurial spirit of individual businesspeople. In short, multiple factors played significant roles in postwar economic development, along the lines of what one Ministry official termed a 'plan-orientated market economy'.

Japanese businesses also forged links with American firms, which facilitated the transfer of technology and production techniques (such as the 'just-in-time' parts delivery system and quality control techniques). American aid also funded the visits of hundreds of Japanese to the USA to study new technologies and production systems. The information they acquired was able to be utilised immediately because of the relatively high educational levels of the workforce in Japan. Productivity in the late 1940s had been low because of much outdated equipment, but as soon as new machinery was available this changed dramatically. Military expenditures being kept to a minimum, usually around the 1 per cent mark, left more money available for use directly in the economy. People were also encouraged to save, the funds so accumulated being used for investment in the economy, precluding a need to rely on foreign loan sources (which would have influenced domestic economic priorities). Tax reforms also encouraged investment. These factors all combined to give industry a massive boost in the late 1950s and 1960s.

Japanese agriculture underwent a similar reconstruction. Farmers began to use new fertilisers, seed strains and machinery and quickly became some of the most efficient agricultural producers in the world. They were aided by substantial returns for their produce. Agriculture was highly protected in the 1950s and 1960s (and remains substantially so today, a continued point of friction with other countries). Japanese consumers therefore paid a high price for foodstuffs, but it allowed the agricultural sector to flourish. To some extent this was also the result of self-interest on the part of government, which was closely connected to agricultural lobby groups for both financial support and votes, and politicians persuaded the public that it was their duty to support Japanese farmers. The lingering fear of starvation left over from the 1940s made such a policy relatively easy to implement. The surprise is that it has continued to resonate with the Japanese public for so many years. At the same time, because of the broad move into industry, the share of the workforce in agriculture dropped substantially between 1950 and 1970, from 48 to 18 per cent.

A combination of the developments just outlined meant that in the early 1950s the Japanese economy grew at 9 per cent per year, rising in the late 1950s through the 1960s to breakneck pace—11 per cent per annum, a sustained growth unmatched by any other major country at any time. During the 1950s Japan's GNP quadrupled.

In terms of international relations, the 1950s were generally years of growing resentment towards the USA. By 1952 the population was, generally speaking, tired of the Occupation but a substantial US military presence was kept in place because of the Cold War and the stalemate in Korea. The continued presence of US troops began to be irritating. Then in 1954, following the US hydrogen bomb test on Bikini Atoll, fish contaminated with radiation arrived in Japan via a fishing boat in the area at the time (radiation had travelled much further than the American scientists had predicted), causing a huge public outcry. Therefore, although trade with the USA grew, and Japan was a recipient of substantial investment associated with the Korean War, the counter-current of anti-American sentiment remained. In some respects the love–hate relationship with the USA today is not dissimilar.

Relations with other countries proceeded slowly. Trade reopened with the People's Republic of China (PRC), albeit at a very low level, in 1953. Trade with Taiwan, however, a country which at the time was officially recognised in Japan (as well as in the USA) as the legitimate government of China, complicated the issue. China forced Japan to choose official trading partners. Under American pressure, Japan chose Taiwan. With China backing North Korea and the USA supporting South Korea, no other choice was possible. The result was that China cut all connections with Japan in 1958. In terms of the USSR, with some of the Kuril Islands north of Hokkaido being a sticking point (both countries claimed ownership), renewing relations was a slow process and it was not until 1956 that diplomatic relations were restored, though no peace treaty was signed at the time. In another move indicative of the country's increasing economic and strategic importance, Japan joined the United Nations in 1956 (after the USSR withdrew its veto on Japan's membership).

The 1960s

The 1960s, like the 1950s, began with substantial civil unrest, this time over the renegotiation of the security treaty with the USA. President Eisenhower was to travel to Japan in 1960 to sign the treaty but widespread demonstrations in May and June (by people from a wide variety of backgrounds) caused the cancellation of the visit and the consequent resignation of Prime Minister Kishi (1957–60). A second dramatic event, minor in scale but taking place in front of television cameras, was the fatal stabbing by a right-wing extremist of the Secretary-General of the Socialist Party, Asanuma Inejiro.

These frictions highlighted both the sociopolitical divisions still evident in Japan and the changing dynamic of US–Japan relations. Japanese often refer to the 1960s, however, as the 'Golden Years'. It was a time when Japanese society, generally speaking, came together to rebuild the country and the result was astounding economic success. Ikeda Hayato (1899–1965), Prime Minister from 1960 to 1964, announced that Japanese would become rich. Japanese incomes would double by 1970 (in fact they did so by 1967), in per capita terms rising between 1960 and 1970 from $421 to $1676. Economic growth gave citizens a clear goal around which they could organise their social institutions—some observers called it 'GNP nationalism'. There was relatively little opposition to this goal. The left wing was unable to mount serious opposition; the new 'Clean Government Party' (*Komeito*), connected to the Buddhist sect *Sōka Gakkai* ('Value Creating Society'), was mostly (as suggested by its name) concerned with limiting corruption in a period of rapid economic growth.

One of the features that allowed Japanese industry to rapidly improve its products was the high expectations of the domestic market. Competition within Japan was generally fierce and people demanded value for money as well as superior service. Those companies that survived in the domestic market often found that selling their products abroad was relatively easy by comparison. A case in point was the American market. In the 1950s and 1960s America was a superpower, both economically and militarily, but along with its preeminent position seems to have come an arrogance—Americans did not have to work hard because they were number one. While Japanese manufacturers were willing to take on any change that would improve their products, American companies often seemed to be complacent. Nor were Japanese companies afraid to borrow ideas from competitors, which also gave them a long-term advantage in trade.

The 1960s saw the consolidation of what some call Japan Inc., the close cooperation of government, bureaucracy and big business. Some Japanese commentators called it the 'bureaucratic–industrial complex', as opposed to the 'military–industrial complex' of the USA. This perception is partly due to the interdependency of these groups. Campaign funds mostly come from business (the figure was about 90 per cent in the 1960s) and business expects favourable policies to follow. These funds are used primarily for 'gifts' to politicians' constituents, and are crucial to keeping them in power. Bureaucrats are also immensely influential in the way in which the economy develops and therefore to the extent to which business or specific commercial activities thrive. Their expertise also tends to make their political masters dependent on them. Furthermore, bureaucrats tend to find employment opportunities in their later careers either in politics or business, so they must make policies with an eye to the future. MITI, for example, can advise on business strategies, facilitate low-interest loans, provide priority access to raw materials and set production quotas. Members of this department have enormous expertise and power, as well as excellent networks throughout industry and the government, so they are in high demand upon retirement. At the same time, businesses join together to present the government with powerful lobby groups. The *Keidanren* (Federation of Economic Organisations), for example, has hundreds of the leading companies in Japan as members. It became particularly influential after independence in 1952 and is a very powerful voice on economic affairs, particularly given its close connections to the ruling LDP. A second such association is the *Nikkeiren* (Japan Federation of Employers' Associations) which was established in 1948 as a counterweight to the rise in union power, and continues to be a vehicle for securing policies favourable to industry.

Japanese industry was also given a boost in the 1960s by the geopolitics of the time. Japan progressively became more important to the USA in strategic terms, especially because of American military bases there and its mounting involvement in Vietnam. In return for defence cooperation, Japan was given special consideration in economic terms. The yen, for example, was held at its 1949 level (¥360 to the US dollar) throughout the 1960s, which made Japanese exports very cheap. Inflation in the US economy because of the Vietnam War also meant that Japan was able to increase its foreign exchange reserves. Preferential access was also given to Japanese products destined for the USA. One example of the impact was in the area of motor vehicles exports to the American market. In 1967, 370 000 vehicles were exported to America; by 1971 the figure had risen to 2.4 million. Total exports to the USA during this five-year period rose in value from $10 billion to $24 billion. It was not until the 1970s that this bargain of military power in exchange for economic power became unacceptable to the American government.

The result of these factors was that Japan joined the group of major industrialised nations—the Organisation of Economic Cooperation and Development (OECD)—as early as 1964, and became the third largest economy in the world (behind the USA and West Germany) by the end of the decade. Heavy industry was the initial vehicle for economic growth. The popular rallying cry was *jū-kō-chō-dai* ('heavy, thick, long, big'). In terms of value of exports, between 1960 and 1970 iron and steel production increased approximately sevenfold; ship-building, metal products and motorcycles fivefold; and automobiles fourfold. In the 1960s Japan became the world's largest ship-builder and third largest iron and steel producer (after the USA and the USSR). Towards the end of the decade Japan was also the world's third largest producer of automobiles, cement, paper and fertilisers. In the 1960s Japan also began to develop its lighter industries. The slogan switched from 'heavy, thick, long, big' to *kei-haku-tan-shō* ('light, thin, short, small'). Between 1960 and 1970 production of watches increased about 35-fold, televisions fourteen fold, and radios and tape recorders fivefold. Japanese products flooded the world and began to gain their current reputation for quality and reliability.

One of the social features of the postwar period in Japan, as in Western countries, was a baby boom. The total fertility rate (the number of children per woman of childbearing age) was 4.5 in 1947 and continued to be relatively high through

The growth of urban areas, Tokyo.

the 1950s, only dropping markedly at the end of the decade (by 1960, the figure was 2.0). The population consequently rose rapidly. In 1945 there were 72 million Japanese, but by 1967 the population had passed the 100 million mark. In part this was a reaction to wartime losses and partly to the traditional practice of farming families being relatively large. The primary factor in changing the fertility rate, however, was what geographers call 'intergenerational wealth flows', in other words whether children are an economic cost or benefit. In early agricultural communities children are a valuable source of cheap labour and insurance for ageing parents, but in a developed economy they tend to be expensive, and unnecessary for long-term financial security. The economic benefit therefore shifts from advantaging the parents to benefiting the children. Hence, while the fertility rate in the 1950s was high, with Japan's spectacular economic growth in the 1960s came much smaller families.

The drop in family size was reinforced by another great

social change, that of urbanisation. This is principally a post-war phenomenon in Japan, with the proportion of the population living in cities increasing from approximately 56 per cent in 1955 to 72 per cent in 1970. The implications have been significant for Japanese society, ranging from the type of employment in which workers engage, to location of services, the expansion of train lines and the rise in numbers of commuters and distances travelled as well as the related factor of the cost and size of family dwellings. The broader social impact was reinforced by the dislocation of the population in the early years following the Pacific War. In agricultural areas communities tended to be closely knit, with strong interpersonal and community ties. These all underwent significant change with the move to cities, especially as it was difficult for grandparents and other relatives to follow, given the restricted size of housing in the urban areas.

The rapidity of urbanisation meant that the development of infrastructure lagged. With the primary goal of industrial growth the Japanese government was loath to direct spending to social welfare, a continuance of past practice. The result was congested roads, poor sanitation facilities, little space for parks, few leisure centres (especially any which might be open to the public) and extremely small living quarters. Housing costs also rose dramatically. Between 1955 and 1970 the value of urban residential land increased fifteen fold on average, and twenty fold in Japan's six largest cities, adding to the burden of their inhabitants.

The rise and then fall of the birthrate had an impact on the educational system. Initially this was, of course, noticeable in the area of primary education. The numbers grew significantly, peaking in 1960. Following on, secondary school and then university enrolments also increased, partly because of more students and partly because of the higher educational levels demanded by an advanced industrial society. While in 1960 there were 630 000 university students, by 1970 the figure had more than doubled, to 1 410 000.

The education system was also steadily recentralised, undoing the Occupation reforms in this area. This began in the late

*A bleak urban park,
Yoyogi district, Tokyo.*

1950s, with a national curriculum established in 1958. The
Ministry of Education (Monbusho) gained substantial influence over curricula and textbooks. Many of the features
identified with the contemporary educational system, such as
its rigid structure, rigorous examination system, the relative
status of educational institutions (though with the expansion
of the university system it was far less elitist than previously)
and ongoing frictions between the Ministry of Education and
the Teachers' Union were set firmly in place in the 1960s.

Religious affiliation, too, changed during this time. With
the move to urban centres the bond with traditional practices
was often broken. New religious groups, such as the Sōka
Gakkai, attracted people who were dissatisfied with their lives
or felt alienated in their new urban surroundings. Membership

of the Sōka Gakkai presents people with a supportive social system designed to make them feel accepted and comfortable in an alien environment. The group's attractiveness is reflected in the growth of its membership—just a few thousand followers in the early 1950s increased to 4.3 million families by 1964. The rapid socioeconomic changes of the time created substantial social dislocation, which continues today. Fewer children and rapidly rising incomes meant a boom in domestic consumption. In the 1960s Japanese went on a buying spree—televisions, stereos and major appliances as well as luxury items. Fostering domestic consumption was government policy, in order to increase the country's industrial output. Consumption levels generally doubled between 1955 and 1970. For example, in the 1960s the number of urban dwellers owning vacuum cleaners increased nearly tenfold, washing machine and television ownership doubled and the number of those purchasing cameras nearly doubled. More was also spent on entertainment, both privately and through the well-known expense accounts. Leisure activities boomed. A bowling craze swept the country. Travel-related expenditures nearly doubled between 1965 and 1970 and there was a concomitant rise in international travel after the lifting of currency restrictions in the mid 1960s.

The XVIIIth Olympic Games, held in Tokyo in October 1964, sent a clear signal that Japan had arrived. They were the first Olympic Games to be held in Japan and, indeed, in Asia. It was a time to show off the new Japan to the world. One of the outstanding images was that of the Olympic Gymnasium, designed by Japanese architect Tange Kenzō. Creative energies were also highlighted by the Nobel Prize for literature in 1968 going to Kawabata Yasunari. This was an unusual event. He was one of only five Japanese ever to receive a Nobel Prize (as of 1999) compared to 193 from the USA, 69 from the UK and 62 from Germany.

The tremendous growth of the economy had a downside, however, in terms of environmental destruction. This is not a surprising development, given the focus on heavy industry, rapidly increasing levels of urbanisation and the location of industry and population along the coasts, especially the eastern seaboard and the Inland Sea. The mega-cities that were emerging in the Tokyo–Nagoya–Osaka–Kobe belt, coupled with growing automobile production and ownership, contributed to serious pollution problems. One of the images from the 1960s is that of the fresh air vending machines at busy intersections in Tokyo, where one could gain a short break from the terrifying air pollution. Policemen directing traffic suffered from lead poisoning, as do those in Bangkok today.

The waterways and oceans adjacent to the large cities were full of industrial effluent. The best-known result of Japan's water pollution was the so-called Minamata disease (named after a bay in Kumamoto Prefecture, Kyushu) which involved mercury poisoning and became public as early as 1953. The first evidence of mercury-poisoned fish came when cats began to convulse and then die. Local people also began showing the results of damaged nervous systems.

The way in which the problem was dealt with reflects the power of big business, the industrial priorities of the government at the time and the powerlessness of private citizens. For years the Nippon Chisso Corporation, which allegedly discharged the by-product methyle mercury during the manufacture of fertiliser, denied any wrongdoing and even went so far as to hire gangsters (*yakuza*) to intimidate protesters. Doctors who investigated the problem saw their findings discredited. A research group from Kumamoto University found its funding cut and its research findings covered up. It was not until widespread demonstrations took place at the plant, coupled with a press campaign and foreign involvement, that the government took action. Even then the comprehensive Pollution Counter-Measures Basic Law passed in 1967 (preceded by a range of more specific laws in the late 1950s and early 1960s) was relatively weak. Only in the 1970s were substantial measures taken to deal with Japan's pollution problems.

Another major pollution scandal was the so-called *itai itai* disease (meaning 'ouch, ouch' or 'it hurts, it hurts'). Cadmium from the Mitsui Mining and Smelting Corporation had allegedly entered the food chain via rice paddies along the Jintsū

River in Toyama-kei (the prefecture next to Nigata), causing people's bones to become brittle and fracture. Reflecting the overriding importance of the government's economic drive, however, a former Chairman of the National Public Safety Commission, Akai Masuo, exhorted people in his electorate to 'have the spirit to eat contaminated rice'. Yet another problem was sulphur dioxide pollution from oil refineries in the Yokkaichi area in 1959, which caused serious asthma problems in the local population. In both these cases the government was very slow to react. Japanese citizens therefore paid a heavy price for their economic miracle.

While there were problems at home, the 1960s was a turbulent time in Asia and proved a difficult time for Japan in terms of international relations. The PRC tested its first atomic bomb in October 1964, sending shock waves through Japan and the rest of the world. The Cultural Revolution began around the same time, sending out images of a China seemingly out of control, though it was also in the 1960s that Japan and China reestablished trade linkages. Thus there were both positive and negative aspects to Sino–Japanese relations over the decade. Vietnam posed another difficulty for the Japanese leaders, given Japan's American connections, in the competition between China, the USSR and the USA. Japan had close defence and trade linkages with America, which were called into question as the war in Vietnam escalated. Relations with the UK, however, steadily improved, and in 1963 the British Foreign Secretary, Lord Home, visited Japan, the first time such a high-level British official had ever come to Japan. In 1965 came a normalisation of relations with South Korea. Generally speaking the decade was a difficult one, however, with Japan treading carefully around Cold War conflicts while ensuring its goal of economic growth was not damaged.

The 1950s and 1960s were important decades in which the foundations were laid for the economic, political and social structures the country has today. Struggles took place between various groups in society to determine which would be more powerful in the new Japan. A range of factors—politics, culture, historical traditions, American influence during the Occupation, anxiety on the part of many citizens over the future and the geopolitical realities of the day—ultimately pushed Japan towards a mild authoritarianism, with economic growth the core of the new nationalism. The relative importance of these different factors, and the consequent reasons for rapid economic growth, continue to be debated by scholars today.

The end result was that most Japanese pulled together to make the country economically powerful beyond most people's dreams. By 1968 Japan had passed West Germany to become the third largest economy in the world. Wealth flowed through much of society, reducing political friction and commanding widespread public support for Japan's new role as manufacturer to the world. This incredible success also put the country in the international spotlight and many outsiders began to take an interest in the new Japan. Such interest, mingled with a little fear, increased as Japan consolidated its economic position in the world over the next two decades.

7
JAPAN AS NUMBER ONE?

THE 1970s OPENED WITH a celebration—the World Exposition at Osaka, where Japan was able to demonstrate to a global audience how far it had come in a mere 25 years. It was as good as the Olympics, and perhaps even better, because the focus was on technology rather than athletic prowess. While the immediate postwar period was a time for rebuilding and the 1960s put in place the basic structure of Japan's rapid economic recovery, the next two decades were a period of consolidation and expansion. What tended to surprise many people, not least the Japanese themselves, was the continuation of strong economic growth in spite of a series of hurdles throughout the twenty-year period. Japan's economy did not fall apart under the so-called 'Nixon (tariff) shock', nor when the Organisation of Petroleum Exporting Countries (OPEC) quadrupled its prices in the early 1970s. Rather, the Japanese showed themselves able to respond rapidly to such problems and pull together to overcome them. Good planning, cooperation, hard work and luck all played their roles once again.

In the 1980s Japan truly came into its own. When the yen skyrocketed in value in the mid 1980s the country's business leaders responded by massively moving industry offshore. The highly valued currency also sent the country on a global buying spree, and from this point we see again the beginning of a perception of Japan as a threat. 'Japan as number one?' unsettled not a few in the region, and even in the USA there was a taste of fear—their vanquished enemy as the next superpower? International relations, particularly with the rapprochement between the USA and China, and the beginning of the end of the USSR, made Japan's role more complex as the country's strategic value was called into question. Was Japan to become America's number one threat? The country seemed unstoppable by the late 1980s, with journalists, scholars and politicians scrambling to explain why it continued to go from strength to strength. There was an explosion of literature on everything, from how the shadowy power-brokers pulled political strings behind the scenes, to the secrets of producing high-quality industrial products, to how the Japanese mind worked. *Nihonjinron*, or the 'discussions of the Japanese', became very popular at this time, as Japanese (either public-spiritedly or smugly) tried to explain to each other as well as to the outside world how different and special they really were. In these heady days before the crash of the 1990s Japan captured the attention of the world.

Except for those fascinated by electoral rolls and voter turnout rates, Japanese postwar politics can look very dull from the outside. Prime ministers change but (almost) never the party. The political agenda remained focused on economic growth and policies stayed highly conservative. Scandals were interesting and there were plenty of those, but none sufficiently outrageous to bring down the government—just ministers or a faction. Political leadership, or at least cooperation, was very important over this period, however. Japan faced a number of crises that required both political will, sound policies and effective cooperation.

The conservative nature of Japanese politics reflects the dynamic tension between different sources of power in Japan. The question 'Who runs Japan?' is often raised, and there is no simple answer. Even in the mid 1990s Karl van Wolferen was able to publish *The Enigma of Japanese Power*, followed by Chalmers Johnson's *Japan: Who Governs?* Conventional wisdom has it that there is an 'iron triangle' of power in the country: big business, bureaucrats and politicians. The three groups need each other, and while competing for influence must also cooperate. Business depends on government to initiate policies that favour its activities, and because of the damage from the war and the need to mobilise people around some kind of nationalistic goal, business has been highly favoured by the country's politicians. Geopolitical priorities have also meant that this group has received priority for many decades. Unfortunately, this is also behind what may arguably be called an exploitation of labour, the decimation of natural resources both in Japan and abroad, and the terrifying pollution problems of the postwar period.

Nowhere is Japan's self-interest more visible than in big business. Politicians, who obtain most of their campaign funds from business, depend on economic growth to legitimise their government. Bureaucrats work closely with business to facilitate these economic goals and, as we saw in the last chapter, often find employment in private enterprise after retirement (*amakudari*, or 'descent from heaven'), using highly developed connections among industrialists, politicians and other bureaucrats. Given the nature of the political system, where politicians are preoccupied with winning the next election, and ministers remain in portfolios for relatively short periods, it is the bureaucrats who have the necessary skills and therefore a disproportionate share of the responsibility in running the country. If a politically driven policy is not supported in the machinery of government, there are many delaying and obfuscating procedures (rather than open conflict) that can be brought into play to make sure it is either watered down or never sees the light of day. Bureaucrats often have an eye on future political careers, so they must be careful not to alienate either their political contacts or the source of future funds—business. Added to this mix are the rivalries within each of the sectors.

In the political and bureaucratic spheres in particular, if a policy is well-established and working at least marginally well, there is no compelling reason to change it. Change in one area means adjustments in others, so there must be pressing need before a policy shift takes place. Even then, because of the interconnectedness of the players, policies are often developed by cooperation, so that all may at least minimise disruption or perhaps share in the benefits. However, when there truly is a need to change, and it is widely supported, the system can alter course relatively quickly and effectively. Moreover, because of the generally close relations between workers and management, the support of labour is usually forthcoming when a company, or more broadly, the economy, is threatened. Japan of the 1970s and 1980s demonstrated these characteristics, as it did in the late nineteenth century and again in the years immediately following the Pacific War.

The first major challenge of the 1970s came with the 'Nixon shock' of 1971. This had to do with Japan's trade surplus with the USA, perhaps the dominant issue in US–Japan relations ever since, and one which has coloured Japan's domestic, international and trade policies for the past 30 years. In the immediate postwar period the USA had provided Japan with massive aid, followed by special procurement orders for the Korean War and preferential access to American markets. This was not, of course, altruism on the part of the Americans. The USA needed Japan to form part of its 'fortress America' in the Pacific to guard against the expansion of communism in Asia. It was an effective trade—Japanese defence co-operation and American bases on Japanese territory in exchange for policies favourable to the country's economic growth. Military power for economic power. The problem was that few expected Japan to become so successful so quickly, certainly not to the point of challenging the USA in economic terms. The rapid and sustained rise of the Japanese economy and exports to the USA prompted a US backlash in the early 1970s, American producers complaining that Japanese businesses were damaging them. The 1949 exchange rate of 360 yen to the dollar was no longer acceptable—it made Japanese products simply too inexpensive in the American market. Hence, President Nixon forced a revaluation of the yen, to

The Mitsubishi Group, like other Japanese keirestu, is comprised of a number of related corporations.

¥308 to the dollar. In February 1973 Japan went to a floating currency, which strengthened the yen further, to ¥272 to the dollar (though it slumped in the ensuing three years). Nixon slapped a 10 per cent surcharge on all imports, in an additional bid to cut the flow from Japan. For the first time since the Pacific War, Japan was beginning to be seen as an enemy.

Part of the problem, as the Americans saw it, was the economic power of the massive Japanese conglomerates, or *keiretsu*.[1] They not only had enormous political clout in Japan (such as maintaining high tariff walls), but were able to marshal their resources to target a particular sector and destroy their competition. We have already seen their formal structure—groups of companies characterised by cross-shareholding, independent financial backing and a trading company at the core. Spreading outward (and downward) from each major corporation in the group are multiple layers of affiliated companies or suppliers which depend on the major companies for orders. The structure is also shot through with informal linkages. The senior executives of the largest companies get together on a regular basis in a group's presidential council (*shacho-kai*) where they discuss issues of mutual concern. Personal contacts and obligation also play a role. The same may be said of the linkages between the larger and sometimes thousands of smaller companies, where long-term associations may take precedence over, for example, lower component prices. There are also informal linkages between companies of a *keiretsu* and independent companies from the outside, under which loans may be arranged or other forms of business cooperation take place. These linkages constitute informal trade barriers that continue to frustrate Japan's competitors.

The economic power that these enterprise groups can bring to bear is enormous. Their sheer size is overwhelming. The six biggest *keiretsu* had 17 per cent of the total paid-in capital of Japan in 1990, as well as 15 per cent of sales and the same proportion of total assets. These figures refer only to the core companies (189 out of about two million Japanese companies in total). If one includes the subsidiary companies, in which the core companies have at least a 10 per cent interest, then the figures become 32 per cent of capital, 25 per cent of sales and 27 per cent of assets. These larger figures still do not include the financial institutions of the *keiretsu* nor the smaller companies over which the *keiretsu* hold informal influence or control.

The power generated by these groups in overseas markets is therefore considerable. In 1990, for example, the Mitsubishi *keiretsu* had more than $1 trillion in assets and $360 billion in sales. The sales figure alone is bigger than the Gross National Product (GNP) of most countries. Because of the linkages, companies can sometimes afford to operate some production lines at a deficit, even for long periods, in an attempt to destroy their competition. Although dumping is illegal, by the time a court case is finalised the damage has often been done. Further, the *keiretsu* are not averse to employing former trade officials in the target countries to argue their cases, and with their vast resources are able to mount substantial legal challenges. Added to these tactics are the high-quality personnel employed by the *keiretsu*. Since the groups' companies provide substantial prestige and benefits, many of the top graduates compete for positions in them. Other advantages include economies of scale in manufacturing, the ability to support high research and development costs and, of course, significant political power in Japan and abroad. Overlaying these considerations is the fact that larger Japanese companies in general are not expected to show short-term profits. Generally speaking, while about half of all US companies will refuse to invest in a project unless profits are seen to be forthcoming within three years, in Japan the proportion that would refuse to invest is only about 10 per cent. Long-term growth and increased market share are seen as much more important than short-term profits. The result in the 1970s and 1980s was that, in the area of consumer electronics—black and white then colour televisions, radios, stereos and the like—Japanese companies systematically destroyed their American competitors, and are today dominant in these areas. Thus the 'Nixon shock' proved not to be a long-term problem.

The second major setback of the 1970s was the 'oil shock' of 1973, with the onset of war in the Middle East and the consequent skyrocketing of the price of crude oil. This issue cut to the heart of Japan's economy—its dependence on resources. Throughout the country's modern period, access to raw materials had been its central preoccupation, leading it into imperialism and war, and eventually into a focus on trade. With nearly 90 per cent of its energy being imported by the 1970s (including 99.7 per cent of its oil), mostly from the Middle East, this was truly a time of crisis. It quickly put an end to the period of supergrowth, with the economy contracting from 9 per cent growth in 1973 to –1.3 per cent in 1974, the first time the economy had experienced negative growth since the Occupation. Japan was, once again, faced with the possibility of a return to relative poverty.

The response was a massive change in the economic structure—a move away from heavy industry into high technology. In a sense the oil crisis simply pushed Japan more quickly in the direction it had already been headed. With the rapid growth of the 1960s and the consequent rise in wages, Japan was finding it much harder to compete against low-wage countries in wage-intensive areas such as heavy industry and labour-intensive assembly lines. Countries like South Korea could provide products of equal quality, such as ships, for much lower cost. Japan was also, in the early 1970s, on the verge of making another technological leap. It was already making products similar in quality and sophistication to those of other developed countries, and since it was so far advanced could no longer depend on technology transfers from countries such as the USA. Additionally, the 'Nixon shock' had made it clear that Japan would have to pull ahead in the technological race if its products were to remain in demand throughout the world. It was no longer good enough to manufacture products of similar quality, even if they were less expensive on world markets. Protective tariffs could undercut this advantage immediately. Finally, it was a natural progression for Japan to move up the technological ladder as its industry became more sophisticated and its competitors were increasingly the leading capitalist countries of the West. The oil shock merely precipitated a change for which pressure had been building for some time. The country rose again to the challenge. By 1976 Japan accounted for 10 per cent of the world's economic output, even though it had only about 3 per cent of the world's population. It is understandable that by 1979 Ezra Vogel could publish his landmark book *Japan as Number One: Lessons for America*.

The central idea of the time was to focus on those industries which did not require huge imports of raw materials. This meant not only lighter manufactures, but also knowledge-intensive industries. The country would have to depend on the creativity and innovation (in addition to the discipline and hard work) of its people. The result was a marshalling of energies in government, academic research centres and industry to a common goal—a focus on such items as numerically controlled machine tools (especially robotics), computers, electronics (especially integrated circuits), semiconductors and biotechnology. To this end the bureaucracy played a role similar to its previous one—the provision of incentives to stimulate development. Some projects were successful while others were not. Mixed examples include the 'Very Large Scale Integration Project', the 'Fifth-generation Computer Project' and the 'Next Generation Basic Technology Project'. The government's role in these initiatives was primarily to set out broad research priorities and provide some of the funding and direction. Usually, however, the application of the findings in commercial terms was done by individual corporations. Hence, Japan's technological successes through the 1970s and 1980s were the result of multiple factors rather than, for example, bureaucratic leadership only.

The government took other measures to deal with the oil shock. Government spending was reduced and loans made to industry to help compensate for the higher energy costs. The money supply was controlled to deal with the inflation caused by the blow-out in oil prices. Exports also grew over the next few years, which helped the balance of payments. This partly offset the twenty-fold increase in the cost of imports from the Middle East due to higher oil prices. Generally speaking, the government did not have to deal with a massive increase in unemployment, which in the West would have been an assumed outcome of such an economic upheaval. Rather, companies bore the brunt of it by retraining workers, transferring them to affiliated companies or encouraging early retirement. This approach received much attention in the Western press. The Japanese response highlights the reciprocal obligation of workers and management, but also underscores the smaller role played by government in dealing with unemployment. In Western countries, if a worker were laid off the government would normally be expected to help in retraining and searching for another job and/or provide substantial unemployment or welfare benefits. In Japan the company takes much of this responsibility; in return, management expects a reduced tax rate as well as other forms of government assistance. In many respects the Japanese system is more efficient since it eliminates another layer of bureaucracy and a huge (and perhaps inefficient) government expenditure on social welfare.

In 1979–80 came a second oil shock, just as the economy was beginning to perform well once again. Growth dropped to about 5 per cent—still relatively high—and unemployment edged up slightly, but otherwise the impact of this oil shock was not nearly as severe as the first one. Partly this was due to measures which had been taken earlier by government, including encouraging the use of less energy. Imports of coal for electrical generation helped, too. In 1970 Japan imported approximately 51 million tonnes of coal; by 1980 this had increased to 72 million tonnes and it continued to rise, to 105 million tonnes by 1990. Nuclear power also took away some of the dependency on imported oil. In 1970 only 0.3 per cent of Japan's energy was provided by nuclear power but by 1980 the proportion had risen to 4.7 per cent. The overall outcome was a lessening dependency on oil, from 71.9 per cent in 1970 to 66.1 per cent in 1980, down to 58.3 per cent in 1990. The result of these changes in industrial structure and energy inputs was that from 1964 to 1984 there was a 60 per cent reduction in the ratio of raw materials per manufactured product.

Another reason Japan was able to overcome the problems it faced in the 1970s was that successive governments deliberately kept defence expenditure to around 1 per cent of GDP. Article 9 of the constitution does not preclude Japan from building up a substantial defence force, but rather forbids its use overseas. By the 1980s the SDF had approximately a quarter of a million personnel, which is substantial for a developed country. Although the Japanese government had come under considerable pressure in the 1950s to rearm, by the 1970s it had generally accepted, as did the USA, that America would provide an adequate defence of the country. That said, Prime Minister Nakasone (1982–87) helped to build up the domestic prestige of the Japanese military (though it still has an image problem), and substantially increased the Japanese contribution to the cost of the American military presence in the country (which he could afford to do since the economy grew so strongly in the 1980s).

This is not to say that the Japanese enjoyed having American bases on their soil, and there was a degree of resistance to the extension of the security treaty in 1970 with demonstrations, mostly by student groups; Tokyo University had to be temporarily closed. The level of resistance was not comparable to that of 1960, however. One factor that lessened tension was the formal return to Japan of the Ryūkyū Islands and especially Okinawa (which the USA had occupied since 1945); this was announced in 1969 and took place in 1972. Generally speaking, therefore, Japan's economy was not burdened by substantial spending on defence. Economic historians enjoy 'what if' types of scenarios, such as 'What if Japan had spent 6 or 7 per cent of its GNP on defence since the Pacific War?' Their findings suggest that this would have meant about a 2 per cent drop in the growth rate over this period—significant but not enough to have substantially changed the 'economic miracle'.

The economy also recovered quickly because of the

widespread support of labour through the 1970s and 1980s. This is understandable given the psychological shocks produced by defeat in war and occupation. National pride needed a new anchor—one which was safer than imperialism—and economic success proved to be effective. The new heroes were successful capitalists. Not everyone shared equally in the benefits of postwar economic growth, however. Larger corporations in particular were better able to provide the so-called 'three sacred treasures'—of lifetime employment, wages tied to seniority (the *nenkō* system, a short form of *nenkō joretsu*, or 'seniority ranking') and enterprise unions. The picture shown to the outside world at this time was of a business as an extended family, with security and substantial benefits being provided in exchange for loyalty, dedication and hard work. It is during this period that the West was bombarded by images of Japanese workers doing morning exercises together, singing company songs and wearing company uniforms. In exchange workers could benefit from company medical plans, live in company-provided accommodation and spend vacations at company-owned resorts. This made good economic sense, since substantial training and support of workers by a company would be rewarded by long-term service, unlike the job-hopping common in the West. By the late 1980s the average staff turnover rate in large Japanese companies was 3.5 per cent per year, while in the USA it was 4 per cent per month. The *nenkō* system also avoids jealousies arising from different rates of advancement or, generally speaking, wages. It also saves the company money with respect to younger employees since they will accept lower wages initially knowing that they will increase steadily over time. In any event, wages are not the only motivation. In 1990 the chief executive officers (CEOs) of American companies were earning on average 119 times the wage of an average worker; the figure for Japan was eighteen times. Many of the rewards of upper level employees take the form of perks, such as chauffeured cars or substantial expense accounts. It was noted by some observers in the 1980s that the amount spent on expense accounts exceeded government expenditure on education. As we have seen, however, these conditions applied to a relatively small proportion of the workforce, though it was these companies that were most visible in the international trading system and which were (overly) focused upon by Japan-watchers at the time.

Employees of larger companies also benefited disproportionately from the shift in Japan's economic structure during the 1970s and 1980s. Especially in the keiretsu there were sufficient resources to retrain workers from older industries or find them alternative employment in another of the group's companies. Workers in smaller companies were faced with much greater problems and suffered substantially, though the larger companies to which they were formally or informally connected sometimes helped them to make the shift and thereby softened the blow.

There was some degree of labour unrest during this time, given the economic changes, though more involving employees in government-owned companies than in private ones. From the 1970s to the 1990s carefully-planned 'spring wage offensives' (shuntō) took place. For at least a brief period each year considerable disruption occurred, particularly in government-owned enterprises such as Japan Airlines (JAL), Nippon Telephone and Telegraph (NTT) and Japan National Railways (JNR). It is not surprising that these organisations later became targets for privatisation. Adding to labour unrest were frictions which had been entrenched since the immediate postwar period, which saw debates over the structure of the new Japan. One of these was evident in the field of education, where the Teachers' Union and the Ministry of Education continued their struggles, the overall result of which was a marked lack of dynamism in the field of education. Hence, while some parts of Japanese society responded quickly and effectively to change, one should not overlook those sectors which continued policies that were out of date and disadvantageous to the country as a whole. Japan today remains characterised by a mix of the highly progressive and efficient, and the backward and inefficient.

What is surprising in postwar Japan, and especially after the country had achieved its remarkable economic growth, is the acceptance of the tremendous expectations of management. Workers are usually organised in an almost military-like manner, with small groups responsible for a specified work load. Mutual responsibility is emphasised, so it is a rare person who will use all of his or her allocated holidays, fail to work overtime, or call in sick, when this means that colleagues will have to compensate by working harder and longer (conversely, when an assigned task is finished early, employees may sometimes simply waste time, since they are expected to put in long hours). Added to this are the often extremely long commuting times on overcrowded public transport necessitated by the high cost of housing in central urban areas. Even then, housing is poor by the standards of many developed countries. Indeed, in 1979 the Japanese were rather shocked to learn of a statement by Sir Roy Denman of the European Commission to the effect that Japan was a nation of 'workaholics living in rabbit-hutches'. More than twenty years later people are still smarting from this observation, suggesting that it was an astute one. The lives of salarymen seemed to be characterised by limited private time for themselves or their families, and severe living conditions in many respects. Therefore, while there were certainly benefits flowing from the rapid economic growth of the time, one could also view the 'miracle' as being the result of labour exploitation, of Japanese workers paying a very heavy price for their country's economic success.

Domestic politics through the 1970s and 1980s continued to be an LDP game. The left, even united, could provide no effective alternative, and by and large maintained visibility by resorting to boycotts or noisy disruptions of the Diet to gain attention. They did increase their following, however, in the wake of the 'Lockheed Scandal'. In 1976 it came to light that the Lockheed Corporation had allegedly bribed officials at All Nippon Airways (ANA) in order to win a contract for the supply of aeroplanes, and the subsequent investigation highlighted the involvement of upper-level bureaucrats, businessmen and politicians. This led to the arrest of, among others, Tanaka Kakeui (Prime Minister 1972–74). Such an event highlights a number of aspects of the power structure in Japan.

One is the argument that in the 'iron triangle' of power there exists a regulatory mechanism. When one element becomes too strong there will be a reaction by the others to pull it back into line. Unfortunately, because there is considerable elasticity in the system, abuses often have to be substantial before this occurs and scandal is often the result. A second point is that the corporation involved in this case was American. The problem may never have come to public attention if it had been a Japanese company, since payoffs and pork-barrelling are routine among the elites and widely accepted. American companies often see things differently, especially if they are the ones missing out on the contracts. Finally, the pressure that the USA can bring to bear on Japan was then (and still is, to some extent) considerable. In fact, Japanese power-brokers often look to American reaction to (inadvertently) support their own political agendas. It enables them to push through policies which they could not otherwise do with their own resources. The phenomenon is so common that it has been given a name in Japan—*gaiatsu*, or 'foreign pressure'.

The Lockheed scandal also highlighted the existence of 'money politics' (*kinken-seiji*) in Japan. Political success and staying power is highly linked to the flow of money from business or lobby groups through politicians to campaigns and individual constituents. The first priority of a politician is to ensure a sufficient inflow of money, in exchange for political favours, and this is where corruption comes into play. On the output side a politician must meet the expectations of those in his (or occasionally her) electorate. It used to be said that a politician needs three *ban* in order to do well in the Japanese political system. The first is the *kaban*, which refers to the briefcase used to carry the money doled out to constituents at various functions such as weddings, funerals, anniversaries and other special occasions. Those helping a politician to identify community needs and organise the flow of funds (as well as help with election campaigns) are the *jiban*, or 'supporters' networks'. If all goes well and the politician is able to provide these financial favours (or semi-financial ones such as helping someone find a job, secure a government contract, or provide

Daikon *(Japanese radish)*, *Hitachi.*

the community with additional infrastructure), he will obtain a *kanban*, or 'reputation'. There is also a vested interest among constituents to keep returning the same person to the Diet, since seniority in the political system (and hence the number and magnitude of favours one can provide to an electorate) is linked to the number of times a politician is elected.

Interest groups also play a significant role in this system. One of the most prominent, because of trade frictions (primarily) with the USA, has been the Nōkyō (a short form of *Nogyo Kyōdō Kumiai*, or 'Agricultural Workers' Cooperative'), a centralised federation of agricultural collectives. Representing more than six million farmers, it is dependent on the government for a continuation of protective tariffs and subsidised inputs (such as seed and fertiliser) and for services such as marketing, insurance and the like. The result is that Japanese consumers pay extremely high costs for agricultural produce. One can imagine how cheap rice imported from, say, Vietnam or Thailand (even if it is of a different type) or even

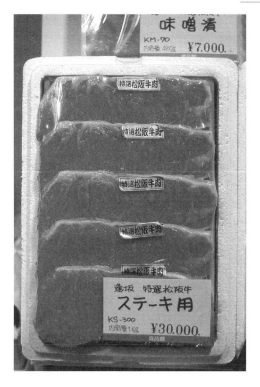

Quality beef for fine steaks comes at a high cost (approx. A$500): Shinjuku district, Tokyo.

Australia (the same type) would be, given Japan's strong currency over the past fifteen years, if there were no tariff barriers. Political support of agriculture keeps this from happening, however. Rice is imported, and it is cheaper than that produced domestically, but it is still subject to tariffs, making it more expensive for consumers. The government buys the domestic rice harvest at inflated prices, hands the money over to the *Nōrin Chūkin* (Central Bank of Agriculture and Forestry), which in turn channels funds back to the *Nōkyō* and thence to Japanese farmers for their lobbying activities. One curious result is the widespread public acceptance of the superior value of Japanese rice, an emotional attachment that transcends rationality. Another, more practical one, is the flow of money back into LDP coffers. The *Nōkyō* supports the LDP politically, and this is especially important given the relative

163

power of the rural vote (following the failure of seats to be allocated to the cities in proportion to the population). Unfortunately, beyond the high prices for agricultural goods domestically, it has also meant a progressive decrease in the efficiency of Japan's agricultural sector. In political terms, however, the cycle of benefit/obligation is complete.

In the 1980s the Japanese economy continued to grow at a reasonable rate for a developed country—generally around 3 to 4 per cent, though it strengthened steadily through the decade (reaching 4.4 per cent by 1990). It was also able to maintain its trade surpluses for a number of reasons. A stronger yen meant that inputs from overseas became less expensive. New energy sources further cut manufacturing costs, as did a steady move into the higher-technology end of manufacturing and the production of more value-added products. Added to this was the enthusiasm of Japanese industry for ensuring high-quality and value-for-money products (through fierce domestic competition), so that the reputation of the country's manufactured goods rose steadily. By the 1980s there was scarcely an area of consumer products that was not either dominated by Japanese companies or being challenged by them. In 1984, for example, Japanese companies had 84 per cent of the world's market share of both 35mm cameras and VCRs, followed by electronic watches (82 per cent), electronic calculators (77 per cent), microwave ovens (71 per cent) and memory chips (67 per cent). By the end of the decade Japan had massive overseas investments, huge trade surpluses and a global manufacturing network.

Japan's current account surplus stood at $5 billion in 1981 and rose steadily to $94 billion in 1987, before falling back to $36 billion in 1990. The US current account started off with a $6 billion surplus in 1981 but this fell to a $7 billion deficit the next year. It bottomed at a massive $144 billion deficit in 1987 before reaching a $92 billion deficit in 1990. The two sets of figures are, of course, connected, especially since by 1990 approximately 30 per cent of Japan's exports went to the USA and 23 per cent of its imports came from there. Indeed, increasing exports brought Japan further into conflict with its major trading partner. Although higher energy costs and Nixon's tariff increase wreaked a degree of havoc in the economy, Japanese products continued to be in high demand throughout the world. The total value of Japanese exports in 1960 was just $4 billion; this had increased massively—to $150.5 billion—by 1981. Although energy problems caused a negative balance of payments in 1979 and 1980, the trade surplus with the USA remained. Through the late 1980s Japan's trade surplus with the USA hovered around the $40–$50 billion range.

By the mid 1980s there was mounting pressure from Japan's trading partners, especially the USA, to deal with the 'surplus problem'. The result was the Plaza Accord of 1985, named after the meeting at the Plaza Hotel in New York of financial advisers from Japan, the USA, the UK, France and Germany. They agreed to push the yen upward in value, and some measures were taken to open Japan's economy to foreign competition. The expectation in terms of the currency was straightforward—a stronger yen meant higher prices for Japanese exports, which meant that fewer people would buy them. Through the early 1980s the yen to US dollar exchange rate had fluctuated between 220 and 240 yen to the dollar. By 1988, however, it had strengthened to about 130, a period that was justifiably called endaka, or 'high yen' (though this high value has generally held ever since, and even strengthened considerably in the mid 1990s). The resilience of Japanese manufacturers, however, was underestimated. As in the early 1970s, the stronger yen again made industrial inputs much cheaper. The continued move of Japanese products up the technological ladder also helped compensate for higher costs. Other products were simplified. Between 1985 and 1986, for example, one could see items such as microwave ovens lose a number of their functions. Japanese manufacturers estimated (accurately, as it turned out) that few people care to bother programming their ovens to start in mid-afternoon to have roasts ready in time for dinner. By eliminating such esoteric functions the cost of the ovens was reduced and the product

The most expensive land in the world: grounds of the emperor's palace, Tokyo.

remained competitive. The result of such innovations was a continued global trade surplus—nearly $107 billion in 1988.

An important consequence of the Plaza Accord was that the Japanese government tried to compensate for the surplus by encouraging domestic consumers to buy more. The situation was such that in 1985 Prime Minister Nakasone went on television to try to persuade Japanese to purchase more foreign (especially American) goods. Unfortunately, few were so inclined. In order to stimulate consumption, both to counter the higher cost of Japanese products abroad and to lessen the trade surplus with the USA, banks provided loans at very low interest rates. As land and buildings were most commonly used as collateral, this naturally led to a surge in land prices, exacerbated by the activities of speculators in the market. By the late 1980s land had become ridiculously expensive. The Western press would run articles which showed a square centimetre diagram and talked about the value of this much land in different parts of Tokyo. Various statistics designed to shock and impress were bandied about, not least by Japanese, who were proud of their new wealth: the grounds of the Imperial Palace were of the same value as the state of California; parts of Tokyo were worth more than ten times that of the business districts of Manhattan; the central Chiyoda district of Tokyo was of the same value as all of the territory in Canada; metropolitan Tokyo had the same worth as the USA; the total value of Japan was equal to 60 per cent of the world's land surface. Other statistics reinforce this picture. For example, between 1960 and 1990 the cost of urban land in Japan increased about 145-fold (wages rose 25-fold over the same period). Unfortunately, such values reflect blatant speculation as well as the involvement of the banks, which were overvaluing land in order to justify overlending to companies which had relatively poor collateral. Increases in the value of real estate did not create new wealth—it merely relied on changes in the perception of land value. A dangerous situation began building up in the banking system. One study of more than 800 companies on the Tokyo Stock Exchange showed that 44 per cent of their assets were in land, as opposed to the usual 4 per cent, and that they had borrowed massively using this land as collateral.

While real estate values showed one side of the speculation boom, the other was speculation in the stockmarket. Companies were being encouraged to grow by the Ministry of Finance (among others) and new shares were being issued in Japan and abroad. With low interest rates and easy terms, private as well as corporate investors borrowed to invest in the stockmarket as well as in real estate. With the rapid rise in the value of the stockmarket ever more people got onto the bandwagon. As in other countries in other times, a bubble was building that would collapse with substantial repercussions for both the domestic and international economies in the early 1990s.

Perhaps the most visible result of the Plaza Accord at the time, however, was the increased movement of Japanese industry offshore. This was not a new development, since Japanese companies had been moving to Europe and the USA since the late 1960s. However, this new round of investment was of much larger scale. It went in two broad directions—to developed countries to protect Japanese companies from increases in tariffs and to access high technology, and to underdeveloped countries to gain the advantage of low labour costs, access to raw materials and dominance in regional markets. Both movements were to have far-reaching implications.

The European and American recipients of Japanese investment viewed it with mixed feelings. On the one hand it created jobs and at least to some extent contributed to the tax base—but there were criticisms, too. One of these concerned the manner in which Japanese companies selected the location of their industries. In the USA it was often the case that states bid against each other to secure investments, which meant substantial tax breaks and other subsidies from the 'winning' state for the Japanese companies. Once an industry was established, components often came directly from plants in Japan and American workers simply assembled them. Thus there was little in the way of technology transfer or spin-off employment or revenue. Eventually this became a point of heated debate with the American government, to the point where proportions of domestically produced components were negotiated. The Japanese complaint was that locally produced components were sometimes of problematic quality. Americans were also critical of the way Japanese companies replicated their industrial structures in the USA, with component suppliers following the parent company. A case in point was Toyota, which set up a factory in Kentucky in the 1980s. Numerous component manufacturers followed, either purchasing local companies or starting up their own production lines. Whichever form they took, they tended to win the supply contracts from Toyota, the result of which was not only local resentment, but profits returned to Japan. The situation was similar in Australia, where Japanese car manufacturers argued that they could only maintain profitability behind high tariff barriers, so Australian consumers wound up subsidising Japanese (and American) companies through high vehicle prices—and again the profits returned to foreigners. The major benefit was employment, a questionable advantage given the high cost of protecting the industry.

Japanese investment patterns also caused friction overseas. Real estate was a particular favourite, especially in tourist destinations that were popular with Japanese travellers. Japanese companies made massive purchases, for example, in Hawaii (Honolulu's Waikiki Beach) and on Queensland's Gold Coast. In the financial year 1987–88, 60 per cent of Japanese investment in Australia went into real estate. Though local realtors, landowners and sellers benefited, the overall result was a substantial increase in property values that hurt other potential entrants to the market. Added to this was the tendency towards vertical integration in the Japanese tourism industry, where networks between or within companies meant that spending by Japanese tourists was channelled through these companies, from the airlines used, to hotels, tour operators, visitors' centres and gift shops. The lack of benefit to locally owned companies inevitably produced a backlash. So too did high-profile purchases. There was a certain irony in having substantial Japanese investment in tourism so close to Pearl Harbor. Other purchases, such as that of Columbia Pictures by Sony Corporation or the Rockefeller Center in New York by Mitsubishi Real Estate, both in the late 1980s, tended to create shock and dismay over the obvious might of the Japanese economy, and a fear of economic imperialism (though, it should be noted, these purchases were made at vastly inflated prices and the buyers lost dearly when they later sold them). There was some cause for concern at the time, however. In 1982 Americans owned more assets abroad than foreigners owned in the USA (about $152 billion). By 1991 the situation had been reversed, with the balance in favour of foreign owners of American assets to the tune of about $757 billion. At one point Japanese owned 4 per cent of the US economy, and it is not surprising that this caused Americans to worry. Of course, this could be said to be the fault of the Americans, who had both borrowed money and sold assets in order to enjoy an artificially high standard of living.

The other side of trade frictions with developed countries lay with the access of foreign companies to Japanese markets. In 1970 total Japanese overseas investment was $3.6 billion; by 1980 it had jumped significantly, to $160 billion, and by 1991 was a whopping $2 trillion, while foreign investment in Japan in 1989 amounted to only $16 billion. With the growth of the US deficit it became imperative that Americans in particular gain greater access to Japanese markets, otherwise they would have to cut spending (and live within their means) or erect higher trade barriers (both damaging trading relationships as well as supporting uncompetitive industries). As we have seen, however, foreign access to the Japanese market is a particularly difficult issue, given the close links between the centres of power in Japan which have created a host of formal and informal barriers to foreign goods. The self-interest within the system meant that considerable pressure had to come from outside the country before any action could be taken—*gaiatsu* making itself felt again. At the same time, highly emotive reactions to the Japanese presence in US markets, and to American attempts to penetrate markets in Japan, made trade negotiations between the two sides extremely difficult.

The Japanese side was particularly adept at presenting both objective and subjective reasons for their reluctance to open markets. Some issues, such as the unsuitability of American goods for Japanese households, were valid. Criticisms included relatively poor quality, appliances being too big or noisy for Japanese homes and the lack of adequate service networks. Other reasons (or stalling methods) were not so convincing, such as the need to 'study the situation' or 'process applications', which might take years. In the area of agriculture one argument presented was that Japan needed to be able to sustain its food-production capacity—this was clearly spurious since self-sufficiency had been lost long ago. Others pointed to the culturally-based 'special qualities' of Japanese rice, including its intimate connections with Shintō and the emperor; even the mystical qualities of sake were cited. Stranger was the claim that Japanese stomachs could not digest foreign rice. Perhaps a more reasoned argument was that imported rice did not suit Japanese dishes such as sushi, but this did not account for restrictions on Japonica rice grown in such countries as the USA and Australia. Some liberalisation eventually did occur in areas such as oranges and beef, but progress was very slow. The USA finally resorted to targeting specific sectors, and invoking tough measures such as Article 301 (the so-called 'super 301') of the US Trade Act, which allowed for harsh retaliation if specific markets remained closed.

Both Japan and the USA, however, were constrained in how far they could go in terms of trade restrictions, for over the years the two economies had become highly interdependent. The reality was that Japan by the late 1980s was the largest creditor nation in the world while the USA, under President Reagan, had become the largest debtor nation. This occurred through a combination of high American interest rates, substantial tax cuts and increased defence spending (the US defence budget doubled in the first half of the 1980s). The first factor attracted substantial foreign currency, which strengthened the US dollar, while the latter two led to significant economic growth, though the cost was a rapid increase in the American deficit. This in turn meant that the USA had to borrow money from somewhere. Japan effectively became America's banker. The USA tended to depend on Japanese banks to purchase such items as American treasury bonds in order to finance the deficit so that interest rates could be held down. If (already high) interest rates had to be increased to attract other bond buyers, the American economy would slow and government spending would have to be cut. This included the defence budget, which had contributed substantially to the deficit in the first place when America attempted to drive the Soviet economy into the ground by forcing high levels of military expenditure. A strong economy in the USA also meant that Americans could continue to buy Japanese products, a fact upon which Japanese manufacturers depended since the USA was by far their largest market. A fundamental point here is that Japanese products were popular with American consumers. In 1970, for example, the Japanese share of the

American automobile market was just 5 per cent; twenty years later this share had increased to 28 per cent. Trade frictions had the potential to severely damage both trading partners, and managing this issue through the 1980s was a preoccupation of both governments. In 1987 things came to a head when the Reagan Administration charged Japanese companies with unfair trading practices and slapped a 100 per cent tariff on selected products. The Japanese government responded by delaying their purchase of treasury bonds the next time they were offered for sale, making the point clearly that Japan's economic power had become formidable and the USA would have to take this into account in future.

The steady integration of European countries over the 1970s and 1980s (into a single market by the end of 1992) meant that Japanese investment there was also important if companies were to avoid potential protectionist policies. For reasons similar to its penetration of the American market, therefore, Japanese investment also flowed to Europe. In the period 1961–70 Japanese investment in Europe totalled only $626 million, but by 1974–80 it had increased to $3.8 billion, and it went up sharply again, to $10 billion, in 1981–86. In high-profile projects Japanese financial institutions were also active. The Eurotunnel, for example, connecting the UK and France, was one-third funded by Japanese investors. In terms of trade, by the late 1980s the countries of the (future) EU were receiving about the same value of Japanese exports as the USA.

With the combination of a strong currency, the need to reduce labour costs in manufacturing and a desire to secure sources of raw materials, investment in Asian countries was a logical step, especially since many of the economies were growing quickly and would provide lucrative opportunities for Japanese companies as well as an increasing market for Japanese products (especially lower-technology ones that were less suitable to Western markets).

Japan's investment in all Asian countries between 1951 and 1990 totalled $47.5 billion. The largest slice went to Indonesia ($11.5 billion) followed by Hong Kong ($9.8 billion),

Japan figures prominently among foreign investors in Ho Chi Minh City.

Singapore ($6.5 billion) and Thailand ($4.4 billion). Over the ten-year period between 1980 and 1990, trade with Asia doubled in value. By the end of the decade Japanese exports to the region were worth $287 billion while imports totalled $235 billion, a massive amount that was also, it should be noted, substantially in Japan's favour. The type of investment varied according to the level of development and resource base of the different countries. In Hong Kong and Singapore, for example, commerce and services received most investment whereas manufacturing dominated in Taiwan, Thailand, Malaysia and the Philippines. Investment in resources was by far the largest sector in Indonesia but was also significant in the Philippines.

Manufacturing in Southeast Asia was predicated on low wages. By 1989 wages in the manufacturing sector in Jakarta and Bangkok were only 4 per cent and 10 per cent of those in Japan, respectively. For labour-intensive industries this was a tremendous advantage. Manufacturing in such countries had other benefits for Japan. One was that Japan itself was the destination for many of the products, particularly through *keiretsu* networks. In 1990 about 60 per cent of exports to Japan from Asia were manufactured products, and these partly helped reduce the cost of inputs for Japan's domestic industries. Another advantage was that it made Japan's trade surpluses look less formidable since exports from these countries were counted in their trade figures rather than in those of Japan. This was an important consideration in the late 1980s, given trade frictions with the USA in particular. Through this investment Japanese companies also gained access to domestic Asian markets, and helped reduce Japan's dependence on the US market. Total trade with Asia between 1985 and 1990 was on a par with the USA, at 28.9 per cent and 29.5 per cent, respectively. By 1990, however, Asia had overtaken the USA as an export destination.

The analogy often used for Japanese investment in Asia through the 1980s was that of 'flying geese', referring to an economic development theory created by Japanese economist Akamatsu Kaname in the 1930s. The proposition was that Japan, as an advanced industrialised country, could provide the developing countries of Asia with capital and technology which would allow their economies to strengthen in both size and technological sophistication. It was a tiered process, however. Japanese companies used selective investments. The countries immediately below Japan in terms of wealth and level of technology were the Newly Industrialising Countries (NICs), also referred to as the Newly Industrialising Economies (NIEs) or the 'Mini-dragons'—Hong Kong, Singapore, Taiwan and South Korea. They received investments appropriate to their existing technological levels, educational systems and broad economic sophistication—in other words, medium to high levels of technological inputs. The next tier, the Association of South East Asian Nations (ASEAN) or 'wannabe NICs' of Thailand, the Philippines, Malaysia and Indonesia (as well as, often, China) received low to medium technological inputs.

Investments in Asian countries were based on carefully

determined comparative advantage—wherever investment would provide the greatest returns. The second part of the 'flying geese' theory argued that countries in each tier would also invest in countries lower down the scale. Indeed, this process has become highly complex, with capital and technology flowing in multiple directions. Japanese firms, for example, may invest in Taiwan, which also invests in Malaysia. Some Malaysian businesses may establish themselves in China or Indonesia, where wealthy companies or individuals may also be investing in the more developed countries of the region. Investment therefore moves up and down the technology ladder. The leader, however, in terms of technological sophistication and wealth, is Japan, spurred on by a high-value yen and the need to locate labour-intensive industries in lower-wage countries.

Given the structure of the Japanese *keiretsu*, it is not surprising that different companies in a group, or even just one such company, will set up shop in different countries, again depending on comparative advantage. Thus components of various electronics devices or automobiles, for example, may be manufactured in many different places. Thailand may make diesel engines, the Philippines transmissions, electronics components may come from Malaysia, and pressed parts from Indonesia. Assembly of the components may take place in part or whole in one of those countries (such as the Proton cars of Malaysia, an operation created by Mitsubishi Motors Corporation). Components or finished products may also be exported back to Japan or to other developed countries. For example, most of the television sets sold under Japanese names in Australia are in fact manufactured partly or completely in Southeast Asia. The result is a veritable web of investment, trade and manufacturing leading to complex intra-regional (indeed global) dependencies. Some observers argue that this is the 'Greater East Asian Co-Prosperity Sphere' revisited, which allows Japanese companies to shop the region for the best value-for-money products. One disadvantage for Asian countries is that the highest level technology is retained in Japan so it can maintain its economic lead. Another is, of course, that if Japan has economic problems the other countries will, too, and more so if investment is diverted back to Japan. This was partly the problem in the 'Asian meltdown' of the late 1990s, which will be looked at in the next chapter.

Australia provides an interesting case of Japanese investment following the principles of ensuring an adequate supply of raw materials and targeting those sectors which will provide the highest returns. As Australia is a relatively high-wage country, investment in manufacturing was either in areas which relied on a high skill level in the workforce and/or where the industry was protected. The presence of Mitsubishi Motors, Toyota and (for a while) Nissan reflects these factors. We have already referred to the massive investments in real estate on the Gold Coast. Finance and insurance, and transport, were areas also favoured by Japanese companies. The other major area of investment in Australia was in natural resources. Japanese companies made substantial purchases in existing coal-extraction companies and in companies connected to forestry products such as pulp and paper. As a result, nine major Japanese trading companies in 1988 accounted for 20 per cent of Australia's exports. In the area of woodchips, the Japanese-dominated industry supplied 6.8 million cubic metres to the world market (the total of which was 14 million cubic metres), and Japan took a whopping 11.8 million cubic metre share. This selective application of investment has caused some scholars to refer to Australia's role as a combination of Japan's playground and its quarry.

By the end of the 1980s Japan's domestic economy and its position in world markets was far more advanced than it had been twenty years earlier. GNP had increased approximately sixfold between 1970 and 1990. Economic growth was the central focus of Japanese efforts for these two decades, which explains the emphasis on the country's commercial activities in this chapter. The result was the dominance of many global markets, from consumer electronics to automobiles, and a massive presence in foreign economies. Japanese financial institutions, too, became both successful and integral players in the global economy. By 1988, 24 of the world's 50 largest banks were Japanese. When Emperor Hirohito died in 1989, Japan was a very different place from the country in which he began his reign in 1926.

Such growth had costs, however, particularly in terms of the lives of Japanese workers. Many foreigners charged the Japanese with being only 'economic animals' who had sacrificed quality of life for financial gain. Since these issues are tied up with current social ills in Japan they are dealt with in the next chapter. The 1990s also saw the end of the Japanese economic juggernaut; by the end of the decade its weaknesses were all too apparent.

8
BURSTING BUBBLES

JAPAN IN THE 1990s presented a very different picture to the world than it had only a few years earlier. In the late 1980s many stood in awe of the country's economic might, with its tentacles seemingly probing into every corner of the globe. Mitsubishi, Panasonic, Sony, Yamaha—these and many more were household names around the world. The country was awash with cash. Foreigners who journeyed to Japan returned with stories of a country where cups of coffee could cost more than $10, dining out required a small bank loan, rents were astronomical, living conditions crowded and often rudimentary and where people were willing to sacrifice all for economic growth.

With the bursting of its 'bubble economy' the media tended to react by describing Japan as suddenly hopeless. Books and articles used words like 'collapse', 'adrift' and 'crisis'. Perhaps this is artistic licence, but it was confusing for those trying to figure out what was actually happening to the economy. How could it be unstoppable one minute and stone-dead the next? In fact, as is often the case, the truth was somewhere in between. Japanese society had characteristics such as close personal business networks, government–business cooperation and Confucianist principles which worked well when the economy was growing but inhibited change when policy adjustments became necessary. The result was a decade of struggle for Japanese business, and many companies are not yet out of the woods. Added to this are a number of social problems that began to manifest themselves in the 1970s and 1980s and came into sharper focus in the 1990s as the media turned the spotlight on 'Japan's problems'. One should avoid, however, the media-like tendency to view Japan in extremes. Substantial problems did arise in a number of areas, but the difficulties should not be overstated.

The end of the bubble economy

Although hindsight is truly 20:20 vision, capitalism is characterised by boom-and-bust cycles, and Japan had had an exceptional run of economic success by the end of the 1980s. Perhaps the Japanese really believed what was being said about them by the rest of the world. They had created an economic miracle and a global industrial empire from almost a standing start (or so it had seemed), so perhaps they thought that their run of good fortune would never end. This belief was, as we now know, misplaced.

The economy at the beginning of the decade had both positive and negative aspects. The high yen following the Plaza Accord pushed Japanese companies overseas where they were usually able to generate good returns on their investments. Manufactured goods from these countries, sold under Japanese brand names but at lower prices because of the reduced wage costs, found their way around the world. The Japanese economy (powered by both overseas investment and domestic demand) grew steadily through the 1980s, hitting 5.3 per cent (GNP) growth in 1990. Following the Ministry of Finance's lead of encouraging economic expansion, Japanese companies engaged in both domestic and foreign share floats. The Bank of Japan kept interest rates down and made borrowing relatively easy to stimulate the economy after the slowdown in the 1970s. This money, easily accessible to both private and corporate investors, tended to find its way into real estate (often used as collateral for the purchase of stocks) and the stockmarket, reinforcing the perception that the economy was on an unstoppable roll. More and more people were caught up in the borrow-buy-sell cycle. The value of the stockmarket doubled between 1986 and 1989. Unfortunately, as we have seen, it was substantially based on speculation. What tended to mislead people caught up in the land and stockmarket booms was that the part of the Japanese economy where they made real products and sold them was doing very well. If people looked around, the evidence of wealth was everywhere. Although some invested their savings or profits from the stockmarket, others engaged in conspicuous consumption— BMWs, Bulgari watches and Louis Vuitton handbags, not to mention first-class tickets to the countries that made these products. The tourism industry boomed, with even the government trying to get people to spend more overseas (and thereby help reduce Japan's trade surpluses). Clearly, the good life had arrived.

At some point in 1990 investors started to look at their portfolios and reflect on their real value. Rents were high but it would take eons before they would pay off the cost of the land upon which the buildings were situated. Stocks were often simply not providing the returns relative to purchase price. Some blamed the new head of the Bank of Japan, Yasushi Mieno, who decided things were getting out of control and raised interest rates to slow the growth rate, but the end was inevitable. Typical of a capitalist economy, when the run started it tended to move as quickly backward as it had forward. The bubble had burst.

There was a tremendous amount of finger-pointing in the months and years that followed, but many different people had contributed to the problem. One could blame foreigners for forcing a higher yen in the mid 1980s or for being so welcoming of Japanese investment, Japanese politicians for over-stimulating growth, bureaucrats for mismanaging the economy, private and corporate speculators for their greed, opportunistic (or dishonest) stockbrokers, securities companies or *yakuza* for overwhelming self-interest. The apportioning of blame did not alter the bleak facts. The stockmarket lost nearly $2.6 trillion before the slide stopped, dropping 60 per cent in value between December 1989 and August 1992. The people especially hurt were those who had climbed on the bandwagon late in the day. Early investors may have finished up with a modest profit since they had invested when the value of stocks and real estate was relatively low. All of this was exacerbated, however, by the fact that money had often been borrowed by the speculators, and since banks are usually substantially funded by the savings of ordinary citizens, ordinary citizens ultimately suffered from the bust even when they were not directly involved.

The problems were felt throughout the economy. Sales of manufactured products fell with the drop in domestic demand, and industrial production consequently declined. Retail businesses also felt the impact immediately, with consumers tending to buy cheaper products provided by newly established 'discount' stores. Many other companies went bankrupt. Japanese banks in particular were in bad shape. As early as 1993 the 21 biggest banks in Japan claimed $145 billion in 'nonperforming' loans, and about one-third of that amount was believed to be lost for good, though later it was discovered that much more debt had been hidden through creative bookkeeping.

As in other economies dealing with recession, unemployment rose. In earlier times, such as the oil shock of the early 1970s, Japanese companies had been reluctant to lay off workers, but this time many felt compelled to do so. Rather than just temporary staff (mostly women) or those in smaller supplier companies being let go, mainstream workers were targeted. Powerful corporations such as Nippon Telephone and Telegraph (NTT), Hitachi and Fujitsu cut permanent staff. The unemployment rate (fraught with problems of calculation and hidden unemployment, and giving artificially low figures) stood at 2.1 per cent in 1990 but had jumped to 5 per cent by the end of the decade, by far the highest since 1960.

Especially hard hit were middle managers, who were usually thought to be secure in the employment system. Tens of thousands were retrenched and others forced to take lower-level positions. The vaunted system of lifetime employment no longer appeared tenable, and this sent shock waves through Japanese society. One immediate impact was to reinforce people's propensity to save. Although savings rates fell through the 1970s and 1980s, they grew in the early 1990s (about 14 per cent in 1991, up to 17 per cent in 1993) and then stabilised in the later part of the decade at about 13 per cent of household income. This was still high compared to, for example, the USA and Canada, both at just over 2 per cent. Household savings grew steadily through the same period, with an average total of $167 000 by 1998. Total Japanese savings by that year amounted to $9.2 trillion. Convincing consumers to spend their savings to rejuvenate the economy, however, was exceedingly difficult in a time of high unemployment and recession.

The situation was made even worse by the widespread shift in perceptions of the economy. Typical of a capitalist system, much of an economy's strength or weakness depends on whether people *believe* it is strong or weak. Reaction is therefore often over-reaction. Because so many people were hurt by the economic downturn, faith in the economy quickly disappeared. Furthermore, when inappropriate practices among those controlling the economy came to light (including corruption, cozy government–corporate relationships, pork-barrelling politics and sheer incompetence), faith in the system as a whole was badly shaken, to the point that at the beginning of the twenty-first century the system, along with the economy has yet to fully recover. This is one of the disadvantages of the interlocked Japanese system. After all, if bureaucrats at the Ministry of Finance were not able to manage the economy, this called into question the educational system that had trained them, the selection process for their positions, the dependence which politicians had on them and their networks of personal relationships (including the notions of reciprocal obligation and mutual dependence). Each of these problems reverberated further through the system to the point where many people threw up their hands in resignation or disgust. How can we fix our problems when they are so immense, widespread and complex?

Along with the economic problems, naturally enough, came political ones. Some argue that with the passing of Emperor Hirohito in early 1989 there was perhaps some concern over cultural continuity, though this would have been more prevalent among older Japanese. If one accepts the argument that the emperor has long been the cultural core of Japanese society, it follows that a younger, more outward-looking emperor might compound the difficulties of losing one who had been a point of stability for such a long time (63 years) and had seen Japan through the worst period in its history. It may be that this change contributed in some small way to the instability of the time; on the other hand, though, the pomp and circumstance of the November 1990 accession ceremonies of the new emperor (Akihito) reinforced rather than challenged the power of the country's cultural traditions.

Certainly at the coalface of Japanese politics changes were taking place. There had been widespread public concern over money politics in Japan for some time, and this came to a head in the late 1980s. The Recruit Scandal of 1989 involved a company which offered stocks to Japanese elites (including politicians, bureaucrats and businessmen) before they were floated on the exchange. As with previous scandals it resulted in the resignation of, among others, Prime Minister Takeshita Noboru, and further undermined public confidence in fundamental Japanese institutions. The economic problems of the early 1990s reinforced the image of an ineffective and corrupt political system. A specific point of concern was the amount spent on election campaigns, one that seems familiar today given the current debate over the issue in the USA. The problem was exacerbated in Japan because of multi-member constituencies, where often the only difference between candidates (since there was often more than one from the LDP) was how much money they could spread around. Eventually this was resolved through the use of proportional representation in these constituencies, but in the short term it contributed to public distrust of the political process.

The government in the early 1990s also had to deal with the pressing issue of tax reform. There were two issues driving it: income tax cuts to stimulate the economy out of its recession and the need for more money in government coffers to fund public works projects and to support a rapidly ageing population. The result had been the introduction of a 3 per cent consumption tax as early as 1989, but there was substantial debate over whether or not it should be increased. It was, to 5 per cent in 1997, but only in the face of substantial popular resistance. There was also considerable debate about the appropriateness of this measure at a time of economic recession.

The end of the bubble economy caused widespread damage and loss of confidence in the economy and government, and political upheaval in the 1990s was to be expected. Money politics contributed to the general disillusionment, where established networks now seemed to interfere with repairing the economy, and electoral reform was superficial at best. Many older Japanese worried about security in old age. While they tended to support the LDP (better the devil you know), there was also substantial popular dissatisfaction. The result was a split in the LDP. The Japan New Party, under the leadership of (former LDP member) Hosokawa Morihiro, combined with seven smaller parties to form a coalition government and for the first time since 1955 the LDP lost power.

Not surprisingly, given the difficult issues faced by the new government and the problems inherent in an eight-party coalition, the new government was short-lived. Hosokawa was made Prime Minister in August 1993 but announced in February 1994 his intention to resign. His successor from April 1994 was Hata Tsutomu, but he lasted only two months. A compromise was subsequently reached in an attempt to end the confusion. In June 1994 a member of the Social Democratic Party of Japan (SDPJ—the renamed Socialist Party), Murayama Tomiichi, became Prime Minister, but in a government where key portfolios were held by members of the LDP.

Then, in 1996 the LDP was returned to power (albeit as part of a coalition), though public apathy showed itself in the lowest-ever voter turnout. Perhaps it was also this apathy that, the year before, had led to two former comedians being elected as the governors of Tokyo and Osaka. Volatility remained a central aspect of Japanese politics through the decade, with eight different Prime Ministers between 1989 and 1999. The situation was neatly summed up by former German Chancellor Helmut Kohl, who allegedly remarked that he was getting tired of meeting new Japanese prime ministers.

The Japanese government attempted to fix its economic problems through the classic approach of public spending. From 1992 onwards various stimulus packages were produced, including massive injections of money ($84 billion in 1992, $119 billion in 1993, $150 billion in 1994, $75 billion in 1995, $123 billion in 1998 and $137 billion in 1999) as well as tax cuts, and financial aid to banks and smaller businesses. Bank bailouts were a particular focus, and the extent of debt and sloppy procedures led to the creation of a new supervisory agency for the banks. The major development here was the establishment by government of a 'bridge bank' in 1998 to take over some $540 billion in bank debt, thereby isolating the problem and eliminating widespread bankruptcies in this sector. Bank mergers were also organised, including ones by Sumitomo and Sakura Banks, and Asahi and Tokai Banks. This may have strengthened the banking sector, but it also led to substantial job losses. While these measures did shore up the growth rate to some extent, they did not serve to restore public confidence or revive the economy. Partly this was because much of the money was spent on infrastructure projects ($183 billion since 1998 alone), and reinforced the cozy relationship between the Japanese government (especially the Ministry of Construction) and construction companies. Fundamental political reform did not seem to be forthcoming.

On the international front the situation was also confusing. The trade surplus grew substantially, from $36 billion in 1990 to $84 billion in 1992 and $109 billion in 1993, partly because Japanese reduced their purchases of foreign luxury goods (which had been a hallmark of the bubble economy) and partly because Japanese companies made special efforts to sell their merchandise abroad to compensate for lower domestic demand. At the same time, many companies shed their overseas investments (especially real estate) in order to bring needed capital home. This meant converting foreign currencies to yen, resulting in a massive increase in the value of the yen. In 1990 the average yearly yen to US dollar exchange rate stood at about 145 but strengthened steadily, to 94 in 1995 (at one point going below 80) before falling to about the 130 mark. The recession in Japan through the first half of the decade therefore had a decidedly odd flavour, with both the balance of trade improving and the currency getting stronger while massive public spending was creating substantial government debt.

The situation was complicated by American dissatisfaction with a trade deficit that was once again growing, to more than $60 billion in the mid 1990s, falling to just over $50 billion by the end of the decade (though the shifting exchange rate plays havoc with figures in US dollars). Given that the Japanese government was having a great deal of difficulty in convincing its citizens to spend more, persuading them to buy American products was a major challenge. With US negotiators targeting specific sectors, sometimes the Japanese government itself brought pressure to bear on its citizens to buy the items.

In other parts of Asia circumstances were different. Goods produced in developing countries in the region were relatively inexpensive, and therefore sold better in a recession-plagued Japan as well as on the world market. Japanese investment in Asia soared, especially in the manufacturing sector. By the mid 1990s, three-quarters of new Japanese projects in this area were either in China, the NICs or the ASEAN Four (Malaysia, the Philippines, Thailand and Indonesia). The total value of Japanese investment in these countries nearly doubled between 1989 and 1994, and increased an additional 50 per cent between 1994 and 1997. In spite of the amount of money flowing offshore, however, the balance of trade remained heavily in Japan's favour.

This growing Japanese presence in Southeast Asia in particular was received, as before, with mixed feelings. The perception in some countries was that Japanese companies were too powerful and could not be trusted. It was certainly the case that the benefits of investment were not evenly spread. While semi-skilled employment was boosted, the benefits flowed primarily to local elites, reinforcing socioeconomic inequities. Where anti-pollution laws existed they were often ignored—in the area of forestry, for example. Japan became the world's largest importer of tropical wood products. The result in the logged areas was erosion, floods, decimation of plant, animal and bird species, and the destruction of the traditional livelihoods of those who lived in the forests. They had little political power, however, compared to Japanese-supported governmental and local elites.

Japan's unwillingness or inability to help its Asian neighbours was brought to light in the Asian meltdown of late 1997. Japanese post-Plaza Accord investment in Asia was largely to blame here, as it had boosted growth rates, especially in the countries of Southeast Asia, to artificially high levels. When Japan's economy faltered, the problems of economic development in these countries were exacerbated, creating substantial 'readjustments'. The important point, however, beyond showing the interconnectedness of the Asian economies, was that Japan could not act as an 'engine of growth' to pull them out of recession. Having had so much difficulty in getting its own financial house in order, it has been unable to rescue others. While most countries are now recovering from this blow, the long-term implications for Japanese and regional trade and investment have yet to be seen.

Another consequence of the degree of Japanese investment offshore, especially in Asia, was its impact on small and medium-sized companies in Japan which now found they had to compete for contracts with low-wage firms in developing countries. In the past, long-term personal associations with larger companies had ameliorated the impact of this effect, but with corporations dealing with recession, low-cost inputs became a priority. Ultimately this led to a degree of 'hollowing-out' of Japanese industry, where firms either went bankrupt or had to move into producing more technologically complex goods of high quality that were not easily manufactured overseas.

The challenge to smaller Japanese companies is likely to become greater with the implementation of regional trade agreements. With European countries consolidating the European Union (EU) in 1992, the US–Canada Free Trade Agreement (FTA) of 1989 and the North American Free Trade Agreement (NAFTA), an extension to the FTA, of 1991, and which included Mexico in 1994, it became apparent to a number of Asian countries, and especially Australia, that some form of new economic grouping was necessary to protect both long-term access to markets and overall economic growth. There had been a number of preliminary moves towards such associations from the 1960s onwards, but the key development was the creation of the Asia–Pacific Economic Cooperation forum (APEC) in 1989, an initiative of Australia's Hawke (Labor) government. Original member nations included Japan, the USA, Canada, Australia and New Zealand, along with China, Taiwan, Hong Kong and six members of the Association of South East Asian Nations (Singapore, Indonesia, Malaysia, Thailand, the Philippines and Brunei). The broad plan was for a progressive reduction in trade barriers (more quickly for developed countries, more slowly for developing ones), facilitation of technology transfers and cooperation in a number of sectors (including telecommunications, energy and transport).

From Japan's point of view an economic grouping such as this presents risks as well as rewards. As in other developed countries, low-technology, high-wage sectors will come under threat from industries in developing countries, but Japan's trade and investment in those countries will be made easier, reinforcing the international production system already created by the *keiretsu*. Access to important markets, such as the USA, will be facilitated, and free trade should have widespread benefits for consumers (and therefore regional economies in general). For Japan the challenge will be to modify its domestic system to allow for greater open competition as well as foreign investment. This is taking place to some extent, with $102 billion in foreign investment coming into Japan in 1998, compared with just $28 billion in 1989. In the banking sector, Merrill Lynch, for example, took over failed Yamaichi Securities, Swiss Bank Corporation tied up with the Long-Term Credit Bank of Japan, and Nippon Bank allied itself with Bankers Trust. Japanese were shocked in 1996, however, when Henry Wallace became President of Mazda in Japan as part of a takeover of the company by Ford. The long-term results will be seen over the coming decades. Above all, Japanese leaders want to avoid substantial trade frictions, which can do a great deal of damage either directly, through protective tariffs, or indirectly, through a global economic downturn.

Japan's changing international role

While economic issues were dominant in Japan's international relations in the 1970s and 1980s, a major change (indeed for much of the world) came about with the end of the Cold War in the late 1980s (popularly dated by the fall of the Berlin Wall in 1989). Suddenly the country's strategic value was called into question. Much of Japan's economic success had had to do with the stand-off between capitalism and communism, and its part in the string of American bases down the western Pacific, but the massive shift in geopolitics made its future strategic role unclear.

For much of the 1980s many people watched Japan's successes with awe and not a little fear. Some speculated whether the country would become a superpower in the military as well as economic sense. Others wondered when it would take a stronger leadership role and, if so, what form this role would take. The decline of the Japanese economy in the 1990s changed these perceptions, though the country still has the second largest economy in the world and the earlier questions are still mostly pertinent.

One of the fundamental characteristics of the Japanese

economy is that it is dependent on raw materials and therefore on trade. Hence an interdependent global trading system is generally to Japan's advantage, and its political manoeuvring tends to support the stability and extension of this system. On the other hand it is, broadly speaking, a relatively inward-looking country with a tightly knit social system, with considerable domestic resistance to letting foreigners become too well-established in their economy. This dynamic tension continues to plague Japan's international relations.

Can Japan be a world leader? Is this what Japan (or others) wants? To date its foreign policies have been characterised by pragmatism, shifting when necessary and tending to be reactive. Unlike the USA, Japan never seems to be out front, leading the way on the basis of principle. While one can argue that all nations are fundamentally governed by self-interest, it appears that Japan is particularly so—the idea of Japan as a 'fragile' superpower reflects this perception. This leads to substantial distrust of Japanese foreign policies among the leaders of other countries, coupled with a sense that Japan has substantial power but is perhaps without a clear purpose save to help itself.

The bargain made with the USA in the early 1950s was an acceptance of the US military presence in exchange for a release from Japan's own military expenditures and special access to American markets. With some frictions and fine-tuning this deal held through the 1980s. Today there are new pressures, and Japan will have to find its way using a more independent foreign policy. With Russia a shadow of its former self, China a key trading partner and even North Korea beginning to show a degree of flexibility, the need for American bases and military personnel in Japan may be dwindling. The passage of time is also allowing Japan's actions in the Pacific War to fade into history, and the time may not be far off when the country takes a more dominant role in global politics. Indeed, for some years Japanese leaders have been lobbying for a permanent seat on the UN Security Council. On the other hand, there is considerable resistance, both at home and abroad, to changing a system that has worked reasonably well for so long. Japan also needs the stability provided by the USA, especially in terms of protecting energy supplies coming from the Middle East, and to deal with regional issues such as the growing power of China, the China–Taiwan conflict and territorial conflicts over oil rights in the South China Sea (involving the Spratley and Paracel island groups).

One of the techniques Japan has used to change its image, especially in Asia, is the use of foreign aid. The Development Assistance Committee (DAC) of the OECD (which Japan joined in 1964) sets 0.7 per cent of GNP as the target for a country's Official Development Assistance (ODA). Japan has never reached this proportion, providing 0.35 per cent in 1999. Though much more than the 0.10 per cent of the USA, it is far less than, for example, Denmark (0.99 per cent), Norway (0.91 per cent) or the Netherlands (0.80 per cent). Because its GNP is so large, however, since 1985 Japan has been the world's largest provider of ODA. In 1999 it gave more than $15 billion in aid, substantially more than the USA ($9.1 billion), France ($5.5 billion) or the UK ($3.3 billion). Japan is also the largest contributor to (and the most powerful member of) the Asian Development Bank (ADB).

There is certainly a measure of altruism in this provision of aid though, as with other countries, considerable self-interest is also apparent. For the past 30 years Japan's aid has effectively followed trade and investment (mostly in the developing countries of Asia), though at a declining rate. In 1970 more than 98 per cent of Japan's ODA went to Asia but today the proportion has dropped to about 60 per cent. The placement of ODA has also been designed to dovetail with the needs of Japan's economy, such as reafforestation projects to replace trees cut down by Japanese companies or building roads and bridges to facilitate the export of goods.

One of the most difficult issues is the role of Japan's Self-Defence Force, which was especially called into question during the Gulf War of 1991. Because two-thirds of Japan's oil came from the Persian Gulf at the time, Japan dithered while Saddam attacked, and the coalition forces counter-attacked. Japan's view was that when one is resource-dependent it is better to wait to see who the victor will be before choosing sides. The USA did not agree. American leaders felt that it was bad enough that US soldiers were in harm's way while Japanese troops were not, but the cost of the war, at $60 billion, was also a major point of contention. Japan pointed once again to its American-designed constitution as a rationale for keeping its soldiers at home (a reason that had lost much of its persuasive power since the 1950s), but agreed to contribute substantially in financial terms (eventually $13 billion). More recently Japan agreed to pay $100 million towards the cost of sending troops from the developing countries of Asia to East Timor. These events have called into question how much longer Japan can continue to avoid military involvement by using 'chequebook diplomacy', though the issue produces mixed emotions in those who remember Japan's role in the Pacific War.

The presence of American bases in Japan is an ongoing issue, though more of the debate is over the cost of running them than whether or not the two countries should be tied in defence terms. One problem here is the poor behaviour of some US troops, recently brought to light by the rape of a 12-year-old school girl on Okinawa in 1996. Public outrage was reflected in an anti-US demonstration which attracted some 850 000 residents. A major base on the island will now be moved to a more remote location, at a cost of about $1 billion. Japan presently pays 61 per cent of the $5 billion cost of the US military presence in Japan—including 47 000 US personnel, 140 aircraft, base operating costs and salaries for Japanese working at the bases. Given the sluggish Japanese economy, this, too, has recently been the subject of debate.

Because Japan's military is not used overseas it tends to receive little public attention (a recent exception being the passage of the 1992 UN Peacekeeping Operations Co-operation Bill which subsequently allowed 600 Japanese troops from an engineering battalion to go to Cambodia). The SDF is formidable, however. Japan's defence budget is nearly $50 billion (including the $5 billion spent on the US military presence), larger than that of China and the biggest in Asia.

Although still only at 0.991 per cent of GDP, partly because Japan's economy grew substantially in the 1980s the defence budget more than doubled between 1980 and 1999. There are today nearly 237 000 troops in the country's military, along with 147 major ships and nearly 1200 major aircraft. Given this level of military strength, it remains to be seen how long Japanese leaders can resist pressure from other major powers to play a more significant defence role overseas.

Intimately associated with the role of the military is the nature of Japanese nationalism. In the postwar decades nationalism was viewed by many, if not most, Japanese as something almost evil that had led them into dire straits in the first half of the century. While ultra-right groups are noisy and visible in the major cities today, they are often viewed as dangerous extremists (though they also have substantial links to big business and conservative politicians). Over the past twenty years, however, a more moderate form of nationalism has begun to reassert itself, which has caused significant concern both in Japan and abroad. One ongoing debate has been in the area of school texts. In 1982, for example, the Ministry of Education (formally entitled the Ministry of Education, Science and Culture) tried to change the perception of the activities of the Japanese military in Asia during the Pacific War, with a replacement of the word 'invasion' by 'advance' and a general moderation of descriptions of atrocities such as the massacre in Nanking. Three years later Prime Minister Nakasone paid an official visit to the Yasukuni Shrine in Tokyo, where Japanese soldiers who died in the Pacific War are enshrined, reinforcing a fear in some of the old link between religion and the state. This was exacerbated by Prime Minister Mori Yoshiro in 2000 when he referred to Japan, during a meeting with a Shintō group, as the country of the gods (*kami no kuni*). Domestic and international reaction to this statement, with its pre-war flavour, was swift and vocal. Finally, a long-standing thorny issue that has become more heated in recent years is the displaying of the national flag (*Hinomaru*) and singing the national song (*Kimigayo*), especially at educational institutions' entrance and graduation ceremonies. Most now use these symbols but there continues to be resistance, especially from the left wing. All of these events suggest a continued sensitivity within Japan, and a wariness among its neighbours, over the nature of nationalism in the country.

The question of national identity is also reflected in the continuing debate argument over how, and how often, Japan should apologise for its actions in the Pacific War. It is frequently an arcane and tiresome debate—which expression of regret is truly an apology? Linguists are heavily involved in the fray. China and Korea are particularly strong on this point, which resurfaced in the 1990s over the issue of the forced use of women as prostitutes for the Japanese military during the war. (The so-called 'comfort women' are estimated to number some 80 000, mostly from Korea but also including Chinese, Filipino, Indonesian, Burmese and Dutch women.) The problem of the 'comfort women' has become complicated by compensation issues, and is a focus for manipulation of levels of aid and trade among Japan's neighbours. At the same time, a reaction has set in among some Japanese who feel that enough is enough and the Pacific War should be consigned to history. The problem is that Japanese nationalism refuses to die, and issues such as the use of national symbols or the military (common enough in other countries) reignite the debate.

This nascent nationalism is partly a result of Japan's economic success in the late 1980s. In 1989 Ishihara Shintarō (now Governor of Tokyo) wrote a book in conjunction with the late Morita Akio, a former chairman of Sony Corporation, entitled *The Japan That Can Say No*. They argued that Japan could flex its muscles now that it was economically powerful, and no longer had to show deference to the USA. Though the book is primarily based on rhetoric, and shot through with flawed arguments, it struck a nationalistic chord with some members of the domestic audience.

The 1980s and 1990s generally produced a more balanced and positive view of Japan's global role, referred to as *kokusaika* ('internationalisation'). In theory this was to provide

Japanese, especially students, with a broader world view and cross-cultural skills to suit a world that was becoming steadily more closely connected. In a general sense the term meant both becoming more outward-looking as well as being accepted by other countries. One of its main supporters was Prime Minister Nakasone, whose 1983 'Seven Point Proposal for Education Reform' promoted the idea. Support came from a number of different sources. It was clear to many in business that, with a significant proportion of their trade and personnel overseas, having employees with some understanding of the languages and cultures of other countries would be advantageous. Government bodies such as MITI also supported the idea. Some writers, however, see this as making a virtue of a necessity, since globalisation will mean greater economic integration and therefore will encourage cooperation.

At least these initiatives were, on the face of it, reasonable. On the other hand, while these forward thinkers were attempting to redefine Japan's international role in the face of economic confusion, *nihonjinron* writing continued to provide its convoluted and misleading message, though not at the level of the vocal 1980s. Although varied in focus and quality of scholarship, compositions in this area are inherently nationalistic as they attempt to explain, mostly to the domestic, but also to a foreign, audience why Japanese are unique, special and different from other cultures. On the positive side such publications may serve to bond people and thus have useful social and economic implications. On the negative side they are exclusionist, and preclude Japanese seeing themselves as part of the global community, with much in common with other human beings. Some of these writings also impart a strong sense of Japanese superiority and, indeed, racism.

One cannot visit Japan today without being on the receiving end of various examples of *nihonjinron* pop psychology, such as 'Westerners are independent because they were originally hunters while Japanese, who were originally rice farmers, are highly cooperative'. Others argue that the Japanese brain is different, using the right cortex (feeling one's way through problems) while Westerners use the left cortex (logical

Youth culture,
Harajuku district,
Tokyo.

analysis). These are perhaps genuine attempts to explain Japanese behaviour and culture, but the acceptance of such superficial explanations is surprising. It is, however, perhaps more satisfying than the common response—'It's the Japanese way'—to questions posed by foreigners.

Social change

The 1980s and especially the 1990s were characterised by a degree of social drift in Japan. The older generation called the newer one *shin-jinrui* ('new persons'). Another term was the 'bean sprout' generation—meaning they grew quickly but had little strength. Although these terms are now generally passé, the point is that once economic success had been achieved young Japanese often found daily life unsatisfying. The economic problems of the 1990s produced both a lack of faith in the existing system and difficulties in securing employment, both of which were destabilising influences on youth.

Younger Japanese have not experienced the deprivations of those who rebuilt Japan after the Pacific War, sacrificing themselves to create the economic miracle of the past 50 years. For the most part they have known only domestic peace, stable education, good health care and the availability of a vast range of consumer goods. They have also faced the severe pressures of competing in the educational system, conforming and succeeding in their employment and coping with highly urbanised and crowded living conditions. Young Japanese are caught in a relatively demanding and inflexible system where traditional beliefs remain relatively strong, social expectations are clearly defined, and they are generally expected to do their duty at particular times, but at the same time they may increasingly see little necessity for this pressure. Their parents or grandparents had a much clearer idea of why they were working so hard, given the exigencies of war and the need to rebuild a devastated country. Young Japanese today are questioning their prescribed roles, examining and investigating alternative types of work and lifestyles in general. This naturally causes some disquiet among older people.

Japan's economic success has been, at least in part, underpinned by its educational system. Its goal has been to produce reasonably well-educated and exceptionally focused, dedicated workers. The system is also, in theory, based on merit, providing a broad-based opportunity for upward social mobility while fulfilling its function of social stratification. Cost does not necessarily play an inhibiting role, as the prestigious national universities charge relatively low fees (private universities are much more expensive). In theory a bright but relatively poor student can aim for a very high-level career, but there is evidence to suggest that those from higher socioeconomic backgrounds generally perform better in the school system, thus inhibiting social mobility for lower income groups. In part this is because of the home environment and in part because wealthier families are better able to afford the costs of better schools and the extra preparatory classes (*juku*) for entrance exams.

The educational system has come under pressure as social conditions have changed. Criticisms have been made of the emphasis on uniformity and standardisation, as well as the strong control of the system by the Ministry of Education. Concerns have also been expressed over the rising level of school violence and the assorted behaviour problems of students. Indeed, the term *futōkō*, or 'school refusal' (a newer version of *tōkōkyohi* or 'school allergy'), has been coined to describe a recent, related problem which has become a serious issue, with an estimated 100 000 high school students refusing to go to school at present. The education system has been very resistant to change, however, in part because of its political structure, where the national Teachers' Union tends to be at loggerheads with the ministry, the result being that new initiatives are difficult to implement. It has also been relatively static, however, partly because of Japan's near-continuous rule by conservative governments since the beginning of the twentieth century.

The university system is especially important in stratifying Japanese society. Given the prestige that is attached to the top universities, graduates are, if not guaranteed a favourable career path, at least given the opportunity to pursue one. There are often specific social functions attached to particular universities, with Tokyo University providing the majority of upper-level bureaucrats, including the foreign service, Waseda University being noted for journalism and Keiō University providing relatively large numbers of business executives. University education is thus closely related to economic function in Japan. Given the economic success to which this system has contributed, it is understandable that any change will take place incrementally. Changing the system would mean making fundamental alterations to the relatively democratic way in which social mobility is determined and society in general is organised.

Given that there is strong resistance to changing the education system, what are the points of stress which can so alienate students? Problems relate to an entrenched Confucianist style of teaching, which includes the lack of emphasis on creative thinking and a focus on rote learning, the undesirable effects of harsh discipline and the pressures to conform, the lack of flexibility in terms of changing educational choices, difficulties with mature-aged entry to the tertiary system and censorship of textbooks. There are criticisms of the structure and quality of the university programs themselves. Perhaps the most serious problem in terms of alienation is the highly competitive nature of the educational system. Competition begins very early, with 40 per cent of the three-year-old population and 90 per cent of four-to five-year-olds enrolled in preschool. The more prestigious preschools select students through entrance examinations, and this has led to the development of an extensive network of *juku* even for these examinations. This aspect has received widespread coverage in the Western press as an example of the intense competition in the Japanese school system.

The competitive entrance exam, an increasingly important aspect of the school system through the higher grade levels, has led to a number of problems. First, there is a strong correlation between the university one attends (and therefore the right junior high and high schools to be in a position to compete effectively for entrance to the prestigious universities) and one's future career. So much hinges on performance in these university entrance examinations that the term *shiken jigoku* ('examination hell') seems particularly apt. With the success rate for the most prestigious universities being as low as one in fifteen or twenty applicants, the pressure is intense. For students who cannot enter the 'narrow gate', there are few choices other than moving down the prestige ladder (to another of the approximately 500 universities, 600 junior colleges or 2500 specialist training schools) or attempting the examinations again. This may mean up to several years of attending special classes in order to improve their marks, the so-called *rōnin* (or 'masterless *samurai*') period in their educational careers. The significance of this group can be seen in the proportion of *rōnin* students sitting entrance examinations—it ranges from 30 to 40 per cent for some prestigious universities. Given the importance of the age cohort in Japanese company structure, however, students cannot delay entry for more than a few years without becoming severely disadvantaged in their search for employment after graduation.

Success in entrance examinations also reflects on a student's family, in particular on the mother. Mothers remain primarily responsible for their children's education and thus play a central role in preparing them for the various examinations they must face. The disparaging term *kyōiku mama* ('education mom') refers to a mother who pushes her children relentlessly to succeed. Failure in examinations means a degree of shame for the family in general, and for the mother in particular.

The entrance examination system, with the severe stress it places on students, is coming under increasing criticism. It skews the educational system, puts too much pressure on young people (with aberrant behaviour sometimes the result) and determines the direction of a person's life at a very young age. Some Japanese are now rejecting the examination system and searching for alternative forms of education. While it largely fulfils its function of controlling social mobility and rewarding talent, the examination system also disadvantages those students who may be very capable but are not adept at written exams. This means that there is a group of talented people who must meet their ambitions in alternative ways, relatively difficult to do in a rigid social system.

The Japanese school system, especially higher education, is focused on men, thus the well-documented problems of excessive competition, rigid uniformity and standardisation had their greatest impact on males. While some changes are becoming evident, most young Japanese males remain locked in an education system that is significantly out of date. The value of a system which subjects them to such intense pressures must be coming into question.

Substantial formal education was historically not thought

to be particularly important for Japanese women, although the literacy rate for girls was an impressive 98 per cent by 1912. Learning traditional arts such as the tea ceremony or flower arranging was thought to add refinement to a girl's education, a part of the *hanayome shugyō* ('bride trainee' program), which preceded marriage (*eikyū shūshoku* or 'eternal employment'). These educational expectations are still, to some extent, in place. While in theory women have equal access to higher levels of education, in practice the picture is different. In 1999, for example, 29 per cent of females who completed high school went on to university; the proportion for males was over 46 per cent. Only about 2 per cent of men went to a junior college; for women the figure was about 20 per cent. Junior colleges usually function as a sort of finishing school for women before they enter the workforce at a relatively low level. However, as with many aspects of Japanese society, change is occurring here. One could argue that, although women still have much less education than men on average, the situation is improving. In 1960 the proportion of women going on to university was under 3 per cent, to a junior college exactly 3 per cent.

The education system for women functions differently from that in the West. While some women go to university to secure qualifications to compete with men in the workforce, many more use their degrees to enhance their marriage potential. Additionally, even in the late 1980s female university graduates had more trouble finding jobs than those men with lower-level qualifications. Attending a tertiary institution was often a chance for a woman to secure the so-called 'three highs', or *sankō*, in a marriage partner—high income, high intelligence and high level of education (this term is somewhat dated). While there is a close relationship between education and a woman's status, the route to status still lies principally through marriage rather than through success in a career, though one could argue that the situation is changing to a degree.

Attitudes to marriage are also changing. There is a great flexibility among young people which allows them to explore their interests without having to be as concerned about the rigid social prescriptions for marrying and establishing families as in the past. There has been an increase in the age of marriage in Japan as well as a slight drop in the proportion of people deciding to marry. In 1996 the average age of first marriage for men was about 30 years, for women approximately 27 years, a substantial increase on the 1950 figures of 26 years for men and 23 years for women. Reasons often given include the greater freedom and lesser responsibility of being single. The trend is more pronounced among people in the larger urban centres and among those with relatively high educational levels. There has also been a marked decline in arranged marriages, or *miai*.

Attitudes towards work are also shifting; it is now often seen as a necessary evil rather than a source of personal satisfaction. There is growing discussion of the phenomenon of *karōshi* ('death from overwork'), which some believe claims approximately 10 000 lives every year in Japan, and whose most recent high-profile victim was Prime Minister Obuchi Keizō early in 2000. The marked increase in unemployment in recent years has led to some rethinking of the value of work and the extent of security a job can provide. While Japanese workers over the past decades tended to remain dedicated to one company, today movement between companies is becoming more common. This also calls into question the ideal of group loyalty and the hierarchical work structure, both part of the bedrock of the postwar employment system. It may be that Japanese companies will have to create a new relationship with their workers which is less rigidly defined.

The role of women in the workplace is also changing, though the pattern of change is less than clear. In the postwar period women were hired at a relatively low level, either as 'window dressing' (enquiries desks, elevator operators and so on) or in a clerical capacity. They were over represented in lower-level jobs in the manufacturing, retailing and services sectors, and under represented in managerial and professional areas. The typical working life profile was the M-curve, with women working in their twenties, quitting in their 30s and

40s to raise children, then returning to work (usually in low-level clerical or service jobs, and often part-time) in their 50s. This led to a female participation rate in the labour force of about 41 per cent in 1997, as opposed to nearly 60 per cent for males. Under the *nenkō* employment system, which ties wages to seniority, women are also disadvantaged. The argument has been, and generally still is, that women usually leave a company after several years to marry and raise children, so any investment in training them has a limited return. With the projected decline in the labour force over the coming decades (due to the falling birthrate), however, this will almost certainly have to change.

In recent years a shift in Japanese employment practices has allowed some women to break through the so-called 'glass ceiling'. Following the passing of the Equal Employment Opportunity Law (EEOL) of 1986 a number of larger companies began to offer the choice of employment streams to their female employees, those of *sōgō shoku* ('comprehensive workers'/'management') or *ippan shoku* ('ordinary workers'). The former gave women the opportunity to fast-track their careers in concert with male colleagues. This system did not function as expected, however, one problem being that it was generally not taken seriously by the companies concerned; it was instituted predominantly as form rather than function. The EEOL was consequently substantially amended in 1999, addressing such issues as sexual harassment, hours of work (including access to late shifts), promotion and the opportunity to work in a wider range of jobs. While providing greater equality for women, it has not lessened, but rather enhanced, the problem of burn-out similar to that experienced by male workers.

Women also continue to face difficulties fitting into Japan's corporate culture. These range from sexual harassment to intense competition with male colleagues. For women with families the significant time Japanese workers spend socialising or working overtime can also be a problem. Although the government has allowed for authorised day-care centres, their numbers and hours of operation are at present limited.

One of the more unusual social developments among young Japanese women is the phenomenon of *enjo-kōsai* ('financially-assisted dating', sometimes shortened to '*enkō*'). This 'Lolita complex' spin-off involves young girls who date older men, often with sex involved, in exchange for money. It is essentially a new form of prostitution (allowed by a loophole in the 1956 Anti-Prostitution Law). It has created some concern in Japanese society because it has become so widespread—it is estimated that some 4 per cent of high school and junior high school girls are involved in the practice. The usual reason given by girls engaged in *enjo-kōsai* is their desire for more spending money with which to buy expensive brand-name goods, an indication of the rampant commercialism among Japanese youth.

The practice of *enjo-kōsai* highlights one of the ways in which contemporary Japanese society has come adrift. Fundamentally, a gap has grown between the sexes. Men generally remain in traditional roles, dominated by securing an education and then dedication to the workplace, while women have new-found freedoms', with high levels of disposable income, independence and time to explore their own interests. The result is that men are often insecure and socially underdeveloped, even feeling themselves emasculated, while women are the opposite. One of the ways this gap is manifested is in the (admittedly minor) phenomenon of older women marrying younger men, known in Japan as *maza-con*, a Japanese–English term for 'mother complex'. Another is the search for females with whom a man can feel powerful, or dominant, generally very young women. Looking at the situation from the perspective of the girls, some Japanese psychologists argue that over the past decades men have become ever more dominated by their work, so that fathers are seldom home. Girls may therefore be seeking a father-type relationship in the practice of *enjo-kōsai*.

The sexual frustrations of men are also reflected in the boom in *manga* (comic books). There is a tremendous range in these, some of them relatively serious reading, but one branch is characterised by sadomasochistic sex. It is argued in their favour that men are able to live out their fantasies through reading them without posing a danger to social order. While this may be true, their existence points to a problem in the way in which young men are socialised in contemporary Japan. Linked to this are the various fetishes and fantasies involving young women, exemplified by shops selling young women's (used) underwear to men, and businesses offering customers simulated sexual fantasies such as molesting women on subways or secretaries in the office. The latter are well-known social problems, but such outlets perhaps reduce their incidence.

A more serious example of social drift in Japan has been the growth in 'new religions'. More than 180 000 religious organisations are formally registered. Some of them, sadly, have turned out to be dangerous cults. The most notorious of these is Aum Shinrikyō, made infamous by its use in March 1995 of sarin gas in Tokyo's subway system, killing twelve people and injuring some 5000 others. The growth of such cults calls into question the direction of Japanese society, and especially the values of its youth. Increasing violence in schools is another issue of concern, with more than 35 000 incidents being reported in the school system in 1999. Suicide, too, is on the increase, with a 35 per cent jump between 1997 and 1998, though the largest rise was not among youth but among middle-aged people affected by the country's economic problems. Recently a Japanese newspaper ran a story about a karaoke bar in Asahigaoka where, for $40 an hour, a person can relieve his stress by smashing dishes, vases and furniture. There is clearly a high frustration level among many Japanese.

The treadmill may be a harsh, though apt, characterisation of the lives of Japanese men, given their very clearly prescribed roles and the sacrifices generally demanded of them by their society. A young Japanese male is usually expected to at least try to gain entrance to the right primary and secondary schools, a process which may begin even before kindergarten, pass the entrance examinations to a good university, join a reputable company, cooperate with his colleagues, marry well and at a reasonable age, and stay with the company until retirement or death, whichever comes first. The competition which exists is generally for the best schools, universities, companies and partners. Hence, there is very little flexibility in the lives of most Japanese men, particularly for those who are especially capable. The drop-outs have much more choice, but this is primarily with respect to which second-rate future they want.

For women there are clear conflicts between tradition and change. In the past there was generally a very rigid set of expectations imposed on women, which prescribed certain duties to be performed at particular times in their lives. Her general role was clear—she was expected to be a 'good wife and wise mother'. While this model is still generally in place, it is now being challenged. The changing role of Japanese women means that the various institutions that have supported such traditions are also being questioned. There is a current debate about how women should be educated, what their employment opportunities should be, when they should get married and what their role should be after marriage. In short, there is today a broad, albeit slow, shift in how Japanese women function in their society.

Urban pressures

Contrary to popular impression, Japan is mostly uncrowded. Its 7000 islands, strung out over some 3000 kilometres, make up a land area of about 378 000 square kilometres. Of this area, about 67 per cent is uninhabited mountains, fields and forests, 13 per cent farmland and 7 per cent under rural roads, rivers, canals and lakes. Only 4.7 per cent is urbanised. Urban areas, especially in central Japan, are relatively high density, with about 43 per cent of the population living within 50 kilometres of the three urban centres of Tokyo, Osaka and Nagoya. If Okinawa is excluded, then almost 54 per cent of the population lives on only 1.7 per cent of its land. Essentially, Japan may not be crowded, but parts of it are, and this results in a number of social pressures.

Although many Japanese now enjoy very high wages, a

The highrise response to crowded urban areas, Shinjuku district, Tokyo.

reasonable social welfare system, and shopping centres in the urban areas provide a seemingly endless display of consumer goods, these gains have had a social cost. Dealing with the pressures of living in crowded urban centres is now one of the great challenges facing society. Such pressures may take a range of forms, but two of the most noticeable, and increasingly problematic, are the lack of adequate housing in the large urban centres and, related to this, the long commuting times required for travel between home and work.

Securing adequate housing is a problem for the person who has decided, or more likely, through the concentration of commercial and government activity in the urban centres, has been forced, to live in the city. Because of the high land prices, compromises must be made with respect to dwelling size and

Crowded East Shinjuku, Tokyo.

location when selecting a home. Houses are relatively small in comparison to those in Western countries. In terms of average floor space per person, the figure for Japan is about 33 square metres but for the USA it is 60. Housing in the urban centres is also expensive. The cost of a home as a multiple of annual income is about 13 for metropolitan Tokyo and 10 for Osaka, compared to approximately 3 for New York and Paris, and 7 in London. Those who are fortunate enough to live in homes which have been passed on from generation to generation are greatly envied. The high cost of a house has forced many Japanese into apartment living, and these complexes are a highly visible feature of the urban landscape.

The lifestyle of the urban dweller is also characterised by the difficulties of commuting between home and place of work, more of a dire necessity than a choice for most of those living in cities. High prices, coupled with the congestion of the city, have compelled many people to find housing in outlying areas and the resultant commuting scene is dramatic. The number of passengers using any form of transportation more than doubled between 1970 and 1997, with the figure for the latter year being about 8.5 trillion trips. In 1997 there were 22.3 billion train trips alone, including Japan Railways (JR) and private railways. This extreme congestion, especially in the major cities and at particular times of the day, means that commuting times tend to average about 90 minutes per day for male company employees, adding up to a significant amount of wasted time and money, for the individual as well as for society as a whole. Unpleasant as this must be, public transportation is quite efficient compared to travel in private vehicles. Maintaining a vehicle and finding parking space is a high-cost proposition in Japan's cities, and in addition the toll charges on highways in and out of the urban centres are substantial.

The Japanese economic miracle has been achieved at high social cost, and many of these costs have not been seriously questioned. The generation which rebuilt the country after the Pacific War was initially interested merely in survival and then with ensuring the nation became economically strong again. It may be argued that this drive to increase wealth is now outdated. Certainly there continue to be both domestic and international economic pressures confronting Japan, as it seems unable to substantially lift its growth rate, averaging about 1 per cent through the 1990s. While the Japanese enjoy extremely high incomes and want for little in terms of material possessions, in the 1990s questions were being more frequently asked concerning both the cost of this achievement and the direction ahead.

9
THE WAY AHEAD

THE TWENTIETH CENTURY WAS a tumultuous time for Japan. It emerged as a world power in the early decades, experimented with imperialism, experienced war and its aftermath. Virtually every aspect of its society and economy underwent change, and then further change. Indeed, coping with change, and the rising and falling of fortunes, may be the central theme of the century, while anxiety may have been the predominant emotion. The twenty-first century promises to be no different. The challenges facing Japan are enormous, not only in terms of new developments, but in coping with trends already apparent. What role will Japan play on the international stage? Will it become a true military-backed superpower? Will the Japan of the new century be a country to be feared? Can it sustain its economic power in the face of rapidly changing social and commercial currents? These questions are on the minds of Japanese and, because of the country's importance in the global economy, on the minds of many others as well.

What is particularly evident in Japanese society today are the stresses between tradition and change. Two of the key aspects of tradition are social cohesion and the capacity of different people, and parts of the system, to work together.

While this gives Japan a great advantage over countries which are socially or culturally divided, it also means that change is difficult unless there is widespread support for new practices. The interrelationships between the different parts of Japanese society also mean that any significant change in one part of the system will have an impact on the other parts. Can Japan make these adjustments as the world changes? There is, naturally, no little fear among policy-makers in introducing new practices. The existing system has served the country extremely well, especially in economic terms, for 50 years. Conservative values are also generally held by the people in power, but the extent to which the Japanese government can respond effectively to contemporary pressures will have a major impact on the country's domestic and international prosperity well into this century.

The ageing population

One of the major challenges facing Japan over the coming decades is its ageing population. By the middle of this century Japan will have the most aged society in the world, with approximately one in three citizens being 65 years of age or older. The population by then will have shrunk to about 100 million. As early as 2010, 22 per cent of the population will be aged 65 years or more (compared with, for example, 13 per cent in the USA), an increase of 6 per cent since 1998. This is the result of several factors, the first being the rapid rise in the birthrate following the Pacific War; the second the currently falling birthrate, now less than 1.4 children per woman of child-bearing age (the replacement figure is about 2.1). The birthrate is expected to fall still further, to about 1.1 by 2020. The third factor is longevity—the Japanese live longer than any other nation in the world, at 77 years for men and 84 for women. Taken together these factors predicate a massive population problem which will affect virtually every aspect of the country's social, political and economic organisation. Some have called it Japan's 'demographic time bomb'.

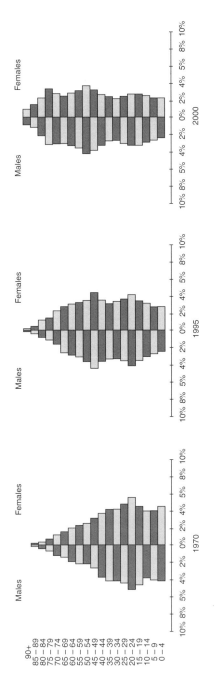

Japan's changing population pyramid clearly shows the country's rapidly ageing population.

In the coming decades one of the major challenges will be to deal with the costs of supporting the ageing population. Funding of basic pensions is the most immediate problem, and pressure will increase steadily here. At present Japan spends only about 7 per cent of GDP on pensions; by 2020 the cost of providing pensions will amount to 14 per cent of GDP, about three times that of the USA. The government has recently introduced legislation to force younger citizens to start saving for their retirement from age 40. These funds can be used in the short term to support this increasing group of pensioners. The fundamental problem is that there will be fewer and fewer younger people to support the elderly. At present there are about five working people per retiree, but this will reduce to about 2.5 workers by 2010, according to government projections. Other costs will also rise. Outlays for medical care will go up given that, with people living longer, there will be a greater need for intensive medical care over a longer period of time. As more funding goes into this sector there will be less available for investment in the economy, and with fewer people working there will also be less savings available as a source of funding. Higher costs mean that the tax base will have to be increased, at the same time that there are fewer younger people entering the workforce. The labour shortage will mean rising labour costs, and Japan will become less competitive as the cost of production increases. Almost certainly more and more industry will be forced to locate offshore in lower-wage countries.

On the domestic front this leaves Japan's policy-makers with few options. One is to keep older people working longer, and a number of companies are now allowing their workers to do this. It may be that the retirement age will simply be steadily increased, with people being asked to work to the age of, say, 70 years. Already the age of eligibility for public pensions is going up, from 60 years to 65 by 2014. It is ironic that those who sacrificed their youth to produce Japan's economic miracle are being asked for further sacrifices in old age.

A second option is to increase the number of immigrants, a common policy option in the West, especially in North

America and Australia. The problem in Japan's case is that it is not an immigrant country; on the contrary, it has had a tendency to be exclusionist. Only about 2 per cent of Japan's population are migrants. It deals poorly with its ethnic minorities (such as Koreans and small numbers of Vietnamese and Chinese). So much of Japan's culture has revolved around being isolationist and resistant to having large numbers of foreigners in the land, that its people often find it difficult to interact with those from different cultural backgrounds. One compromise has been to facilitate the entry of Brazilians of Japanese descent, and there are now about 270 000 in the country. Many more migrants are needed, however. UN estimates are that as many as 600 000 immigrants are needed per year on a continuing basis to sustain Japan's economic growth. If such a recommendation were to be followed (and there is overwhelming popular resistance to it), it would put pressure on the government to treat immigrants more equitably. It was only in 1999 that foreigners staying in Japan for more than a year ceased to be fingerprinted as if they were criminals. The government may compromise further on this issue, and allow more foreigners into the country on temporary work permits. However, 'guest workers' may eventually demand greater concessions from the government (as they have done in Germany), and no doubt the Japanese leadership is considering this problem carefully.

A third option in dealing with the ageing population is to change the way in which Japanese women are treated in the workplace. To date their labour is largely wasted. Many are well-educated but not supported to the point where they can rise to the level of their abilities. Others might have preferred a higher level of education, but since the employment system does not support them they have opted for relatively poor qualifications. The ageing of the population will, however, force changes in women's employment. Circumstances will provide them with a greater range of employment alternatives. As their labour is needed more, there may be a continuation of the move away from career interruptions and towards higher-level employment as they remain longer in the labour force. Indeed, to remain economically competitive Japan will be forced to utilise female labour more effectively. One indication that this is already happening is the 1999 modification of the Equal Employment Opportunity Law.

Changing women's role in the workforce, however, will reverberate through society as a whole. The socialisation of females will have to change, along with the education system, support services such as the availability of day-care for children, more comprehensive programs of maternity leave and care for the elderly (a traditional function of Japanese women), as well as men's roles within the family. If men's roles change, so too must the employment system for men, which in turn will cause a chain reaction throughout the economic system. The present employment system in Japan is seriously out of date, and the coming labour shortage will arguably create a new system that looks more familiar to Westerners, with a much higher degree of flexibility in the workplace for both men and women.

International relations

What are the pressures in the international arena that are likely to be brought to bear on Japan? As the ageing population leads to an increasing proportion of its industry being located offshore, this will in turn force Japan to be more interactive with other countries, and especially the developing countries of Asia. Effective diplomacy will be needed even more than now, and this may mean a final resolution to the lingering problems caused by the Pacific War. While the receiving countries have thus far been relatively dependent on Japanese investment, they may in future play a more powerful role in these agreements. As throughout modern Japanese history, the country remains dependent on others. While this has been principally in the area of raw materials, it will increasingly be extended to include labour.

Given the idea that force is another aspect of diplomacy, with Japan's increasing vulnerability in the economic sphere its military may have a more substantial role to play, supported by a stronger sense of national identity. The safety of shipping routes and energy supplies, and the stability of countries where there is substantial Japanese investment, will all become more crucial to Japan's economic health, and this may mean that military power will be increased and be available for use off-shore. Pressure from other countries, notably the USA, to play a more significant role in conflicts around the world will almost certainly increase, and this will bring more pressure to bear on the Japanese government to revise its constitution. If Japan succeeds in gaining a seat on the UN Security Council the pressure in this regard will also be raised. The fragile superpower may need its military to give it strength.

Productive international relations, as well as economic growth, can only be achieved if the country's political system can be overhauled. There is still considerable instability here, with ten different prime ministers in the past twelve years. There are continuing criticisms in a range of areas, from backroom deals to lack of transparency in the policy-making process, corruption and inflexible policies. Leadership is desperately needed to solve Japan's problems, but at present it does not appear to be forthcoming. Although the June 2000 elections showed a strong increase in support for the Democratic Party of Japan, the LDP remains in power, primarily because of the backing of the rural conservative vote.

Economic development

In terms of trade with other countries, Japanese corporate leaders have already been contemplating the idea that excessive competition is destructive. With manufacturing being located increasingly offshore, and the greater integration of Japanese companies in regional economies, there is likely to be more emphasis on cooperation. Reductions in trade barriers may also contribute to a move in this direction, where unfair trade practices will not be tolerated, and the capacity for retaliation by a number of countries over a specific issue will be increased. Japan will have to become a more responsible regional player. Japan remains the driving force behind regional economies, with the IMF estimating that about 70 per cent of the GDP of Asia comes from Japan. The decisions taken in this country therefore have significant regional, indeed global, implications. While some observers have tended to downplay Japan's role while focusing on that of China, this is shortsighted. Existing production systems and investment alone will make Japan's economy extremely important in the future, regardless of whether or not it recovers in the short term.

This is not to say that the decision-makers in government and business can be complacent. There remains substantial corporate, as well as public, debt, and reforms are badly needed if Japan's economy is to pull itself out of the doldrums. At present the country's economic malaise, particularly noticeable in the banking sector and the widespread bankruptcies of small businesses, is having a powerful, adverse effect on the social system. High levels of unemployment and increasing numbers of homeless people are two visible examples. Temporary government measures must be replaced by long-term, effective policies if the economy is to substantially recover.

The ageing population, while posing several long-term economic hurdles, is also presenting short-term ones. With older people saving money for their retirement, there is insufficient domestic stimulation of the economy. They are not buying foreign products either, and this will mean an increasing trade surplus for at least the next decade, an ongoing issue that the Japanese leadership will have to deal with.

Along with growing international connections, there is already a greater demand for more, and more effective, English language instruction. To date English is learned as an examination subject, which gives Japanese an outstanding command of the more obscure points of English grammar, but is not effective in teaching them useful communication skills. Already there are plans to begin teaching children English in the lower school years, but it remains to be seen if this will mean more applied ability. The growth of the Internet is also driving this change, as approximately 80 per cent of global users communicate in English. Japan lags significantly in Internet usage, partly because of this dominance of English. The country has about 1700 net users per 10 000 people, where the figure for Australia is 3600 and for the USA 4500. The proportion of GDP due to the Information Technology sector is only 5 per cent in Japan compared to 7.3 per cent in the USA, but Japanese adaptation to the New Economy is beginning to make itself felt.

On the domestic front business cooperation will have to be enhanced if the economy is going to deal effectively with the challenges posed by competitor countries as well as by its declining workforce. To date such cooperation has generally been enhanced by government, as strong competition has been the norm between Japanese companies. While this has resulted in very high-quality products, in future it may become more worthwhile to cooperate, sharing research and development as well as production costs. A recent example has been the seconding of 160 employees to Toyota from Toshiba, Fujitsu and Ishikawajimaharima Heavy Industries for the creation of a new motor vehicle. This trend will almost certainly increase, reinforced by the mutual obligations which such transfers of employees or technologies will entail. At the same time, many of the best graduates (including women) are opting for employment in the increasing number of foreign corporations in Japan, which will force some reassessment of traditional employment practices.

Social issues

Japan's social system is a virtual cauldron of bubbling issues. There are many different cross-currents, some undermining social cohesion, others reinforcing it. One of the overriding issues is that of quality of life. In 1996 Gavan McCormack wrote *The Emptiness of Japanese Affluence*, which effectively raised the question of whether or not the Japanese are poor people in a rich country. Will Japanese, especially young ones,

*Limited parking space
for bicycles, Tokyo.*

be content with the lives their parents had? There are different pressures now. On the one hand, the present high levels of unemployment seem to be generating a return to an earlier work ethic. One can only speculate as to whether or not this will last when, in a few years, the current labour surplus becomes a shortage. There will certainly be more significant social pressures on the young to support the elderly and keep the economy going while paying higher taxes. Will they rise to this challenge or demand more concessions from their employers? It may be that more concessions will be in everyone's interests.

The concentration of economic activity and population in a few massive urban centres is an outdated practice. The decentralisation of economic functions, facilitated by contemporary changes in communications technology, would mean better housing, a less congested and polluted urban environment and shorter commuting times (and therefore much less wasted time and energy). Lower costs associated with locating in less concentrated urban areas would also allow for higher wages for workers and much better working conditions. Decentralisation has been a topic of serious discussion for three decades, but the political will to activate existing plans has been lacking. Younger workers, however, may demand a change in future.

The aimlessness of many young people may be reduced in the Japan of the future as they find a role where they are needed—but this depends on changes taking place in the education and employment systems. Refusal to attend school and school-related violence are symptoms of a system that is arguably becoming dysfunctional. The pressures of the examination system are questionable given that some of those who have performed best have not necessarily done particularly well in their subsequent jobs—many key decision-makers made poor choices in the late 1980s, letting the economic system get out of control. University education in the non-technical areas is also often a wasteful exercise, with students working hard to enter an eminent educational institution and then coasting for four years. Japanese society may have to demand more of the education system as labour becomes more valuable. Education may also have more of a role to play for mature-aged workers, as part of a lifelong learning system. Linked to this is the issue of creativity. While Japanese have shown themselves to be remarkable adaptors of technology, can the education system shift to enhancing the creativity of its students while retaining the advantages of focus and discipline?

There is a good argument to be made that Japanese are indeed creative, and that their history shows a tremendous ability to take ideas or technologies and improve upon them. Japanese successes in consumer electronics are evident everywhere. In recent years we have also seen the emergence of Japanese writers and film-makers who have been successful both at home and abroad—Mishima Yukio, Murakami Haruki and Kurosawa Akira spring to mind. Japanese popular music is making vast inroads throughout Asia. Japanese designers are beginning to achieve high status in the fashion field, and architects such as Ando Takao and Kurosawa Kishio are well known in their field. The name of Nintendo is famous in the computer games industry. Japanese food is becoming popular throughout Asia and the West. Karaoke bars seem to be everywhere. Clearly, Japanese culture is making significant inroads in many countries.

With exposure to the rest of the world through overseas travel (nearly 17 million Japanese travelled abroad in 2000 alone), and through the Internet, Japanese are coming to see that there are many different ways of organising social systems. Some of these models offer better alternatives, others worse ones. In the past Japanese leaders have been adept at selectively choosing outstanding practices from around the world and adapting them to a domestic context. If historical experience holds true, the Japanese people will rise to the challenge of improving out-of-date social practices. At the same time they may begin to view themselves less and less as unusual, with more in common with the rest of the world than they might have thought. Already there is evidence that Japanese are becoming increasingly global citizens, with the young in particular demonstrating significant knowledge of other countries and cultures.

Japan in the early twenty-first century presents a remarkable mixture of attributes. Although its economy is growing only slowly, it remains an incredibly powerful global force, and Japanese products continue to be in demand around the world. The employment and education systems are showing some wear and tear, but remain largely intact and, indeed, are shifting (albeit slowly) to meet the new demands being placed upon them. There is a degree of social dislocation, but this is natural enough when a new direction is being sought. Indeed, because Japan has a relatively controlled society (*kanri shakai*), changes are perhaps more noticeable than they are in other countries, and are frequently overstated. Much of the strength of Japanese society still exists, and the hard work of earlier generations will carry the country forward as its social and economic problems are resolved.

Japan is a very special country. It has few natural resources, but its people have shown themselves to be capable of producing an exceptionally vibrant culture in spite of (or because of) its natural poverty and isolation. When required, Japanese have shown that they can adapt quickly, while holding on to their core values. There is a strength and determination in Japanese society that has often been underestimated by outsiders. Although Japan has many hurdles ahead, especially in reorganising its economic structures (and it is sometimes said that 'optimism is usually the product of intellectual error'), a dynamic future could await it. If we consider Japan's historical response to challenges, the country can look forward to the coming years with confidence.

GLOSSARY

amakudari	descent from heaven (usually bureaucrats joining the business sector)
aware	the sadness of things
baku-han	centralised feudalism
bakufu	tent headquarters (military government)
be	early occupational category (e.g. weavers, potters, armourers)
burakumin	modern group which includes former *eta* and *hinin*
bushidō	way of the (samurai) warrior
corvée	system of extracting unpaid labour
Dai Butsu	bronze statue of Amida Buddha in Kamakura, cast in 1252
daimyō	feudal lord
Dajōkan	Meiji-era council of state
Emishi	barbarians (early Japanese term for people living in outlying regions of Japan)
endaka	period of high yen value
enjo-kōsai	financially-assisted dating
eta	feudal outcast group (worked with dead animals and made leather goods)

fudai	house *daimyō* (early vassals of Tokugawa Ieyasu)
fukoku-kyōhei	rich country, strong army
futōkō	school refusal (i.e. refusing to attend school)
gaiatsu	foreign pressure
Ginkakuji	Silver Pavilion
gokenin	housemen (vassals)
gyōsei shido	administrative guidance (bureaucratic influence on business)
haiku	short formalised Japanese poem
hakama	skirt-like traditional male pants
han	feudal domain (i.e. principality)
haniwa	pottery used to decorate *kofun* (burial mounds)
hinin	non people (feudal outcasts through occupation, including beggars, executioners, etc.)
Hinomaru	national flag
hiragana	phonetic Japanese alphabet
honne/tatamae	inner reality/outward appearance
Jieitai	Japan's self defence forces (SDF)
jingikan	formal Shintō office established in 1869
jinrikisha	human-powered vehicle
jinushi	feudal usurer—landlords
jitō	land stewards
Jiyūtō	Meiji-era Liberal Party
Joei Code	legal code of AD 1232
juku	cram school
Kaishintō	Meiji-era Progressive Party
kami	various gods, or spirits, of the Shintō religion
kamikaze	divine wind
kanji	Japanese written language based on Chinese characters
kanpaku	feudal-era civil dictator
kanri shakai	controlled society
karōshi	death from overwork (chronic exhaustion)

katakana	phonetic Japanese alphabet
Keidanren	Federation of Economic Organisations
keiretsu kigyo (or *keiretsu*)	aligned companies (industrial combines modelled on the earlier *zaibatsu*)
kempeitai	wartime military police
Kimigayo	national anthem
Kinkakuji	Golden Pavilion
kinken-seiji	money politics
kofun	burial mounds for Japanese leaders (c. AD 300–700)
Kojiki	Records of Ancient Matters (AD 712)
kokusaika	internationalisation
Komeito	Clean Government Party
kondei	stalwart youths
kurōdo-dokoro	household treasury office (AD 810)
kuromaku	black curtain (power-brokers who operate invisibly behind the scenes)
kyōiku mama	education mom
manga	comic books
maza-con	Japanese–English term for 'mother complex'
miai	arranged marriages
Monbusho	Ministry of Education
nenkō joretsu	(usually shortened to *nenkō*) seniority ranking system in Japanese companies
nihonjinron	discussions of the Japanese (literature on what it means to be Japanese)
Nihon Shoki	*Chronicles of Japan* (AD 720)
Nikkeiren	Japan Federation of Employers' Associations
Nikkyōso	left-wing Teachers' Union
Nōkyō	short form of *Nogyo Kyōdō Kumiai*, or Agricultural Workers' Cooperative
o'kimi	great king
ritsuryō	codified system of criminal and civil law statutes
rōnin	masterless samurai

saburahi	old Japanese word meaning 'to serve', referring to mounted warriors; early form of the word *samurai*
sakoku	national seclusion (Japan's feudal isolation policy)
sankin-kōtai	alternate attendance (formal, feudal hostage system used by Japanese leaders)
seii tai-shōgun	long form of *shōgun*, meaning 'barbarian-suppressing supreme general'
Sengoku-Jidai	Age of Warring States
senpai/kōhai	senior/junior relationships
seppuku	ritual suicide
sesshō	regent
shiken jigoku	examination hell (university entrance exam period)
shin-jinrui	new persons (i.e. the younger generation)
shinpan	collateral *daimyō* (related to the Tokugawa family)
Shintō	the way of the gods (Japan's animistic religion)
shōen	land system of private estates
shōsha	trading company
Shōwa	Enlightened Peace (era name for Emperor Hirohito)
shugo	provincial military governors
shuntō	spring wage offensives (seasonal strikes)
Sōka Gakkai	Value-Creating Society (modern Buddhist sect)
sonnō-jōi	honour the emperor—expel the barbarians
Taika	Great Change (political) Reform of AD 645
taikō	retired regent
Teiseitō	Meiji-era Imperial Government Party
Tenno	Japanese emperor (from the Chinese term)
tōkōkyohi	school allergy (i.e. not wanting to attend school)
tokuju	special procurements (US orders for war matériel during the Korean war)

tozama	outside houses (feudal vassals opposed to Tokugawa Ieyasu)
ukiyo-e	sexually explicit 'pictures of the floating world'
uji	Japanese clan
yakuza	Japanese gangsters
Yamatai	the earliest agglomeration of about 30 Japanese settlements or 'kingdoms'
za	feudal merchant association
zaibatsu	family-owned industrial combines

NOTES

Chapter 2 In the beginning

1 At least sufficiently for Japanese to have celebrated, for example, the 2600th anniversary of their state in 1940.

2 It was common practice for Japanese leaders to take or be given new names at times of important changes in their lives, and this can be confusing for Western historians. Fujiwara no Kamatari, for example, was born Nakatomi no Kamatari.

3 In the seventh century Japan had abandoned its substantial presence in Korea, so the influence of that country had also declined.

4 The illustrated handscrolls of the 'Tale of Genji' are featured on the 2000-yen note released in 2000.

Chapter 3 Chaos to unity: Feudalism in Japan

1 Because Minamoto no Yoritomo gained power over a period of time, seven different dates are used by Japanese historians for the start of the Kamakura *Bakufu* (between 1180 and 1192).

2 It was not unusual at this time for women to hold positions of power, in both upper and lower classes. Property could also be held by women and passed on through the female line.

3 This period is sometimes known as the Azuchi-Momoyama period, reflecting the (numerous) moves of the headquarters of the *bakufu* at this time (Azuchi is near Nagoya while Momoyama is outside Kyoto).

Given the difficulty of grounding the name in a geographical location the period has also come to be known as Shokuho-Seiken, meaning the political age of Oda Nobunaga and Toyotomi Hideyoshi.

4 The 'cake' in the story is actually an uncooked sweet called *mochi*; Nobunaga mixed the dough, Hideyoshi pounded the dough and Ieyasu ate the result.

5 During this time of conflict with Korea and China, many Korean artisans were brought to Japan and settled mostly in the south of the country.

6 The visibility in the West of this period of battle for succession is relatively well known as a result of the success of James Clavell's book *Shōgun* and the subsequent film. The tale is based on the story of an English pilot of a Dutch ship that reached Japan in 1600. His long friendship with Ieyasu makes fascinating reading, though of course entertainment is often substituted for accuracy.

7 A very careful and patient man, as indicated by the stories handed down about him, Ieyasu was also ruthless. For example, when his first wife fell under suspicion of plotting against Nobunaga, Ieyasu had her put to death and forced his first son to commit suicide. Clearly, this was a determined man.

8 The Yoshiwara district itself was an area set aside for drinking establishments and prostitution. It was here that *geisha*, for example, were active. The artistic developments associated with Yoshiwara actually did not come from this area, since it was illegal to establish other types of businesses there, but from adjoining districts. Their inspiration may well have come from Yoshiwara.

Chapter 4 Modernisation and imperialism

1 Technically speaking, Turkey established the first representative government in Asia with its 1876 constitution, but it lasted for less than a year.

2 Itō was the first Prime Minister of Japan (1885–88), leaving the office in order to concentrate on formulating the Meiji Constitution.

3 Along with new agricultural techniques in Hokkaido came new crops, including grains and potatoes. Hokkaido was also important for mining, especially coal, which was used for the production of steel and operating steam trains.

4 Other *zaibatsu* had been established during the Edo period. Mitsui, for example, as noted in Chapter 3, was founded in the early seventeenth century, but now dramatically increased in size with the purchase of silk spinning mills and coal mines from the government, later expanding

into heavy industry. The well-known Mitsukoshi department store, owned by the Mitsui family, also dates from this time.

Chapter 5   War and peace

1   All dollar figures in this book refer to US currency.

Chapter 7   Japan as number one?

1   There are two types of *keiretsu*, vertical and horizontal. The former are like any vertically integrated business, with one company controlling others through the production cycle of design-production-retail. There are numerous examples of this type in Japan, as there are throughout the world. The horizontal *keiretsu*, on the other hand, is more commonly focused upon in Japan. These are groups of companies, making many different products, that cooperate loosely with each other and are linked through formal and informal mechanisms. The Big Six are Mitsui, Mitsubishi, Sumitomo, Fuyō, Sanwa and Dai-Ichi Kangyō Bank (DKB). Complicating the issue is the fact that within the horizontal *keiretsu* there are many vertical ones, with smaller and smaller companies sitting under the larger ones in a pyramid shape.

SELECTED FURTHER READING

There is a rich body of reference material to choose from covering virtually every aspect of Japan. Numerous articles in scholarly journals deal with a range of different topics, but there are far too many to list here. The following are but a few of the better-known books available.

There are some outstanding scholarly works in the field, led by those of George Sansom. He has published several volumes covering different periods in Japanese history, including *A History of Japan to 1334* and *A History of Japan 1615–1867*. He has also written a comprehensive book entitled *Japan: A Short Cultural History*, which focuses on religious change and the intellectual currents and social institutions which have played a role in Japanese history. Many other writers make reference to his works, an indication of their enduring value. One should not miss *The Cambridge History of Japan*, in six edited volumes, which is an astonishingly detailed comprehensive coverage of Japanese history. Finally, a very good book on the feudal period onwards is that edited by Tim Megarry entitled *The Making of Modern Japan: A Reader*.

It is interesting to take a look at W. G. Aston's translation of the *Nihongi*, the chronicle of earliest Japan, written in 720.

The book comprises more than 800 pages of detailed events, both real and imagined. A comprehensive archaeological coverage is provided in a number of chapters in *Multicultural Japan: Palaeolithic to Postmodern*, edited by Donald Denoon et al. The recent book by Mark Hudson, *Ruins of Identity: Ethnogenesis in the Japanese Islands*, is particularly thorough on this topic.

There are a number of excellent general Japanese histories. Two well-known ones are Edwin O. Reischauer's *The Japanese Today*, and Reischauer and Albert Craig's *Japan: Tradition and Transformation*. They provide only a light treatment of Japan's early years, however, in keeping with their contemporary focus. Hugh Cortazzi's *The Japanese Achievement* provides excellent coverage of Japan's early years, as does Kenneth Henshall's *A History of Japan*. Conrad Schirokauer's *A Brief History of Chinese and Japanese Civilizations* compares developments in the two countries from the beginnings of the two societies, and contains sections on artistic and literary developments to complement his political and economic coverage. Other works providing a broad view are W. Scott Morton's *Japan: Its History and Culture*, Mason and Caiger's *A History of Japan* and Kenneth Latourette's *The History of Japan*. Finally, although his treatment of the early years is relatively brief, Richard Storry's *A History of Modern Japan* is highly readable.

For more focused coverage of early Japanese civilisation, a useful book is David John Lu's *Sources of Japanese History* (volume 1). *The World of the Shining Prince: Court Life in Ancient Japan*, by Ivan Morris, examines the Heian period. Those interested in the Japanese imperial family could peruse *Sons of Heaven: A Portrait of the Japanese Monarchy*, by Jerrold M. Packard. Readers who would like to get a sense of the underlying geography of the country are referred to Donald MacDonald's *A Geography of Modern Japan* or the volume edited by Graham Chapman and Kathleen Baker entitled *The Changing Geography of Asia*.

There is a rich literature on the history of religion in Japan as well, including *History of Japanese Religion* by Masaharu Anesaki. For a focus on Buddhism only, see *A History of*

Japanese Buddhism by Shinsho Hanayama and J. Edward Kidder's *Early Buddhist Japan*.

Those interested in the Momoyama period could have a look at the novel *Taiko: An Epic Novel of War and Glory in Feudal Japan* by Yoshikawa Eiji, which gives the reader some flavour of the time. Japan's feudal period and its antecedents are covered in John Whitney Hall's *Government and Local Power in Japan: 500 to 1700*. Perry Anderson also presents persuasive arguments in the chapter on Japanese feudalism in his book entitled *Lineages of the Absolutist State*. For the Tokugawa period in particular, *Tokugawa Japan: The Social and Economic Antecedents of Modern Japan*, edited by Nakane and Oishi, examines a range of economic, political and social developments during that period.

A view emphasising popular movements rather than elite policies is given in Ann Waswo's *Modern Japanese Society 1868–1994*. Tessa Morris-Suzuki's book *The Technological Transformation of Japan* covers the topic from the seventeenth century through to the present. A more detailed work in this area is that edited by Yamada Keiji, entitled *The Transfer of Science and Technology between Europe and Asia, 1780–1880*.

A thorough account of the Pacific War is provided in *The Origins of the Second World War in Asia and the Pacific* by Akiro Iriye. A very readable semi-novelised version appears in John Toland's *The Rising Sun: The Decline and Fall of the Japanese Empire 1936–1945*. A controversial book, the most recent of a number of similar works, calling into question the level of knowledge about Japanese activities by American leaders in the lead-up to Pearl Harbor, is Robert Stinnett's *Day of Deceit: The Truth About FDR and Pearl Harbor*.

Japan's economic successes have resulted in a plethora of books. These include *Japan's Capitalism* by Tsuru Shigeto and *The Economic Emergence of Modern Japan* by Yamamura Kozo. Numerous books examine specific aspects of Japan's economy. Among these are *Keiretsu: Inside the Hidden Japanese Conglomerates* by Miyashita Kenichi and David Russell, and Arthur Whitehill's *Japanese Management: Tradition and*

Transition. There are also many books which examine the growth of Asia's economies in general, and which contain chapters or sections on Japan, including Gerald Segal's *Rethinking the Pacific* and *The Asian Pacific: Political and Economic Development in a Global Context* by Vera Simone and Ann Thompson Feraru. *Pacific Century*, edited by Mark Borthwick is good, while another useful volume is *Pacific Economic Relations in the 1990s: Cooperation or Conflict?* edited by Richard Higgott, Richard Leaver and John Ravenhill. Others in this area include Grahame Thompson's *Economic Dynamism in the Asia-Pacific*, *Asia-Pacific in the New World Order* by Anthony McGrew and Christopher Brook, *Negotiating the Pacific Century* by Roger Bell, Tim McDonald and Alan Tidwell and *The Rise of East Asia* by Mark Berger and Douglas Borer. Problems in Japan's economy in the early 1990s led to a number of authors re-examining the situation rather pessimistically. Works here include Jon Woronoff's easily readable *The Japanese Economic Crisis* and *Japan as Anything but Number One*. A carefully constructed argument is presented by Brian Reading in *Japan: The Coming Collapse*, and Bill Emmott examines Japan's flow of capital offshore in *Japan's Global Reach*.

Good books focusing on Japan's political structure include *Japan: Who Governs?* by Chalmers Johnson, *Politics in Modern Japan* by Kishimoto Kōichi, and *Japanese Politics Today*, edited by Purnendra Jain and Takashi Inoguchi. A landmark title in this field is J. A. A. Stockwin's *Governing Japan*. Two good books on recent foreign relations are *Japan's Foreign Policy After the Cold War*, edited by Gerald Curtis, and *US–Japan Alliance Diplomacy 1945–1990* by Roger Buckley. Finally, an interesting volume which examines Japan's bureaucracy from an insider's perspective is the highly readable *Straitjacket Society* by Miyamoto Masao.

Books which deal with Japan's foreign trade include *Regionalism and Rivalry: Japan and the United States in Pacific Asia*, edited by Jeffrey Frankel and Miles Kahler, *The United States, Japan, and Asia* by Gerald L. Curtis and Lester Thurow's *Head to Head: The Coming Economic Battle Among Japan, Europe and America*. Two very good books which examine Japan's trade connections with Asia are *Asia in Japan's Embrace* by Walter Hatch and Yamamura Kozo and *Japan in Asia*, produced by the *Far Eastern Economic Review* and edited by Nigel Holloway. A number of books examine Japan thematically, with a focus on the contemporary period. A well-known volume here is *Understanding Japanese Society* by Joy Hendry, who looks at developments in the educational system, religious influences and socialisation. Others include Roger Buckley's *Japan Today*, a useful book that takes the reader up to the late 1980s, and Janet Hunter's *The Emergence of Modern Japan*. One book which challenges some of the generalisations made about Japan is entitled *The Myth of Japanese Uniqueness* by Peter Dale. Critical views of the way in which Japan's social, economic and political systems function appear in the highly readable and persuasive *The Enigma of Japanese Power*, by Karel van Wolferen, and in Jared Taylor's *Shadows of the Rising Sun*. A nicely written volume that is particularly good for newcomers to the study of Japan is Steven Reed's *Making Common Sense of Japan*.

There are a number of very good books around on the Japanese educational system. These include Leonard Schoppa's *Education Reform in Japan*, Michael Stephens' *Education and the Future of Japan* and the volume edited by James Shields Jr entitled *Japanese Schooling*.

Useful books which look at women's roles in Japan are also available. One of the best known is Iwao Sumiko's *The Japanese Woman: Traditional Image and Changing Reality*. Jane Condon's *A Half Step Behind: Japanese Women Today* examines various aspects of the lives of Japanese women while *Japanese Women Working*, edited by Janet Hunter, examines the history of women's employment.

Recent social developments in Japan have been addressed in a number of works. These include *Japanese Society* by Sugimoto Yoshio, *Dimensions of Japanese Society* by Kenneth Henshall, and *The Japanese Social Crisis* by John Woronoff. Two very good volumes are *The Worlds of Japanese Popular Culture*, edited by D. P. Martinez, and *Japanese Society Today*, edited by Ishido Kotaku and David Myers.

BIBLIOGRAPHY

Anderson, P. (1979). *Lineages of the Absolutist State*. London, NLB.
Anesaki, M. (1983). *History of Japanese Religion*. Tokyo, Charles E. Tuttle.
Aston, W. G. (1988). *Nihongi: Chronicles of Japan from the Earliest Times to A.D. 697*. Tokyo, Charles E. Tuttle.
Bell, R., T. McDonald et al., eds (1996). *Negotiating the Pacific Century*. Sydney, Allen & Unwin.
Benedict, R. (1989). *The Chrysanthemum and the Sword*. Boston, Houghton Mifflin.
Berger, M. and D. Borer, eds (1997). *The Rise of East Asia*. London, Routledge.
Borthwick, M. (1998). *Pacific Century*. Boulder, Westview Press.
Buckley, R. (1990). *Japan Today*. Cambridge, Cambridge University Press.
——(1995). *US–Japan Alliance Diplomacy 1945–1990*. Cambridge, Cambridge University Press.
Chapman, G. and K. Baker, eds (1995). *The Changing Geography of Asia*. London, Routledge.
Condon, J. (1992). *A Half Step Behind: Japanese Women Today*. Tokyo, Charles E. Tuttle.
Cortazzi, H. (1990). *The Japanese Achievement*. London, Sidgwick Jackson.
Curtis, G., ed. (1993). *Japan's Foreign Policy After the Cold War*. Armonk, M.E. Sharpe.
Curtis, G. L., ed. (1994). *The United States, Japan, and Asia*. New York, W.W. Norton.
Dale, P. (1995). *The Myth of Japanese Uniqueness*. London, Routledge.
Denoon, D., M. Hudson et al., eds (1996). *Multicultural Japan: Palaeolithic to Postmodern*. Cambridge, Cambridge University Press.

Emmott, B. (1993). *Japan's Global Reach*. London, Random House.

Frankel, J. and M. Kahler (1993). *Regionalism and Rivalry: Japan and the United States in Pacific Asia*. Chicago, University of Chicago Press.

Hall, J. W. (1966). *Government and Local Power in Japan: 500 to 1700*. Princeton, Princeton University Press.

Hanayama, S. (1966). *A History of Japanese Buddhism*. Tokyo, Bukkyo Dendo Kyokai.

Harris, S. H. (1994). *Factories of Death: Japanese Biological Warfare, 1932–45, and the American Cover-Up*. London, Routledge.

Hatch, W. and Y. Kozo (1996). *Asia in Japan's Embrace*. Cambridge, Cambridge University Press.

Hendry, J. (1995). *Understanding Japanese Society*. London, Routledge.

Henshall, K. (1999). *Dimensions of Japanese Society*. London, Macmillan.

Henshall, K. G. (1999). *A History of Japan: From Stone Age to Superpower*. London, Macmillan.

Higgott, R., R. Leaver et al., eds (1993). *Pacific Economic Relations in the 1990s: Cooperation or Conflict?* Sydney, Allen & Unwin.

Holloway, N., ed. (1991). *Japan in Asia*. Hong Kong, Review Publishing.

Hudson, M. (1999). *Ruins of Identity: Ethnogenesis in the Japanese Islands*. Honolulu, University of Hawaii Press.

Hunter, J. (1991). *The Emergence of Modern Japan*. London, Longman.

——ed. (1995). *Japanese Women Working*. London, Routledge.

Iriye, A. (1987). *The Origins of the Second World War in Asia and the Pacific*. London, Longman.

Ishido, K. and D. Myers, eds (1995). *Japanese Society Today*. Rockhampton, Central Queensland University Press.

Iwao, S. (1993). *The Japanese Woman: Traditional Image and Changing Reality*. New York, The Free Press.

Jain, P. and I. Takashi, eds (1997). *Japanese Politics Today*. Melbourne, Macmillan.

Johnson, C. (1995). *Japan: Who Governs?* New York, W.W. Norton.

Kidder, J. E. (1972). *Early Buddhist Japan*. Southampton, Thames and Hudson.

Kishimoto, K. (1997). *Politics in Modern Japan*. Tokyo, Japan Echo.

Latourette, K. S. (1957). *The History of Japan*. New York, Macmillan.

Lu, D. J. (1974). *Sources of Japanese History*. New York, McGraw-Hill.

MacDonald, D. (1985). *A Geography of Modern Japan*. Woodchurch, Paul Norbury Publications.

Martinez, D. P., ed. (1998). *The Worlds of Japanese Popular Culture*. Contemporary Japanese Society. Cambridge, Cambridge University Press.

Mason, R. H. P. and J. G. Caiger (1972). *A History of Japan*. Melbourne, Cassell.

McCormack, G. (1996). *The Emptiness of Japanese Affluence*. Sydney, Allen & Unwin.

McGrew, A. and C. Brook, eds (1998). *Asia-Pacific in the New World Order*. London, Routledge.

Megarry, T., ed. (1995). *The Making of Modern Japan: A Reader*. Dartford, Greenwich University Press.

Miyamoto, M. (1994). *Straitjacket Society*. Tokyo, Kodansha International.

Miyashita, K. and D. Russell (1994). *Keiretsu: Inside the Hidden Japanese Conglomerates*. New York, McGraw-Hill.

Morris, I. (1979). *The World of the Shining Prince*. Harmondsworth, Penguin Books.

Morris-Suzuki, T. (1994). *The Technological Transformation of Japan*. Cambridge, Cambridge University Press.

Morton, W. S. (1970). *Japan: Its History and Culture*. Melbourne, Wren Publishing.

Nakane, C. and S. Oishi (1991). *Tokugawa Japan: The Social and Economic Antecedents of Modern Japan*. Tokyo, University of Tokyo Press.

Packard, J. M. (1998). *Sons of Heaven: A Portrait of the Japanese Monarchy*. London, Macdonald Queen Anne Press.

Reading, B. (1993). *Japan: The Coming Collapse*. London, Orion Books.

Reed, S. (1993). *Making Common Sense of Japan*. Pittsburgh, University of Pittsburgh Press.

Reischauer, E. O. (1993). *The Japanese Today: Change and Continuity*. Tokyo, Charles E. Tuttle.

Reischauer, E. O. and A. M. Craig (1989). *Japan: Tradition and Transformation*. Sydney, Allen & Unwin.

Sansom, G. (1958). *A History of Japan to 1334*. Stanford, Stanford University Press.

——(1963). *A History of Japan 1615–1867*. Stanford, Stanford University Press.

——(1976). *Japan: A Short Cultural History*. London, Barrie & Jenkins.

Schirokauer, C. (1989). *A Brief History of Chinese and Japanese Civilizations*. San Diego, Harcourt Brace Jovanovich.

Schoppa, L. (1991). *Education Reform in Japan*. London, Routledge.

Segal, G. (1990). *Rethinking the Pacific*. Oxford, Clarendon Press.

Shields, J. Jr, (1993). *Japanese Schooling*. University Park, Pennsylvania State University Press.

Shively, D. H. and W. H. McCullough, eds (1999). *The Cambridge History of Japan*. Cambridge, Cambridge University Press.

Simone, V. and A. T. Feraru (1995). *The Asian Pacific: Political and Economic Development in a Global Context*. London, Longman.

Smiles, S. (1880). *Self-help*. London, John Murray.

Stephens, M. (1991). *Education and the Future of Japan*. Sandgate, Japan Library.

Stinnett, R. (1999). *Day of Deceit: The Truth About FDR and Pearl Harbor*. New York, Free Press.

Stockwin, J. A. A. (1999). *Governing Japan*. Oxford, Blackwell.

Storry, R. (1990). *A History of Modern Japan*. London, Penguin Books.

Sugimoto, Y. (1997). *Japanese Society*. Cambridge, Cambridge University Press.

Taylor, J. (1993). *Shadows of the Rising Sun*. Tokyo, Charles E. Tuttle.

Thompson, G., ed. (1998). *Economic Dynamism in the Asia-Pacific*. London, Routledge.

Thurow, L. (1993). *Head to Head: The Coming Economic Battle Among Japan, Europe and America*. Sydney, Allen & Unwin.

Toland, J. (1970). *The Rising Sun: The Decline and Fall of the Japanese Empire 1936–1945*. New York, Random House.

Tsuru, S. (1996). *Japan's Capitalism*. Cambridge, Cambridge University Press.

United Nations (1996). *Population Ageing in Asia and the Pacific*. New York, UN.

Vogel, E. (1979). *Japan as Number One: Lessons for America*. Cambridge, Mass., Harvard University Press.

Waswo, A. (1996). *Modern Japanese Society 1868–1994*. Oxford, Oxford University Press.

Whitehill, A. (1991). *Japanese Management: Tradition and Transition*. London, Routledge.

Wolferen, K. van (1993). *The Enigma of Japanese Power*. Tokyo, Charles E. Tuttle.

Woronoff, J. (1996). *Japan as Anything but Number One*. London, Macmillan.

——(1996). *The Japanese Economic Crisis*. London, Macmillan.

——(1997). *The Japanese Social Crisis*. London, Macmillan.

Yamada, K., ed. (1992). *The Transfer of Science and Technology between Europe and Asia, 1780–1880*. Kyoto, International Research Center for Japanese Studies.

Yamamura, K. (1997). *The Economic Emergence of Modern Japan*. Cambridge, Cambridge University Press.

Yoshikawa, E. (1992). *Taiko: An Epic Novel of War and Glory in Feudal Japan*. Tokyo, Kodansha International.

SOURCES

All photographs in the book are courtesy of the author. The map and diagram credits are as follows:

p. ii   Buckley 1990, p. xiv

p. 23   Denoon et al. 1996, p. 27; adapted from N. Saitou, K. Tokunaga and K. Omoto, 'Genetic affinities of human populations', in D.L. Roberts, N. Jujita and K. Torizuka (eds), *Isolation and Migration*, Cambridge University Press, 1992, pp. 20–30

p. 26   Mason and Caiger 1972

p. 27   Reischauer and Craig 1989, p. 9

p. 33   Reischauer and Craig 1989, p. 37

p. 37   Schirokauer 1989, p. 132

p. 74   Schirokauer 1989, p. 412

p. 95   Mason and Caiger 1972, p. 222

p. 101   Reischauer and Craig 1989, p. 235

p. 151   Miyashita and Russell 1994, p. 89

p. 212   United Nations 1996

INDEX

Page numbers in *italics* refer to illustrations and page numbers suffixed with m refer to maps.

kunigae, 62, 65
Kuomintang, 97, 106
Kurile Islands, 22–3, 136
kuromaku, 51
Kurosawa Akira, 221
Kurosawa Kishio, 221
Kwangtung Army, 101–2
Kyoto, 39, 54, 56, 116; Heian era, 40,
42, 45, 46
Kyushu, 17, 23, 24, 25, 34, 144

labour: agricultural sector, 135, 140,
162–4; and capital, 130–2, 133,
150; exploitation, 11–12, 149, 160;
forced, 114, 115, 119; gender
differences, 5–7, 206–7; low-wage
countries, 154, 168, 175, 187, 213;
offshore, 168–9, 173–4, 175, 176,
187, 213; shortages, 5, 13, 203,
213, 215, 219; women, 5–6, 13, 98,
133, 202–3, 206, 214–15; *see also*
employment system; trade unions;
unemployment
land values, 141, 166–7, 169, 207–8
landholding, 36; feudal period, 49–50,
51, 58, 61, 62, 67; Heian era, 43–5;
Meiji era, 81, 87, 90; postwar, 120–1
language, 64, 84; instruction, 195,
217–8; writing system, 34–5
language barrier, 12, 113, 119
League of Nations, 97–8, 102
legal codes, 34, 36, 52, 58, 65, 67–8,
70, 77, 92, 120; *see also*
constitutions
Liaison Council, 108
Liaotung (Liaodong) Peninsula, 93,
94–5, 96
Liberal Democratic Party (LDP), 2,
129–30, 131, 138, 160, 163–4,
184–5, 216
Liberal Party (*Jiyūtō*), 87–8, 122,
129–30
Lockheed Corporation, 160–1
London Disarmament Conference
(1930), 108
Long-Term Credit Bank of Japan, 189

MacArthur, General Douglas, 118–19,
120–1, 123
McCormack, Gavan, 219
Mahayana Buddhism, 31
Malaya/Malaysia, 112, 115, 173
Manchuria, 102, 105, 108, 117, 123

Manchurian Incident (1931), 101–2,
103
Manchurian Industrial Development
Corporation, 108
manga, 204–5
manufacturing, 124, 125, 188, 216;
1950s and 1960s, 132–4, 137, 146;
1970s and 1980s, 153–7, 164–9,
172–6; offshore, 147, 167–9, 173–4,
175, 216; technology, 154–5, 164–6,
168, 175, 188; *see also* raw materials
Marco Polo Bridge, 103, 106
marriage, 5–6, 28, 41, 70, 200, 201–2
Matsui Iwane, 106
Matsuo Bashō, 72
maza-con, 204
Mazda, 3, 189
meat, 12, 30, 84, *163*
media, 86, 102, 178–9
Meiji constitution, 88–9, 93, 229n1,
229n2
Meiji era, 78–96, 128; art and culture,
84–5, 86; economy and finance, 81,
85–6, 89–91, 92, 129; education
system, 82–3, 87; foreign relations,
79, 82, 93–6; nationalism, 78, 79,
82–3, 87, 92–4, 96, 122; political
system, 19, 79, 80–1, 87–8, 89;
religion, 92–3; Westernisation, 80,
82–5, 87–8, 90, 92
men, 6–7, 11, 99, 200, 201, 204–6
merchant class, 68, 71–2, 73, 91
mercury poisoning, 144
Merrill Lynch, 189
Middle East, 154, 156, 182, 191
migration, 22, 24, 35, 48, 213–14
military, 29; constitutional limitations,
120, 126, 157, 192, 216; current
debates, 191–3, 216; defence
expenditure, 95, 106, 157, 164,
171, 190, 192–3; feudal era, 48–50,
58, 60–3, 65, 75–6; Heian era,
45–6; Kwangtung Army, 101–2;
Meiji era, 81, 91–6; nationalism, 93,
94, 99, 101, 112, 193, 194; political
influence, 46, 48, 49, 54, 58, 91,
94, 99, 105, 108; Taisho era, 99,
100–2, 103; US–Japan defence
cooperation, 138–9, 150, 190; War
and Navy ministers, 94, 99; *see also*
bakufu; conscription; military bases;
samurai; Self Defence Forces (SDF);
war